WITH HEARTS EXPANDED

WITH HEARTS EXPANDED

Transformations in the Lives of
Benedictine Women
St. Joseph, Minnesota
1957 to 2000

Co-authored by:

Evin Rademacher, O.S.B.
Emmanuel Renner, O.S.B.
Olivia Forster, O.S.B.
Carol Berg, O.S.B.

NORTH STAR PRESS OF ST. CLOUD, INC.

Cover design: Johanna Becker, O.S.B.

Title Context: "For as we advance in the religious life and in faith, our hearts expand and we run the way of God's commandments with unspeakable sweetness of love."
St. Benedict's Rule for Monasteries, Leonard Doyle, trans.
(The Liturgical Press: Collegeville, Minnesota, 1948)

ISBN: 0-87839-155-X Cloth
ISBN: 0-87839-156-8 Paper

First Edition: December 2000

Printed in the United States of America by Versa Press, Inc., East Peoria, Illinois.

Published by
North Star Press of St. Cloud, Inc.
P.O. Box 451
St. Cloud, Minnesota 56302

DEDICATION

This book is dedicated to the two prioresses, Mother Richarda Peters and Mother Henrita Osendorf who gave insightful and courageous leadership to the development of Saint Benedict's Monastery in the last half of the twentieth century.

Mother Richarda Peters, O.S.B.
Born: October 2, 1895
Professed: July 11, 1914
Entered Eternal Life:
July 5, 1972

Mother Richarda Peters' career as an educator and her doctoral studies in psychology and in psychiatry preeminently prepared her for her providential service of leading the sisters of Saint Benedict's Monastery (1949 to 1961) into one of the most remarkable periods of renewal in the history of the Church and of religious life.

Mother Henrita Osendorf, O.S.B.
Born: August 22, 1906
Professed: July 11, 1925
Entered Eternal Life:
February 12, 1992

Mother Henrita Osendorf stood as a firm rock amid strong winds of change in her leadership of St. Benedict's community (1961 to 1973). Through the challenges of post-Vatican II renewal which brought the sisters into readiness for a new age, she offered them motivation and encouragement to remain true to their monastic Benedictine vocation.

Dear Sisters, we need not be unduly distressed by the winds if we strive diligently to arrive at a better under-standing of the scriptural and theo-logical basis of religious life. . . . It will safeguard us from being swept off our feet and losing our balance. . . . Calm and tranquillity of spirit are the characteristics of religious whose preoccupation is with basic elements. They do not fear change because they know that they have penetrated to the heart of the matter and are secure in that knowledge.

(Saint Benedict's Monastery Archives: Osendorf, Circular Letters, 1965-1967, RG 5-10-2, f 6.)

FOREWORD

When Pope John Paul II proclaimed the year 2000 as the Great Jubilee of Jesus Christ, he conjured up for all Catholic Christians the potent meanings of what it meant to observe "a year of jubilee" in the Hebrew Scriptures (Leviticus 25: 10-12). Rooted in the notion of "sabbath," the jubilee year was permeated by a sense of the goodness of creation together with a compassionate acknowlegement that all creatures are dependent and share the common lot of the human family. The biblical jubilee began with a call to reconciliation, signaling a time of liberation and the renewal of relationships with family, the community, and nature itself. It was meant to be a time of return to former ideals—a time of remembering and a time for new vision.

Someone once called jubilees and anniversaries "icons of time" through which we enter into another dimension of reality. They are like landmarks that give direction and point out the way we have come on the journey of life. They are myth-making moments in the sense that they can provide for us an overarching sense of meaning. Remembering and commemorating are the heart of the biblical story and define the worship of the Christian community.

It is eminently fitting then that in this year of Great Jubilee, we, the Sisters of the Order of Saint Benedict in St. Joseph, Minnesota, are remembering in this book the first half of the second century of our history as a community of American Benedictine monastic women. Ours is a compelling story, alongside all the equally poignant accounts of other sisterhoods founded in this country during the nineteenth century. These stories are shot through with evidences of the remarkable workings of the Holy Spirit in the lives of women whose only desire was to love and to serve God by being of service to God's people in whatever circumstances they found themselves.

Sister Grace McDonald, in our centennial history, *With Lamps Burning*, told the story that comprised the first three stages in what some sociologists refer to as the "life cycles" of a religious community—stages of foundation, expansion, and stabilization. The story resumes in this volume at the brink of a new stage in the life cycle, a critical period of transition and reidentification. The reader is quickly ushered into the story's dynamics of dramatic change and astounding transformations, during an historical period marked by widespread cultural upheavel and religious unrest. The past fifty years of our community's history clearly parallel the phenomena of rapid change and paradigmatic shifting that have been occurring in the society at large during the last half of the twentieth century.

The community of Saint Benedict's Monastery has, indeed, been shaken during the recent decades of change and transition but not uprooted. The same indomitable spirit of the "ardent women" about whom Sister Grace McDonald wrote, has lived on and flourished in the women the reader will meet between these pages. As this story goes to press in the first year of a new millennium, let it be remembered that in the 143-year history of our community, 2,445 women have entered the novitiate in this place, in search of a God who does not disappoint. During the same time period, 990 of our members have gone home to God and intercede for us still among the "communion of saints."

The authors of this book have accomplished what I sometimes feared could not be done. They have effectively captured the spirit and zest of one of the most complex, challenging, and formative periods in our history. In this year of Great Jubilee, they have gifted us with an "icon of time," an anniversary story of ever-renewing vision and overarching meaning. They have given us a landmark that points out the way our Benedictine community has come on the journey of life.

Sister Ephrem Hollermann, O.S.B., Prioress
Saint Benedict's Monastery, St. Joseph, Minnesota

August 15, 2000
Assumption of Mary

TABLE OF CONTENTS

ACKNOWLEDGMENTS

In keeping with the spirit of post-Vatican II renewal, this sequel is the result of a collegial process. The research was done by Sisters Shaun O'Meara (Community Renewal Programs before and after Vatican Council II), Carol Berg (Native American Missions, Dependent Priories, New Ministries), Emmanuel Renner (College of Saint Benedict), and Olivia Forster (Health Care). Sister Kathleen Kalinowski's compilation of community affairs regarding the separate incorporation of community-owned institutions, the dependent priories, and the community's demographics and resources, served as a valuable resource. Sister Evin Rademacher organized the researched materials and wrote the narrative of Part I and Part II. Her lived experience in Saint Benedict's Monastery beginning in 1941 enabled her to transform the information into a living history. The essays regarding St. Benedict's long-standing institutions of ministry in Part III were written by the sisters who researched the respective areas as indicated in the outline and in the titles.

Special mention should be made of: Sister Carol Berg's unflagging enthusiasm in chairing the committee; the former prioresses, Sisters Evin Rademacher, Katherine Howard, Mary Reuter, and present prioress, Ephrem Hollermann, for their willingness to be consultants to the committee; the community archivists, especially Sister Ruth Boedigheimer for assistance in researching and selecting photographs; Sisters Sheila Rausch and Nancy Hynes for pruning first drafts; the readers for their encouragement and suggestions regarding style and content, especially Sister Jeannette Klassen; Sister Thomasette Scheeler for preparing the photographs; Norma Koetter and Sister Malachy Hurley for secretarial services; the editor, Sister Stefanie Weisgram, who shaped the work of this committee into its final book form; Studium for giving space, encouragement, and expertise in seeing the publication to its completion; and all the sisters who submitted suggestions for a title.

This book, and Saint Benedict's Monastery, would not be but for the Sisters of St. Benedict whose commitment and dedication to the work of God shaped this history. In gratitude, all members of this community as of August 2000, are named in the Membership List. The cloud of witnesses whose spirit continues to bless and inspire this community are remembered in the Necrology as a conclusion to this sequel. The numbers after names indicate page reference(s).

Co-authors (seated), Sisters Emmanuel Renner, Carol Berg, Olivia Forster, and Evin Rademacher, with Sister Stefanie Weisgram, editor, and Sister Shaun O'Meara, researcher.

PART I

INTERNAL COMMUNITY TRANSFORMATIONS

by
Evin Rademacher, O.S.B.

Saint Benedict's Monastery/Academy (High School)/College campus in 1957. The new Mary Hall Commons and one residence wing, beginning the south campus, are shown on the extreme left.

INTRODUCTION

In *With Lamps Burning*, Sister Grace McDonald traced the growth of Saint Benedict's Monastery from its establishment in Minnesota in 1857 to its centennial in 1957. It is the purpose of this sequel to capture the exciting and often troublesome challenges that faced this community in the last half of the twentieth century. It is a story of moving from a stable and predictable era to an explosive era of expanded knowledge, information, and communications that resulted in irreversible societal changes effected by such grassroots movements as civil rights, women's rights, and environmental concerns, and by a Christian religious tranformation called for by Vatican Council II. The story of the community's struggles and achievements in responding to the call to renew itself and set its face toward the third millennium needs to be told: most people, observing only the external manifestations of the changes, were not privy to the sacredness of the transformations taking place. This book offers the community's self-disclosure in the hope that it will help its readers find meaning for the challenges with which God also shapes their lives.

(A Glossary is included before the Index for those unfamiliar with monastic terminology.)

"Long black lines of sisters wending their way, in rank of seniority, to Mary Hall . . . marked the centennial celebrations . . ."

1
CHANGE ON THE HORIZON

Centennial Celebrations

Long black lines of sisters wending their way, in rank of seniority, to Mary Hall on the south end of the monastery-college campus marked the centennial celebrations of Saint Benedict's Monastery.[1] In 1957 the Sisters of the Order of Saint Benedict commemorated the centenary of the arrival of the Benedictine sisters in Minnesota, with celebrations spread throughout that year. Little did they realize that this occasion was one of the last times they would give public witness in full traditional garb to their community's monastic commitment.

A challenging and forward-looking message for the celebration of a century of monastic life at Saint Benedict's Monastery was delivered by Abbot Baldwin Dworschak, O.S.B., from Saint John's Abbey. In his homily at the opening Pontifical High Mass on January 1, he congratulated the sisters for their one hundred years of service, offering encouragement as they faced their second century. He urged more attention to the future than to the past, successful as it was, and to a rededication to the sacred purpose for which the community had been founded. In a prophetic stance, he concluded:

5

> The blessings of the future are going to depend entirely on what you do now in preparing for the future, in the foundation you now lay for the blessings of the future. . . . Review the lessons that can be learned from monastic history, lessons which will show us our Holy Rule in the proper perspective. [You] must also, I think, examine the traditions of this particular community, traditions that have grown up over a 100 years, some of them undoubtedly very good traditions, some of them probably traditions that should be questioned.[2]

Neither he nor the sisters could have imagined the amount of questioning that would occur within the next fifty years. Nor could they have seen on the horizon the national and the global earth-shaking events that would deeply influence their futures

A second special celebration occurred that year upon the arrival of Lady Abbess Augustina Weihermueller, O.S.B., of St. Walburga Abbey in Eichstätt, Bavaria. She presided at the Divine Office (now more commonly known as the Liturgy of the Hours) in the Sacred Heart Chapel on the feast of St. Scholastica, patroness of the sisters of St. Benedict. Her presence renewed a spiritual and physical link with the original founding motherhouse from which the first sister-pioneers had set out for the United States a century earlier. Informal contacts with St. Walburga Abbey have since been maintained to the mutual benefit of both communities.

A third centennial event occurred on August 19, 1957, when the sisters hosted a public celebration, inviting representative clergy, religious, and laity to Eucharist, dinner, and tours of the grounds. In her letter of invitation to this event, Mother Richarda Peters, prioress (1949 to 1961), paid tribute to the monastic foundresses:

> We realize that our mere existence gives a witness to a continuity of their spirit, possible only by God's grace. . . . While we rejoice and thank God for the past achievements of our sisters, we likewise feel obliged to extend their zeal and labors in the apostolate, and to perpetuate their hymn of praise and worship offered to God from this area of [God's] kingdom.[3]

Two histories were published for the centennial year highlighting the lives and work of the sisters of Saint Benedict's Monastery: *Harvest*, a pictorial panorama, edited by Sister Mariella Gable, professor of English at the College of Saint Benedict and, still in print, *With Lamps Burning*, a narrative history by Sister Grace McDonald, professor of history at the College of Saint Benedict. However, a new history began to unfold very quickly in the next fifty years.

Symbolic of the threshold of the new age on which the sisters were standing was the launching of Sputnik in the year 1957—the space age was born. Within ten years of that event, Vatican Council II had taken place, the United States was mired in the Vietnam War, two Kennedys and Martin Luther King, Jr., were assassinated, the Cold War and the space program pitted superpowers Russia and the United States against one another, and Saint Benedict's Monastery was deeply involved in renewal—a word that would capture the attention of religious communities for the remainder of the century. To use Dickens' opening words in the *Tale of Two Cities*: "It was the best of times, it was the worst of times." The tale of how the forces of Church and society impacted the sisters' lives as they strove to be faithful to their Benedictine call to "listen" to God working with the "signs of the times," needs to be told. The women who lived through these tumultuous years of searching and change need to have their historic efforts chronicled and kept alive as inspiration for the next generations.

Sister Formation Movement

Prior to and immediately after the centennial, monastic life at Saint Benedict's Monastery seemed to go on as usual. There was little indication of pending change in the community's traditional religious life. If anything, old customs were strongly reaffirmed. For example, minutes of the December 28th superiors' meeting in 1951 record that Mother Richarda Peters emphasized the Book of Customs as she urged the local missions to careful observance of monastic practices. Among many other rules and customs, limits were placed on correspondence, visiting and eating with relatives, and even trips by sisters to other local missions or to the motherhouse. Regarding the latter "privilege," Mother Richarda stated: "A sister should ordinarily not have permission to come to the motherhouse during the year. In an emergency, a superior may grant this permission."[4] Traveling was not an easily available option since most sisters were neither permitted to drive nor had access to a community car.

The content of sisters' initial formation and their ongoing formation through retreats and reading, both personal and communal (table reading and common periods of *lectio divina* or spiritual reading), remained very similar to that of late nineteenth-century religious life. Recommended for their meditation were such authors as Columba Marmion, Pius Parsch, Romano Guardini, and Cuthbert Butler. Suggested journals included *Review for Religious* and *Sponsa Regis* (later *Sisters Today*). Rarely did these works question the basic structure or customs of religious life.

Seeds of new thinking sprouted during Mother Richarda's second term, 1955 to 1961. To give the sisters the education they needed to understand better the theological and spiritual basis of their vowed life and to carry out their ministry professionally, she sent sisters to various schools across the nation to earn their degrees. To encourage the educational updating of the sisters, she initiated education programs within the community, such as study clubs, in which every sister was expected to participate, and she suggested an extension of the community's initial formation program. She proposed a two-year novitiate and urged that the sisters remain at the home monastery during their first year in triennial vows. She recommended to Bishop Peter Bartholome that the sisters withdraw from teaching kindergarten to help relieve the pressure to send the young sisters out to teach as quickly as possible. She added that the community did not wish to staff any new schools at this time, or, if new schools were opened, that sisters be withdrawn from existing schools and be replaced by lay teachers: "The urgent requests for teachers have forced us to send out sisters who are not adequately prepared professionally nor spiritually to assume the responsibilities of a teaching position, with the result that they frequently become discouraged and waver in their vocation."[5]

The inspiration for Mother Richarda's zeal for the sisters' proper formation and education stemmed from her involvement with the Sister Formation Conference. This conference was formed in 1954 under the aegis of the National Catholic Education Association (NCEA) as a result of a survey that a graduate student, Sister Mary Richardine Quirk, B.V.M., sent to women's religious communities to gather information for her thesis. The survey revealed communities' current practices and problems relative to the education of sisters. The Sister Formation Conference's leader, Sister Mary Emil Penet, I.H.M., worked tirelessly to alleviate some of these problems by promoting the cause of education for sisters, especially the young. Likewise, Mother Richarda's dream was to provide every sister with the preparation she needed for her life as a religious and her life's work. She also advised each mission community to subscribe to the *Sister Formation Bulletin* which Sister Mary Emil edited to keep sisters abreast of what was happening nationwide on behalf of sisters' education. Mother Richarda encouraged convent libraries to make available current books, periodicals, and newspapers. Among the latter, the diocesan weekly paper, *The New York Times, America, Commonweal,* and the *London Tablet* were highly recommended—certainly a departure from the permitted reading lists of the past.[6]

Women Religious Uniting

Simultaneous with the developments of the Sister Formation Movement in the 1950s, Pope Pius XII encouraged religious superiors to organize national conferences of women religious. He saw the sisters as a powerful healing force in the world and wanted a concerted voice that would reflect mutual assistance among communities. Inspired by such leadership from the Vatican, as well as by the leadership of American sister-educators of the Sister Formation Conference, the superiors of women religious held their first American Congress in 1952. They organized the Conference of Major Superiors of Women Religious (CMSW) that eventually developed into the Leadership Conference of Women Religious (LCWR), a body that continues to be active.

Likewise, as early as 1951 the Benedictine prioresses began to collaborate on a regular basis for retreats, workshops, and common projects, such as planning an institute of theology. They formed an informal association in 1963, with the presidents of the four pontifical Benedictine women's Congregations (Federations) acting as a governing board with Mother Richarda Peters as the chairperson. In 1965 this board initiated the formal organization of the association of prioresses known as the Conference of American Benedictine Prioresses (CABP).[7]

Sisters found strength, new resources, new visions, and a unifying bond in these organizations. It was a welcome departure from the competitive isolation from each other that had often been the case in the pre-Vatican II era.

Benedictine Institute of Sacred Theology

An example of the benefits of these national associations among religious was the establishment of the Benedictine Institute of Sacred Theology (BIST) in the summer of 1958. The American prioresses had searched for a program to enrich the spiritual formation of sisters. Mother Richarda envisioned the development of such a program at the College of Saint Benedict and arranged with Saint John's Abbey to have Father Paschal Botz, O.S.B., as director of the program and Sister Mary Anthony Wagner as co-director. The first session of BIST held at St. Benedict's enrolled sixty sisters from twenty-seven monasteries and twenty states. The majority of the participants were engaged in formation work in their respective monasteries. BIST envisioned educating sisters in a five-summer sequence of courses in dogmatic and moral theology, in sacred scripture, and in ecclesiastical and Benedictine monastic spirituality.[8] Within four years, BIST was moved to Saint John's University, partly because of its library's richer theological resources at that time. Sister Mary Anthony continued to serve as its co-director until BIST evolved into the Graduate School of Theology at St. John's for which she then served in the role of dean for five years.

Rumblings of New Visions

Mother Richarda, Sister Mary Emil, and Pius XII probably did not anticipate the open discussion of tensions that sisters felt. The difference between the traditional convent culture of uniformity and conformity and the new intellectual vistas the sisters encountered through their educational and intercommunity experiences called into question many irrelevant practices. Sister Mary Ewens, O.P., described this dilemma well:

> . . . the whole system [of "convent culture"] was thrown open to critical examination and the buttresses began to crack. The effort to achieve integration of all aspects of a sister's life certainly exposed areas of disharmony. . . . Sisters trained in the liberal arts with critical thinking skills and a solid historical and theological base were prepared to look at religious life and separate the essentials from the nonessentials. They could make allowances for historical circumstances, different schools of theology, and the various ideologies that have dominated the thinking of various epochs. A knowledge of developmental psychology would alert one to elements of religious life that did or did not promote a healthy personality.[9]

In the process of obtaining their education, the sisters were exposed to aspirations and struggles of other movements such as the Women's Movement and Civil Rights Movement, ecological and environmental concerns, and social justice and peace issues. These issues were discussed at the College of Saint Benedict, where most sisters were educated, but exposure to these movements at larger schools and universities with students from all over the nation had an even greater impact. As individual sisters returned from summer schools and workshops, their new insights and experiences rippled throughout the community. Of all the movements, the Sister Formation Conference is singled out here because it most directly effected the community's readiness for the monumental changes that would soon be called for by Vatican Council II.

It was a questioning community ready for change that elected Mother Henrita Osendorf, well known for her charism of leadership, to lead the sisters through the troubled times of doubts, expectations, fears, and excitement of the next twelve years, 1961 to 1973. Because she had served as the community's novice director for seventeen years, 435 sisters knew first hand of her love for religious life, her sound theological background, and her regard for persons. Having served as subprioress with Mother Richarda the year prior to her election, she was well aware of the seeds of change that had been planted. She too encouraged the sisters to keep abreast of national and world events, and she granted "permission" to watch television. Challenged by discussions of Cardinal Leon-Joseph Suenens' book, *The Nun in the World*,[10] at a meeting of religious superiors in Chicago in 1963, Mother Henrita offered the book for table reading in the monastic dining room. Every local community of sisters did likewise, and it generated much interest and discussion throughout the community. Cardinal Suenens urged that religious be faithful to their constitutions and collaborate with lay people in their apostolic work by opening the doors and windows of the convents, not to let the world in but to let their spirit out.

Beginning where Mother Richarda left off, Mother Henrita strengthened the community's initial and ongoing formation programs as described in the next section. The leadership of these two prioresses had the sisters well on the way to meet the call to adaptation issued by Vatican II even before its documents were promulgated.

The 1957 novitiate class of thirty-nine novices, one of the last of such classes.

Impact on Community Formation

From her seventeen years of service as novice director, and later from the hours she spent in consultation with sisters discerning their departure from the community, Mother Henrita Osendorf was convinced that preparation of candidates should be the primary concern of the community. She, as had Mother Richarda Peters, began to attend to the problems surrounding formation by experimenting with the time parameters. However, the length of time spent in formation was not the crucial issue. The traditional concept of novitiate became more and more problematic. Formation patterns retained some of the ideologies of medieval culture even as they were brought to America. The novitiate had little resemblance to the life of ministry the sister would encounter once she completed the formation program.

An example that illustrates an anachronistic adherence to traditional practices of formation was the strict enclosure that segregated the novices even from the sisters of the community with whom they would be sharing their lives. Visits with the professed sisters were limited to once a month; more frequent visits were allowed only by special permission. The enclosure included living in separate quarters, sharing only the dining room (where they had a separate table) and the chapel. This was strictly enforced, so novices and sisters passed one another in a shroud of silence. Enclosure applied even more strictly to family and friends. A family visit was allowed once during the novitiate year. The exchange of letters was limited and censored. Ordinarily novices did not attend family weddings or funerals. Even the length of time spent in a hospital could jeopardize the canonicity of a novice's formation, so that she would have to repeat her novitiate.

There was a time when young women found the rigors of the formation program exciting and a challenging way to give themselves completely to God in prayer and work, in obedience and humility, in asceticism and self-denial. As the twentieth century moved into its last phase, candidates came from a society sophisticated in its psycho-sexual-social-spiritual development. Practices that stemmed from maternalism, legalism, and elitism were no longer held as sacred. In fact, religious life was not held in high regard. It was indeed a challenge for religious communities to evaluate their manner of directing formation, but Vatican Council II was clear in its mandate to adapt religious life to the changing conditions of modern life.

The formation directors of Saint Benedict's Monastery did not lag behind the national movement to update the formation program and to help the community take a new approach to formation. At the August 1968 Chapter meeting, they suggested that the major objectives of the formation program shift from an emphasis on rules and practices to scriptural-liturgical spirituality, community-oriented life, and a conversion of life involving both separation from and union with the world. The directors noted four major trends developing in initial formation among sisters nationwide: having formation teams rather than single directors for each stage, putting greater emphasis on the person, stressing community service to the Church and the world, and increasing opportunities for dialogue. The key word now was "flexibility"—in regard to both the age of candidates and to their progression through the stages. The directors quoted Father Roger Vossberg, director of vocations in the Diocese of St. Cloud: "The Holy Spirit is speaking to us through the vocation shortage to restructure religious life today in such a way that it will be meaningful to young people."[11] By fall of 1968, the proposals made at the August Chapter meeting were implemented, but despite all efforts, the number of candidates dropped severely. The last two large classes of thirty-nine novices were in 1957 and 1958. Instead of the envisioned continued growth in membership for which the community had expanded the novitiate in 1958, the number of novices dwindled from an average of twenty-five per year from 1958 to 1967, to an average of three per year from 1968 to 1978, notwithstanding an updated formation program.

The Sister Formation Movement within the nation and the community, followed by the mandates of Vatican Council II, laid the foundation for a holistic approach to religious life. It may not have produced the fruit of increased vocations that the sisters had anticipated, but it helped the sisters make the work of renewal a transformative experience rather than a mere rejection of oppressive structures and traditions. Mere rejection would not have given the community the insights and energizing force necessary to move creatively into the future that transformation gave them.

Vatican Council II[12]

In some ways Vatican Council II effected a re-creation of Christendom. The age-old silence between Church and the world, the Catholic Church and other faiths, and hierarchy and laity exploded into a dynamic dialogue. Pope John XXIII surprised the world by his sudden announcement on January 25, 1959, that he would convene an assembly, an ecumenical council of all the bishops in the world. This would be the first council since 1870 and the twenty-first in the history of the Church. He had complete confidence that the Holy Spirit was guiding him and that the time was ripe for an open dialogue to discern the church's role and method for preaching the Good News in the modern world. His simple, calm response to critics prior to the Council was: "The prophets of doom always talk as though the present, in comparison to the past, is becoming worse and worse. But I see [humankind] as entering upon a new order and perceive in this a divine mandate."[13]

That John XXIII was visionary in trusting his intuition about the Council was attested to by Dr. Albert C. Outler, an observer for the World Methodist Council who attended every session. In *Reluctant Dissenter*, James Patrick Shannon, one of the youngest bishops to attend Vatican Council II, shared Outler's eloquent testimony at a dinner honoring the observer delegates and the American bishops at the close of the Council:

> Here we are, virtually at the end of the most epochal event in modern church history, already in the initial stages of a new era, on the verge of the enormous undertakings [and confusions] of the postconciliar era. . . . There will be no more meetings of this sort again in our lifetime. Our ways from here lie in a thousand directions all in God's keeping. . . . The splendors of Vatican II— this strange interlude when we have been so strangely one—will fade and be filed in the archives of our memories. But a new advent of the Holy Spirit has happened in our world in our time—an epiphany of love that has stirred men's hearts wherever they have glimpsed it incarnate.[14]

A New Perspective of the Church

While Vatican II did not change fundamental Catholic doctrine, it did call for dramatic changes in Catholic culture—its worship, its dealing with other Christians and with non-Christians, its relationship to human/world culture, its evangelization, the role of its bishops, and its understanding of pluralism, diversity, and human freedom. It called for the development of new ministries and an expanded role of the laity in the Church. In fact, one of the most masterful strokes of genius of this Council was the new definition it gave to "Church" as "the People of God" in dialogue. This perspective was basic to all of its documents and effected a wide range of change in the postconciliar renewal of the Church. The conversion of hearts and the transformation of religious practices called for by Vatican II placed enormous strain on even the most zealous Catholics. With very little preparation, they were asked to modify deeply ingrained traditions of religious piety and practice. The adjournment of Vatican II in Rome marked the beginning of a vastly more difficult second phase, that of making the decrees of the Council intelligible and attractive to the People of God. This task was probably far more taxing than even the most far-sighted bishops anticipated as they left Rome in December 1965.

Implementing the renewal mapped out by Vatican II was taxing for American women religious, including those of Saint Benedict's Monastery, but thanks to Mother Richarda Peters and Mother Henrita Osendorf, when Pope John XXIII convoked Vatican Council II, many sisters were ready for it. They eagerly studied each document as it was released, particularly those affecting religious life. Many sisters found the new theological and scriptural nuances life-giving and in keeping with what they had experienced in their own lives and in working with the People of God. Some felt discomfort in the questioning of long-held customs and the crumbling of Church and convent mores, which to them seemed essential for the continued existence of the Church and religious life. For a number of sisters, changes were to come too late; for others they came too fast. Mother Henrita's charism was keeping her finger on the pulse of the community and quite accurately ascertaining its readiness to move into changes. She motivated the sisters to use this time of renewal as an opportunity for true conversion of heart and a return to the Benedictine charism and gospel values. What follows is a history of events in the process of renewal in which the sisters of Saint Benedict's Monastery engaged after Vatican II. It is also an acknowledgment of the ways in which the Holy Spirit empowers the grassroots with wisdom, goodness, and energy; imbues leadership with compassion, conviction, and courage; and creates a new community in the fusion of these two creative forces, grassroots and leadership. It does not happen easily or without pain. More than a result of conscious planning, a renewed community is a gift from God.

The People of God bless the 1998 golden jubilarians' renewal of religious profession.

2
MOVEMENTS OF CHANGE WITHIN COMMUNITY

Liturgy of the Hours

For many reasons the changes Vatican II proposed in liturgy or worship received priority in Saint Benedict's Monastery's renewal program. The aspect that most uniquely affected St. Benedict's was the change in the Liturgy of the Hours (the Divine Office or in monastic parlance, the *Opus Dei*, terms which may be used interchangeably). This prayer of the Church is at the heart of monastic life, but the sisters had experienced a constant struggle in their communal prayer from the time they set foot on American soil. In her book, *With Lamps Burning*, Sister Grace McDonald traced the sisters' struggle between the full recitation of the Liturgy of the Hours as they knew it in St. Walburga Abbey in Eichstätt, Bavaria, and the praying of the Little Office of the Blessed Virgin in the Minnesota foundation.

> In 1858 Abbot Boniface Wimmer, O.S.B., after establishing the American foundations, ordered the sisters to pray the Little Office of the Blessed Virgin to give them more time for their apostolates.
>
> By 1860 with increased numbers, the sisters returned to chanting the full Divine Office.

19

In 1865 Abbot Wimmer again interfered. He requested and received permission from Rome for the sisters to
pray the Little Office on all ferial (week) days.

In 1880 Mother Scholastica Kerst abolished the Divine Office altogether. The Little Office was to suppplant
the Divine Office at all times, ferial and festal days.

On November 1, 1926, the daily praying of the Divine
Office was reinstated by Mother Louisa Walz.

For nearly seventy years the sisters were able to keep
alive their yearning for the full Divine Office. The Liturgical
Movement in the 1920s gave them the necessary impetus to
restore their long-lost love, the Divine Office. Sister Grace
observed: "The love of the *Opus Dei* had never died out in the
community for down through the years many of the older
members lamented and regretted that they could not join
the Church in its official prayer."[15] Some sisters feared that
they were not true Benedictines because they did not pray
the Divine Office. Certainly their struggle is a manifestation
of the work of the Holy Spirit in creating and maintaining a
grassroots ground swell of enthusiasm for liturgical prayer
even at times of contrary legislation from leadership.

Sister Urban Gertken and the sisters' choir, 1956.

The chant text "Gaudeamus" often sung at the opening of the Eucharistic celebrations on feast days.

For fifty years after the restoration of the Divine Office, Sister Urban Gertken, choir director, worked with the sisters to maintain a manner of recitation befitting the praise of God. She also directed the study of Gregorian chant which was sung at liturgical services. Sisters still remember the many hours spent in choir practice. Saint Benedict's Monastery became well-known for its nearly perfect rendition of chant and has produced several recordings by the choir.

Though the sisters felt privileged to be deputed to pray the official prayer of the Church, the Divine Office posed two major problems: its language and its structure. Considered the official prayer of the Church, it was required to be prayed in the Church's official language, Latin. The structure of the Divine Office was inherited from the early monastics who interspersed their prayer hours throughout the day and night in order to fulfill the sacred number of praying seven times a day. Because it was reverenced as "the prayer of the Church," no one tampered with its content or style.

Sister Cecile Gertken, age ninety-eight, shares her love of chant with Novice Janine Mettling.

Prayer Language

Twenty years before Vatican Council II, the sisters decided to address the problem of Latin language. Their desire to understand what they were praying resulted in the translation of the entire Divine Office into English. The 1945-1946 class of novices typed and proofread the manuscript presenting the Divine Office in two parallel columns, Latin and English. When the manuscript was published by H. Dessain, Belgium Publishing House, as *The Monastic Diurnal* in August 1948, the community approached the Liturgy of the

Hours with a new fervor. Now it was possible to glance at the translation as the monastic choir prayed the Divine Office antiphonally or to pray it in English when one was not able to join the choir. Later on, as preparations were being made for Vatican Council II, the sisters got sneak previews of the document on the liturgy through Father Godfrey Diekmann, O.S.B., from Saint John's Abbey, one of the Council's *periti* (experts) on liturgy. The community was fully prepared, then, to make its first major change in the area of liturgy by praying the Liturgy of the Hours in English on December 4, 1963, using the translation given in *The Monastic Diurnal*. The sisters experienced the vernacular at their Eucharistic celebration on the first Sunday of Advent in 1964, as did many parishes throughout the United States. At the same time, the vernacular was also gradually introduced in the community's rituals of investiture of novices, profession of vows, and installation of the prioress.

There were sisters who felt that moving into the vernacular stripped the sense of the "mystery of God" from their experience of prayer. In fact, a strong minority of sisters believed that dropping the Latin meant that the Divine Office no longer held its traditional role and status. In a letter to Bishop Paul Leonard Hagarty, O.S.B., monk of Saint John's Abbey and bishop of the Bahamas, who was in Rome at the time, Mother Henrita Osendorf asked: "Does reciting the Divine Office in the vernacular still constitute saying the official prayer of the church? . . . This question has caused great unrest in the Community, with strong feelings on both sides, as you know."[16] Bishop Hagarty reassured her that Vatican II had wholeheartedly endorsed the use of the vernacular in the official prayer of the Church.

The next problem with language came very soon after the community had created its new Resource Book which served as the basis for experimentation with the Liturgy of the Hours. The general growing sensitivity to sexist, militaristic, and culture-bound words demanded a change in prayer-language. Prayer is the privileged time for attitudes of non-violence and peace, inclusivity and solidarity, and a loving relationship with God to grow in the hearts of those who pray. The first step taken to alleviate this problem in the 1970s and 1980s entailed the tedious crossing out of undesirable words and writing in substitute words. The translations used in the new Prayer Books in 1990 were alert to the language problem. Language evolves so rapidly, however, that it continued to offer challenges, and not all sisters agreed on the importance of language sensitivity in praying the Liturgy of the Hours.

Prayer Structures

The problem of the structure of the Divine Office was just as challenging as its language. The sisters had to wait for Rome to make changes if they wished to pray the official prayer of the Church. The Office consisted of multiple prayer "hours"—Lauds, the Little Hours of Prime, Terce, Sext, and None, Vespers, Compline, and Matins—which were to be interspersed throughout the day and night. Demands of professional schedules had resulted in the grouping of prayer hours and excusing those not living at the motherhouse from praying Matins, the longest of the prayer hours, which was formerly prayed as a vigil or before dawn.

Vatican II's *Constitution on the Liturgy* changed this legalistic and inflexible approach and simplified the structure of the Divine Office. Article 89 of the *Constitution on the Liturgy* declared that Lauds as morning prayer and Vespers as evening prayer were the hinges on which the daily Office turns. They were defined as the chief hours and were to be celebrated as such. Article 91 also addressed the number of psalms to be said, no longer requiring that the entire Book of Psalms be prayed in one week but be distributed over longer periods of time. In response to these guidelines, monastic communities tended to gather at least three times daily for prayer and to pray seventy-five to 100 psalms weekly.

The sisters on the local missions welcomed the opportunity to experiment with restructuring the Liturgy of the

Hours to fit their situations. The order and number of psalms and the choice of readings were left to their discretion. As a result, individual sisters created prayers to replace the Liturgy of the Hours that many sisters questioned as appropriate substitutions for public communal prayer. The experimentation also became a tedious work as the sisters prepared an Office for each week. For this reason, the Community Council set up the Liturgy Committee (operative to the present) to study Church directives on liturgy, to inform the sisters about these directives, and to guide the implementation of liturgical changes. Following these guidelines in their work of restructuring the Liturgy of the Hours, the committee announced in 1968 that there would be one Office for all of the sisters, with two major Hours being celebrated in each house—Morning Praise and Evening Praise. In addition, Vigil or Noon Prayer was to be prayed at the motherhouse.

Since creating an Office Book demands a great deal of research, the Liturgy Committee first prepared a Resource Book in the 1970s, which contained psalms and canticles from which sisters constructed their daily morning and evening prayer. It was indeed a day for rejoicing when in 1990 the sisters finally had Morning, Evening, and Noon Prayer in Office Books including the chant and familiar hymnody that were tailored specifically for Saint Benedict's Monastery. The experience of renewing the prayer of the Church rejuvenated the sisters' appreciation for communal prayer, which continues to be the heart of their monastic life. Throughout the renewal period, the Liturgy Committee and leadership reminded the community of the core meaning of the Church's call to transform its official prayer: "The reform is not an emphasis on how many psalms are to be said, but rather on the psalms as *lectio divina,* and the stress on contemplation."[17] The renewed Liturgy of the Hours was to create a better balance between prayer and work. Mother Henrita assured the community: "the aim sought in all liturgical change is not less prayer, but better prayer."[18]

The community assembles three times daily to praise God.

New Liturgical Understandings

Because of the sisters' experience of adapting the Liturgy of the Hours, the changes regarding the celebration of the Eucharist were, no doubt, less painful for the community than they were for parishes throughout the United States. November 1967 marked the first Eucharist celebrated with the priest facing the community. It took another year before the sisters received communion in the hand and under both species. In 1970 sisters served as Eucharistic ministers. Because liturgical functions are often the setting of important community rituals, it was not difficult to introduce the practice of sisters giving the homilies, a welcome and common practice. It must be acknowledged that the community had what many parishes did not have, chaplains like Fathers Michael Marx, O.S.B., (1956 to 1962) and Vitus Bucher, O.S.B., (1969 to 1978) both from Saint John's Abbey, whose gift of teaching and relating to the sisters won

Sister Celine Kraker, the first sister commissioned as a Eucharistic minister in the Diocese of St. Cloud, serving St. Michael's Parish in Buckman, 1970.

their trust. These two chaplains carefully prepared the sisters for liturgical changes.

The rationale for the changes in liturgy can be traced to the new perspective that Vatican II proposed, the perspective of the Church as the People of God. That fundamental concept had exciting and far-reaching consequences. It changed the traditional hierarchical model of Church to a circular image of community. All members of the Church were now recognized as members through baptism, having equal responsibility for living its inner life and carrying out its mission. The basic purpose of all liturgical renewal was, and continues to be, the strengthening of this social awareness and its attending social responsibilities. Worship of God must flow into actions of love, justice, and peace. Actually, a path for these new liturgical understandings was paved by the reforms of Pope Pius X in 1903, and the Liturgical Movement in the 1920s. Pius X had made the word of God in scripture and sacrament more accessible to the faithful. Father Virgil Michel, O.S.B., from Saint John's Abbey, devoted his life's energies, to raising awareness of such concepts of Church as the "Mystical Body of Christ" and "universal priesthood." These concepts became even more meaningful to the sisters when one of their members, Sister Jeremy Hall, described Father Virgil's contributions to this movement in her book, *The Full Stature of Christ*, in 1976.

Because the Liturgical Movement had already introduced the sisters to the new understandings later promulgated by Vatican II, they welcomed the Council's stamp of approval on changes in liturgical practices that flowed from these understandings. Changing to the vernacular, creating a circle-community around the Eucharistic table, and sharing more fully in the ministry of the word were simply external manifestations of the profundity of the mystery of Church, a mystery which has not yet been fully plumbed, nor have the social implications been fully grasped. The sisters have worked assiduously in creating liturgies that celebrate the mystery of the Church as People of God. Hence, many are finding the liturgical worship in Sacred Heart Chapel, and the welcoming environment provided by the sisters, a true experience of Church and of God in their times of daily or weekly worship and in accepting liturgy's challenge to live in love, justice, and peace.

Worshippers moving from the introductory liturgy in the Gathering Place into the Chapel.

Community Life Styles

Some changes since the 1960s "just seemed to happen." There were no directives in the documents of Vatican II to guide the community in its plunge into changing life styles and changing styles of governance. There was simply the grassroots' feeling of dissonance in the life they had been experiencing. The Sister Formation Conference exposed them to changing principles of theology, spirituality, and psychology that they shared with sisters across the nation through the conference's bulletin. The conference questioned why there should be such a tension or dichotomy between the sisters' spiritual and intellectual formation and between their lives as religious and as professionals as they served the needs of the Church.

Twenty years before Vatican Council II, Pope Pius XII had offered a glimmer of hope, which gradually freed religious to question seriously the "convent culture" that seemed to be such a bastion of immutable structures. He cautioned sisters to make sure that outdated customs and asceticism did not form barriers to religious vocations. In 1954 in an encyclical, *Sacra Virginitas*, he spoke of the life dedicated to virginity and what it could mean in the context of the present world.[19] Having opened the door to change and having encouraged the formation of national conferences for collaboration among religious orders, Pope Pius XII had set the stage for the renewal programs that swept across the American scene when Vatican II convened from 1963 to 1965.

No doubt membership and participation in the national leadership conferences gave Mother Henrita Osendorf the wisdom to listen to the rising strong concerns for more human and collegial living situations. The structured convent life style was certainly one of the barriers to attracting religious vocations. Traditionally, the sisters at the motherhouse and large local missions lived in close quarters, often sleeping in dormitory arrangements, six to ten in a room, or, if they were lucky, with two or three in a room. At times of "recreation" (that is, conversation) the entire community gathered together, with small-group interaction possible only sporadically. For most of the day and certainly at night, their times together were spent in silence. Their meals too were generally taken in silence or with table reading. Strong friendships between individuals were not encouraged, and even visits to each other's local mission or to the motherhouse were discouraged. Most sisters simply accepted these anachronistic practices as part of the life they had chosen in order to dedicate themselves to a life of prayer and service to the Church. Though the regime of discipline left some psychological scars, it also offered entertainment years later as the sisters shared their stories of how common sense and humor allowed them to "beat the system." Most sisters did not judge their past experiences as "wrong." Their experience of religious life was not that different from their traditional German family life, their Catholic education, and their experience as women in a society and Church that had been inculturated to "protect the weaker sex" and to expect a "ladylike" compliance. The problem was simply that some past structures and disciplines no longer fit twentieth century American culture.

Experimental Community Living Groups

Questions of life style, authority, obedience, and decision-making became urgent in the late 1960s. In response, Mother Henrita established a Restructuring Committee in December 1967 to consult with her and her council on studying, evaluating and directing ways of helping the community face and implement changes in these areas. Programs such as *Interact* and *Building Faith Community* were initiated to strengthen relationships so that a dialogue of sharing ideas, hopes, and concerns would deepen the sisters' appreciation for the growing diversity within its membership.[20] The rapidity of the changes might otherwise have polarized the community. Surveys and questionnaires were also used to keep the sisters connected with one another

Sister Leonore Mandernach.

Sister Janelle Sietsema.

Small community groups provide a base for community discussions and provide parties and pancakes for the motherhouse community.

and with administration. A subcommittee on Collegial Living Experimentation was appointed to evaluate the expectations and options for living situations.

The first subgroup to request experimentation at Saint Benedict's Monastery came from Caedmon House in 1968. This group of eight sisters requested separate housing with collegial living and shared leadership in which to experience a life style that would encourage individual responsibility, facilitate personal development, and strengthen relationships. Though they would have community events in their own group, they planned to attend Eucharist and to share some meals and some of the Liturgy of the Hours with the total motherhouse community. A similar request followed in the spring of 1969 from sisters who would form Riverside community in St. Cloud. Both requests were granted in the summer of 1969.[21]

The following spring, new guidelines were established for providing leadership on local missions. Traditionally the prioress had appointed superiors for each group. Sisters were now given the option of electing the coordinator or having a team approach. In the 1970s, guidelines were in place to enable subgroupings within the large community of sisters living at the motherhouse. The requests for small-group living outnumbered suitable living quarters at the motherhouse by 1973. That initiated a gradual renovation of living areas at the motherhouse, providing for a lounge, kitchenette, and neighboring bedrooms for subgroups, and a gradual division of the entire community into small groups with the understanding that each sister would be affiliated with a group. While these groups formed a more intimate "home base" for the sisters, the total community at the motherhouse maintained its prayer, meals, and work schedule in common.

The innovation of small groups within the community brought blessings and challenges: the blessings of increased community bonding and dialogue, and the challenges of moving in and out of these groups. A deeper concern for some sisters, however, was the question of the compatibility of small-group living with Benedictine spirituality. These sisters felt that the authority of a superior was a necessary component for every community group. Others felt that the community already had that necessary component by electing a prioress to whom all were ultimately accountable. To allay fears in this regard, Sister Evin Rademacher, prioress (1973 to 1981), appointed deans as Benedict suggested in his rule (RB 21:1) to act as liaisons between the leadership and local groups. Her successor, Sister Katherine Howard, continued that practice. In addition, the custom of referring to the prioress as "mother" was then discontinued because "sister" more aptly described the interdependent relationship of membership and leadership.

Questions about authority and obedience began to take on a different perspective as the sisters experienced the demands of listening with "the ear of the heart" (RB Prologue: 1) while participating in community meetings aimed at reflection and discernment. Arriving at collegial decisions both in their local groups and in Chapter meetings took time and called for faith and patience. The sisters were much more accustomed to giving a spiritual motivation to the functional and utilitarian value of authority and obedience in maintaining order within community. They may have been surprised by the discipline and motivation required in the listening, participation, consultation, and subsidiarity demanded by discernment. In fact, though, they were merely claiming more fully the Benedictine principle that every member of the community is to have a voice in its decision-making process.

Community Decision-Making Process

The Rule of Benedict is amazing in its legislation concerning the community's decision-making process: "As often as anything important is to be done in the monastery, the [prioress] shall call the whole community together and [her]self explain what the business is. . . . The reason why we have said all should be called for counsel is that the Lord often reveals what is better to the younger" (RB 3:1-2). Having experienced the opportunity of taking more personal responsibility in their community groupings, the sisters began to look for ways of becoming more involved in over-all community affairs and decision-making. To clarify the community's decision-making processes, Dr. William Sexton, instructor on Human Relations and Management at the University of Notre Dame, was invited to speak to the Chapter. He urged the sisters to work on a collegial process, to identify attitudes and to get the pulse of the community by providing opportunities for sharing values. He expressed enthusiasm for what he saw as a trend in religious communities to use the discernment process.[22] Sister Evin Rademacher followed up on his suggestions by initiating area meetings between Chapter meetings so that the communication could filter from the grassroots to the Administration and among the sisters themselves.

There had been a growing concern in the 1960s among community members that important matters were sometimes decided by the Council rather than by the Chapter, such as moving from ownership to sponsorship (See Part II). Under the leadership of Sister Evin, a Community Synod was formed in 1974 to allow for grassroots' gathering of information, ascertaining readiness for action, and making recommendations regarding concerns voiced by community members. Important concerns surfaced, such as the manner of placement of sisters in work situations, the sisters' work-oriented mentality, the development of simple life styles, the development of potential leadership in community, and the sisters' image and role in the changing world. Even though the sisters found the Synod meetings informative and life-giving in the dialogue and bonding that occurred there, they also found the growing number of meetings taxing. The number of Chapter meetings a year had doubled in the renewal period, and often there was need for small group and regional meetings to prepare for the Chapter meetings. It was also difficult to coordinate the

Synod and Chapter agendas, so the Synod was discontinued in 1980 with some regret concerning the loss of collegiality and subsidiarity that it had provided.

Discovering the Discernment Approach to Decision-making

For large groups, such as Saint Benedict's Monastery, a gap can easily exist between theoretical and real opportunities for members to have a voice at the Chapter meetings. To further close that gap, Sister Evin suggested a study of the discernment process: "Our goal is a condition in which, in a spirit of prayerful discernment and mindful of the good of the whole, each sister, leader, living group, and total Community understand the various areas of decision-making responsibility and freely act accordingly."[23] It took some years and earnest practice before that goal began to be realized.

During Sister Katherine Howard's term as prioress (1981 to 1989), the Chapter formally adopted the discernment process of shared wisdom as the process to be used at Chapters of election of prioress, to which a three-day period was allotted. The revised process was used for the first time in the election of Sister Mary Reuter as prioress on April 30, 1989. The Election Committee reminded the sisters about the mode and pace of discernment:

> [It] is indicative of slowness, gentleness, tentativeness, and collaboration, as opposed to speed and efficiency, absoluteness, competition, and control. . . . Discernment, particularly [in the] early stage of the total process, is not so much about content as about formation. . . . As we create an atmosphere of prayerful reflection, of silence and surrender, we make a space where the Spirit can touch us deeply.[24]

Calling forth leadership qualities from a broader segment of the community received a major boost in the early 1990s when, under Sister Mary's leadership, the discernment process was also applied to the election of council members and Federation delegates. The process provided opportunities for the members of the Chapter to discuss and reach a consensus in small groups, preparing a slate of nominees for these roles. Before 1990, the same names tended to appear on the slate year after year, but this new process achieved its purpose of surfacing names that had not been considered previously. The variety of personalities and backgrounds enlarged considerably, along with a wider age spread. An adaptation of the discernment process continues to be used in making other important Chapter decisions such as setting directions for the Community.

Model of Decision-making in the Monastery

In closing her term, Sister Mary reported that decision-making issues needed further clarification:

> Understanding the nature of decision-making is important. It is often a process occurring over time rather than a discrete occurrence. The participation in arriving at a decision varies depending on the issue. The process needs to be appropriate so it does not become paralyzed by unrealistic expectations. Questions such as, who makes what decisions, what does it mean that the chapter is the governing body, are challenging us and need resolution.[25]

Shortly after her election as prioress in 1995, Sister Ephrem Hollermann and the Council responded to this challenge by appointing a committee to study the documents governing the monastery's decision-making process and to make recommendations for necessary clarifications. Taking the Gospel, the *Rule of St. Benedict*, and *Upon This Tradition* (document of the American Benedictine Prioresses, 1975) as the foundational guidelines, the committee studied the *General and Specific Norms of the Federation of St. Benedict and Its Member Monasteries* and the monastery's *Handbook of Monastic Norms*. They prepared a statement to clarify the interrelatedness of the monastery's governance system, which consists of the prioress, the Chapter, the Council, the Leadership Team/Staff, the Program and Department Directors, Committees, Task Teams and *Ad Hoc* Groups, and the individual sisters. This statement was discussed in community groups and at area and Chapter meetings. The final statement, *Model of Decision-Making in the Monastery: An Interrelated Governance System*, was presented to the Chapter in August 1999 and received the final approval of the Chapter in January 2000. This allowance of time and of membership participation witnesses to the importance the sisters have placed on their decision-making responsibilities.

Many influences converge to effect change, but often there is a cornerstone upon which the whole structure depends. The one most effective influence in changing the way sisters lived together in community, made decisions and developed a deeper understanding of authority and obedience, was again Vatican II's definition of the Church as the People of God. Before Vatican II, spiritual writers had spoken of a Benedictine community as a "little church," so the former hierarchical model of Church aptly described the structures of authority and obedience that characterized religious life in the mid-twentieth century. As soon as this pyramid-image collapsed into the circle-image, authority found its rightful place within the circle of the People of God at the service of God and the community. This began to have important ramifications in the way the sisters related to one another in community and, as we shall see in **Part II**, in the way they related to others in their services to the Church and to the world.

Witness and Outward Signs of Religious Life

The first change that comes to people's minds when they hear about the post-Vatican II renewal of religious life is the change in clothing. Surprisingly, that change came more slowly and with more pain and labor than did most other changes. This difficulty is understandable when one realizes how the wearing of the religious habit was intimately intertwined with witnessing to the role of religious in the vision of the Church and the world. That role had been an ambivalent one of religious being placed on a pedestal but of having no voice, so, for example, the religious had no role at the Council. Very likely the religious did not expect to have a role, nor did it occur to the Church authorities to give them one. At a meeting in Santo Domingo sponsored by CELAM and the LCWR/CMSM in February 1994, Archbishop Rembert G. Weakland, O.S.B., former Abbot Primate of the Benedictine Order, described the problem of this evolving role of religious:

> Religious, like priests, seemed to have fared less well [than the bishops and laity] in Council documents. In preparing the documents on religious life, religious themselves did not play a significant role. They seemed then to take their historical place in the Church for granted and did not articulate a new vision for themselves. It must be stated that religious welcomed the abolishing of the degrees of perfection, even if such a change may have seemed to diminish their prestige and privileged place within the Church. . . . Neither the section of Lumen Gentium that dealt with religious life . . . nor Perfectae Caritatis . . . came to terms with [how] the new perspectives that make up the whole of the Council's vision [impacted on the reality of religious life]. Just as the priesthood did not receive from the Council a new impetus, so the image of religious life did not shine forth as totally integrated into a newly defined mission of the Church.[26]

The lack of clarity concerning the role of religious who were not ordained resulted in ambivalent treatment when controversies arose.

For religious themselves to come to a new vision of their life in the Church was a long hard road. It began slowly when in 1952 Pope Pius XII issued the challenges to religious to adapt their lives to contemporary needs.[27] Also, the question of dichotomies that the Sister Formation Conference had raised in the mid-1950s demanded a new vision of religious life.

However, Mother Richarda Peters' response to the growing unrest was to reaffirm the traditional ideals of religious life. Thus, she urged the sisters to intensify their striving for perfection by renewed faithfulness to the monastic practices, especially of poverty and reverence for one another. Mother Richarda's insistence on the cultivation of a monastic spirit was credible because she herself was an exemplary religious and a model of decorum lightened by a wry sense of humor. In her firm commitment to religious life, she pursued introducing the ritual of Consecration of Virgins at Saint Benedict's Monastery in 1954. The Church's prayer in this ceremony reassured the sisters of their privileged status as religious. By 1975 when it was discontinued, seventeen groups had renewed their vowed commitments in this ancient ritual. By then, it was recognized by many that the language of the ritual seemed to set religious on a pedestal that did not resonate well with the new perspective of Church promulgated by Vatican II.

Mother Richarda's request for the Consecration of Virgins at St. Benedict's reminded authorities in Rome that the American Benedictine women had indeed achieved a unique character and were considered *moniales* even though they professed simple vows. Rome's long-held and unfortunate distinction between *sorores* (sisters in simple vows engaged in apostolic services) and *moniales* (sisters in solemn vows living a contemplative life withdrawn from the world in papal enclosure) had separated Benedictine women with these different monastic orientations. It also created an apparent dichotomy between "contemplation" and "action" in general. The Consecration of Virgins ritual had been a privilege reserved for enclosed religious in solemn vows. In her own way, Mother Richarda was able to cut to the heart of the problem and convince Rome that simple vows were not that different from solemn vows, though she was not ready for Pope Pius XII's more radical approach in examining the validity of traditions related to enclosure.

Rather than endorsing the status quo, Pope Pius XII cautioned religious in 1952 to examine outdated customs and asceticism and thus called into question the concept of enclosure and the various ways of expressing it. In this context he suggested a simplification of the religious habit.[28] The ground work was laid, ten years prior to Vatican II, for the sisters' growing discomfort with the perception of religious life as a "state of perfection" and the questioning of the religious clothing that set them apart. Serious discussion among sisters about the religious habit as a necessary, even though often misunderstood, witness of religious life, gradually emerged all over the nation. Mother Henrita Osendorf had barely begun her term as prioress in 1961 when she recognized the need to deal with the issue.

Modifying the Religious Habit

Since it was easier for the religious superiors to discuss the question of clothing among themselves first, the prioresses asked to have the question on the agenda of the Federation General Chapter in July 1963. They decided that each priory should appoint a committee to study simplification of the habit. Mother Henrita and the Community Council immediately appointed a committee to survey other communities also considering a clothing change and to study options for a modified headdress. It was a challenge to invent ways of keeping the veil on the head without pinning it on the head pieces, the coif, and band. The latter two were considered particularly undesirable for health reasons. No prescriptions were included in Rome's mandates to modify the habit, but some communities were advised that the head and ears should not be tightly covered because of many reports of resulting scalp and ear problems. Little did the authorities realize the far greater damage to the human, feminine psyche in having one wardrobe for all seasons, activities, and occasions, hiding the identity and individuality of the sisters in yards of serge.

More than any other change, the change in clothing aroused fear and emotion. Some saw the habit as a hin-

Try sports in long skirts and flowing scapulars.

drance to realizing the contemporary role of religious in the Church; others saw it as a necessary witness, a symbol that had become a part of their identity. To keep the occurring changes in perspective, Mother Henrita challenged the sisters to live lives of continual conversion, renewed from within through a deeper union with Christ. She especially urged faithful adherence to the Benedictine values and observance of personal poverty. At a Chapter meeting in 1965, she advised the sisters: "The worst thing that could happen to the community is . . . that its members become spiritually bankrupt." Later she cautioned: " Sometimes we can suffer greater anguish over changes in superficial things than over essentials."[29] Because the habit had been so closely linked to the identity of a religious, Mother Henrita waited three years to allow the sisters to adjust to the notion of a change in the habit. First, the Chapter approved experimentation with the headdress on December 29, 1966. One year later, it also approved experimentation with a modified habit, limiting the colors to gray, white, and black.

At St. Benedict's, controversy over the veil as the minimal symbol of religious profession lasted until 1977 when it was discontinued as the symbol of consecration to God. The community accepted the wearing of the distinctive ring as the official outward sign of religious life. Optional wearing of the veil was allowed before then, but it was expected that the veil would be worn on special days, such as profession of vows and jubilees. This requirement for the occasion of their jubilee celebrations caused no end of anxiety and anger for some sisters who had already chosen not to wear the veil. The decision of 1977 finally brought peace and ended the community's struggles concerning the religious habit.

This summary is, of course, an over-simplification of all the intervening events, both serious and humorous, that occurred between the first and last stages of experimentation with changes of clothing. The tension was interspersed with laughter over style shows that offered options for modification of the habit and the quandary of the Habit Committee because a sister had worn a black-and-white polka-dot blouse for Easter! Was that within the intention of the community in limiting colors to gray, white, or black?

The saving feature of this period of experimentation with clothing was the insistence of the community and the Leadership that change in the habit be optional as it continues to be to the present. Observing the variety in dress among the sisters may seem strange to outsiders, but to community members that sensitivity to an individual sister's preferences is an important symbol of the acceptance of diversity, an acceptance which had grown during the period of transition.

Through it all, Mother Henrita's guiding principle was that "[t]he ultimate question in regard to the clothing of religious is not the kind of dress a religious should wear, but why she wears it, and what she and the world in which she lives expect from it."[30] For the early monastics, wearing the clothing provided by the monastery symbolized the complete dispossession required of those entering the community. The sisters realized that in former ages monastics did not wear complicated habits; the clothing of the monastery was that of the average middle-class people where they lived. The Benedictine sisters' coif, the pleated tight-fitting headgear, however, originated in society's elite class of the Middle

Sisters Renee Rau, Phyllis Zuzek, Thomas Carey, and Cortona Justen enjoying their diversity of dress.

Ages. People in general did not know this historical background and were puzzled by the sisters' apparent loss of identity. Benedict's expectations regarding dress were clear and simple. Moderation and simplicity were the hallmarks of the *Rule of St. Benedict.* Monastics were not to complain about the color or coarseness of the articles of clothing they received from the monastery but were to be satisfied with what was available in the vicinity at a reasonable cost. When they received new clothing, the old was to be put aside for the poor. That religious were to be set apart by the clothing they wore was part of the gradual and unfortunate elevation of religious life as a special state of perfection superior to all other states, except the priesthood. For many, the change in religious dress signified the realization that religious life is simply one of many ways of living the Gospel, all of which are privileged vocations from God.

During this period of modifying the religious habit, some sisters also returned to their baptismal names, especially if they had received masculine names at the time of their profession of vows. After Vatican II, the growing appreciation of the importance of the rite of initiation or baptism de-emphasized the rite of religious profession as a "second baptism," which had traditionally meant that religious were given a new name. That practice had been another loss of identity, which was considered an important part of the asceticism of religious life. Another principle that guided Mother Henrita in making changes was: "There must be freedom for the Community to grow from within. . . . Evolving changes, as well as radical ones, should always remain a genuine possibility."[31] That their religious community was not a fixed entity and that its unity derived from a deep love rather than from external uniform appearances or loss of individuality, are wise legacies deeply imbedded in the hearts of the sisters.

The most important outcome of the change of dress was the community's grappling with their understanding of their lives as religious in the Church. In the end, religious life remains a mystery, evading legal definitions and never fully grasped because it falls in the category of charisms in the Church. It is a gift from the Holy Spirit for the good of the Church. In examining the implications of this truth, the sisters find inspiration for the living out of religious life today.

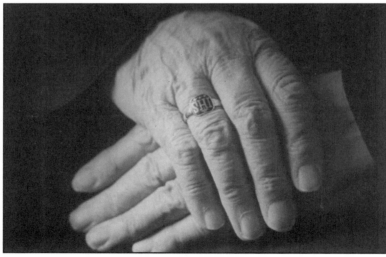

The ring, symbol of the sisters' final profession of vows.

MONASTIC SOURCES REVISITED

Returning to the Founding Charism

The directive from the Vatican II document, *Perfectae Caritatis*, most quoted by religious, was that the charism of the founder/foundress was to be examined so it might again inspire contemporary religious. At first, most apostolic-oriented religious congregations interpreted this directive as a mandate to shed the monastic traditions that had gradually crept into their lives. As the constitutions of these groups had been modified over the years for approval by Rome, they had moved more and more toward the monastic model in regulations of enclosure, the prayer schedule, and other traditions and practices. By the 1990s, however, it was generally recognized that the monastic quest for God is the common impulse of all religious groups.

On the other hand, revisions of the Code of Canon Law had stripped American Benedictine women of their distinctive monastic identity by characterizing them more like a modern apostolic congregation. The sisters of Saint Benedict's Monastery, however, had all along focused on their monastic character, so the burning questions of renewal for them were: "Are these changes in keeping with the Benedictine monastic charism?" and "How can the monastery maintain its Benedictine character in the face of the growing demands made upon it by its apostolic ministries?" These were not new questions for the community.

In her insightful book, *The Reshaping of a Tradition*, Sister Ephrem Hollermann traces the struggles that the Benedictine sisters from Eichstätt had with the question of their monastic identity from their beginnings in America in 1852 to 1881.[32] She shows how American Benedictines forged for themselves new perspectives as they responded to the American experience. They reshaped the essential elements of the traditional monastic way of life into a unique expression of life according to the *Rule of St. Benedict*. In 1981, Sister Incarnata Girgen had published *Behind the Beginnings*, the heart-rending letters of Mother Benedicta Riepp in her struggle with authorities to maintain the autonomy of the sisters' true identity as monastics.[33] For the sisters, then, the mandate to return to their sources included an invitation to return to the faith and courage of their foremothers, Mother Benedicta Riepp, venerated as the foundress of the American foundation of Benedictine women from Eichstätt, and Mother Willibalda Scherbauer, the first prioress (1857 to 1868) of the Minnesota foundation. Mother Benedicta and Mother Willibalda are both buried in St. Benedict's cemetery in St. Joseph, Minnesota. Their death anniversaries are marked by special prayers. On Heritage Day, July 22, the anniversary of their coming to Minnesota, the sisters celebrate their foremothers with special prayers and a procession to the cemetery. On several Heritage Days, a group of sisters took a boat ride up the Mississippi River from Min-

Mother Willibalda Scherbauer, first prioress of the Minnesota Benedictine foundation.

neapolis-St. Paul to replicate the experience of Mother Willibalda with three sisters and two candidates aboard the *North Star* on the last lap of their journey to St. Cloud. On the 140th anniversary of their coming to Minnesota, citizens of Waal, Germany, homeplace of Mother Benedicta, came to celebrate with the community. Previously, the citizens of Waal had invited sisters for the dedication of a monument to Mother Benedicta in Waal. There resulted not only a Mon-astery-Waal relationship, but also a sister-city relationship between St. Joseph and Waal. All these events keep the spir-it of the foundresses alive in the hearts of the sisters.

Mother Benedicta Riepp's grave marker in St. Benedict's cemetery.

Discerning Monastic Identity

The question concerning their monastic identity is an on-going search for the sisters, requiring faith, honesty, courage, confrontation, and charity. That search was nurtured throughout the last half of the twentieth century by the prioresses' concern for monastic observance, skillful guidance of the renewal to focus on monastic life, and the call for a commitment to make St. Benedict's primarily a monastic center. The community experienced a continual reinforcement of the monastic charism through conferences, workshops, and in setting community goals, objectives, and directions for the future.

Sister Katherine Howard summarized the community's outreach and strong, vital internal life on missioning day of August 2, 1986. She observed that Vatican II's mandate to renew religious life called the sisters to two simultaneous processes: a continuous return to the sources of all Christian life and to the original inspiration behind a given community, and an adjustment to the changed conditions of the time. She affirmed the community's renewal process: "We have been deeply involved in both [goals] and have been making conscious efforts to re-appropriate and articulate the charism of our community as a monastic community of Benedictines from Europe re-founded in America."[34] Continuing the summary, Sister Katherine pointed to the community and Council goals and objectives along with the Lifelong Formation programs of the twenty years after Vatican II and observed that:

> Our common programs including lectures, retreats, workshops, courses, and conferences have been designed to try to help us integrate those values within our lives, individually and as a community, in our development, whether of personal or communal development, in our contemporary world . . . and [especially in] our own development as women.[35]

The first of such total community retreat/workshops was planned in 1972 by Sister Norita Lanners, the renewal

Mother Henrita and Sister Norita Lanners enjoying the success of the first total-community Renewal Week.

director. In a week-long experience of reflection and relaxation, the sisters reveled in being together for such an extended time and in sharing the insights into scriptural and Benedictine spirituality given by Father Demetrius Dumm, O.S.B., of St. Vincent Archabbey, Latrobe, Pennsylvania. Over six hundred sisters attended this community event and often thereafter referred to the "field of flowers," the Gospel image of God's providential love that characterized Father Demetrius' presentations. Another retreat/workshop conducted by Father Colman Grabert, O.S.B., of St. Meinrad's Abbey, St. Meinrad, Indiana, is remembered as the first critical study of the *Rule of St. Benedict* undertaken as a community. Sister Katherine continued to nurture communal development by initiating the practice of the prioress giving conferences on a regular basis. Her talks were oriented to contemplative prayer and the inner transformations effected by monastic tradition and practices.

The sisters had carefully scrutinized every change of the postconciliar renewal with the question, "Is it Benedictine?" and realized that the search for identity must go on in every age to keep it relevant for the contemporary work of furthering the reign of God in that age. Still, they hoped for some blueprint of the past to guide them through the challenges of the twentieth century, which was swiftly moving into the twenty-first century.

Revision of Constitutions

Perhaps the blueprint and the security for which some sisters were looking in order to answer their questions about their monastic identity were the directives given them by their constitutional documents. These directives were also being challenged. Therefore, another incentive for the sisters to revisit their monastic tradition for wisdom and inspiration in adapting to the contemporary scene came from the mandate given in the Vatican II document, *Perfectae Caritatis*: ". . . Constitutions, directories . . . and similar compilations are to be suitably revised and brought into harmony with the documents of this sacred synod. This task will require the suppression of outmoded regulations."

Constitutions are important because Rome's approval of the constitutions of religious communities formally establish them as ecclesial institutions. In the past, Rome had looked for an assurance in these documents that practices traditionally espoused by religious were observed. Thus, the constitutions had become notoriously legalistic and detailed in their description of and prescriptions for religious life. For example, one community noted that in their constitutions thirty acts were mentioned explicitly for which their sisters needed the permission of the local or general superior. Obviously, there was little freedom for sisters to make their own decisions.

At last the responsibility for their documents rested with the sisters themselves. Here was their opportunity to give expression to the vision that too often lay buried under legalistic definitions. Here too was their challenge to come to a consensus in describing their identity as monastic women. The document that governed the sisters of Saint Benedict's Monastery, *Declarations and Constitutions*, was the general one that governed all the member priories of the Federation of St. Benedict. The first edition had been submitted in the mid-1940s as part of the process of establishing the Congregation of St. Benedict. The Decree of Praise, issued in March 1947, gave the approval of Pope Pius XII for the establishment of the congregation and approved its document, *Declarations and Constitutions*, for a trial period of seven years. It had been revised and submitted to Rome for approval in 1956 under the direction of Mother Richarda Peters, president of the congregation. After Vatican II, the responsibility for its second revision again rested with the General Chapter of the Federation. In the mid-1960s under the direction of Mother Athanasius Braegelman, O.S.B., member of St. Scholastica Priory in Duluth and president of the Federation, the General Chapter, appointed a committee to begin the project. The committee consisted of one member from each priory. Sister Evin Rademacher was the representative of St. Benedict's on this committee. The committee members met summer after summer and each year took back to their respective priories the fruit of their labor for the sisters' study and response.

Creating Life-giving Documents

The *Declarations and Constitutions* had an interesting format. It combined the aspects of spirituality and canonicity into declarations on every passage of the *Rule of St. Benedict* that needed explanation, specification, or adaptation. Hence, the layout of the *Rule* determined the framework of the document. Though this framework was interesting and effective in some respects, Mother Athanasius identified a problem in embedding the theological elements within the juridic elements. She felt that the document lost "soul" or spirit in doing so. She asked the committee to separate the two elements in order to give each one its proper importance. At first it was a painstaking process of cutting out and pasting elements of the former *Declarations* into two separate sections to make certain that all aspects would be considered in the revision. The end result was an interim document, *Adaptations of the Rule of Saint Benedict*, accepted by the General Chapter in 1970. The three fresh approaches of this document that were most freeing for the sisters were:

> referring to the theology of monastic vowed living as the "Beatitudinal Life"

> viewing monastic observance, not as legalistic prescriptions, but as aspects of the monastic vocation, namely, community life, meaningful separation from the world, and a scriptural-liturgical spirituality

> allowing for the principle of subsidiarity in designating juridic areas to be determined by each priory.

Meanwhile, sensing that individual priories and congregations were agonizing over the revision of their documents, Sister Joan Chittister, O.S.B., president of the Conference of American Benedictine Prioresses, organized a process whereby all of the American Benedictine sisters would have a voice in articulating a common vision. The conference produced five outstanding documents:

Upon This Tradition, identifying once again the elements of the Benedictine tradition, 1975;

Of Time Made Holy, identifying American Benedictine women as communities of worship, 1978;

Of All Good Gifts, identifying monastic stewardship and the monastic heritage of contemplative vision and community, as ways of meeting obligations to creation and to life itself at this time in history, 1980;

Toward Full Discipleship, Benedictine women taking a position that is life-giving for both men and women on the issue of women in Church and society, 1984;

With a Listening Heart, exploring the implications of discernment in the lives of Benedictine women, 1996.

In the mid-1970s, the experimentation time for interim documents was running out. Sister Enid Smith, president of the Federation of St. Benedict, gathered the resources of the Federation to draw up the final draft of its constitutional document to be submitted to Rome for approval. Learning from other religious communities' difficulties in getting their documents approved, Sister Enid enlisted Sister Mary David Olheiser from St. Benedict's, who had just completed a degree in Canon Law, and canonist, Father Kevin Seasoltz, O.S.B., to assist in formulating the document in acceptable canonical language.

The Federation retained the concept of a separate spiritual document, as well as the process of involvement of the member priories. By July 1981, With Hearts Inclined, the spiritual elements of the constitution, was adopted by the General Chapter, and in another six years the final constitutional document containing all the juridic norms regarding the governance of the monasteries was adopted. *With Hearts Inclined* effectively placed the mystery of the monastic vocation within the mystery of the Church and her mission to the world.

It took longer to revise the juridic elements because each priory was required to revise its own handbook to spell out its specifications of those general document's norms, which allowed some freedom for the uniqueness of each monastery or priory. These handbooks needed to accompany the Federation document when it was sent to Rome. The final approval of the document containing both the theological and juridic elements, the *General and Specific Norms of the Federation of St. Benedict and Its Member Monasteries*, was given at Rome on the feast of St. Benedict, July 11, 1987. Tedious as these processes of document revision seemed, they were no doubt the most productive tool in involving each sister, each monastery, and American Benedictine women as a whole, in revisiting the sources basic to their Benedictine way of life.

The crowning point of study, probing, and celebrating the Benedictine monastic charism came for Benedictines in 1980 in the world-wide sesquimillennial celebration of that charism's existence for 1,500 years. The sisters changed the focus of their questions—"Is this new structure Benedictine?" or "Do I look like a Benedictine?"—to "Are we living up to our heritage and tradition, a tradition that in the past created an entire alternative society as a result of its commitment to living the full Gospel? Can we be as radical?"

Sesquimillennial Celebrations[36]

"This is the biggest birthday party I've ever been invited to," remarked Sister Joan Chittister, O.S.B., prioress of St. Mary's Priory, Erie, Pennsylvania, as she opened her keynote address for the sesquimillennial celebration at St. Benedict's. For St. Benedict's, it was the biggest birthday party it had ever hosted. Because 480 is commonly held to be the year of the birth of Benedict and his twin sister Scholastica, 1980 became a memorable event for all Benedictines of the world as they commemorated the 1,500 years of existence of their order. In the United States and Canada, Benedictine women and men were divided into regions, and each region was to organize a congress to celebrate this important event. The Midwest fell into Region VI and Saint Benedict's Monastery and Saint John's Abbey hosted the Region VI Congress on June 19-21, 1980.

Twelve hundred Benedictine women and men gathered in the Benedicta Arts Center of the College of Saint Benedict on June 20 for Sister Joan's keynote address. She challenged her monastic audience to live fully their call as Benedictines and to reassess their potential for change. After outlining the contemporary world conditions, not unlike those of Benedict's time, she suggested: "Benedictinism has never been more relevant. It has never been as much obliged to look at the world in a new and creative way. The history of Benedictinism is the history of a thousand beginnings and this is the time to begin again."[37]

Twelve hundred Benedictines gathered for Region VI Sesquimillennial celebrations. (The Lutgen family in center foreground: Sisters Philomene and Carolissa and Brother Bernard.)

The next day the twelve hundred Benedictines gathered at Saint John's Abbey Church to celebrate a Solemn High Mass at which Cardinal Basil Hume, O.S.B., Archbishop of Westminster, England, officiated. In his homily, Cardinal Hume emphasized the opportunity for Benedictines to "choose life!" by renewed fidelity to their vows. He also stressed the need to maintain a strong loyalty to the Church.

Other events highlighted the festivity. There was a great outdoor picnic, a Benedictine talent show, the Liturgy of the Hours prayed together as if all present had always been one choir, and a procession to the cemetery for a prayer service at the grave of Mother Benedicta Riepp. The celebration was a joyful experience of solidarity in gratefulness for the tradition and heritage handed down and a resolve to pass it on to future generations.

Praying to Mother Benedicta Riepp at her grave site marked by a flaming urn.

Much publicity was devoted to the sesquimillennial celebration locally and regionally. The *St. Cloud Times*, the *St.
Cloud Visitor* (diocesan paper), and the *Minneapolis Star* covered the Region VI Congress quite thoroughly. Writing for an
issue of *The Crusader*, a student paper for Cathedral High
School in St. Cloud, Sister Evin Rademacher stressed the
community purpose of the Sesquimillennial celebrations:

> For us this is a profound moment, a radical questioning
> of what it is that we can hope to become, not only in and
> for ourselves, but also as part of our fragmented, pollut-
> ed, war-torn world. For us this is the task to live anew
> the call to the Benedictine way of non-violence, of peace,
> of mutual obedience and regard, and reverence for all of
> life and creation.[38]

For St. Benedict's community, the Sesquimillennial Congress was the apex of its postconciliar renewal experience. It
began a series of events honoring past and present Benedictines and motivated further probing of the community's
ongoing vitality. In her keynote address, Sister Joan had
reminded her audience of Benedict's simple and direct
approach to his vocation to do something about the deca-
dent Roman Empire; she challenged Benedictines today to
live in the spirit of that tradition. She described the
Benedictine vocation as the decision to live a gospel life and
to invite others to a meaningful, God-centered life that was
communal—holding all persons as equal—and that was
well-ordered and productive, without being competitive or
self-centered. She added: "The *Rule of St. Benedict* brings to
consciousness the big questions of life—power, person,
acquisition, community, and union with God. . . . Benedict
changed his society. Why do we think we can't change
ours?"[39]

Symbolic of that question burning in the hearts of
Benedictines throughout 1,500 years, the sisters had placed
a large flaming urn on the grave of Mother Benedicta Riepp,
who had brought the Benedictine flame to America and to
St. Joseph, Minnesota. Sister Joan's concluding keynote
remarks captured the spirit that had enabled Mother

Benedicta to persevere and that would enable the sisters to face the consequences of their diminishing numbers and the diminishments of aging while still nurturing a vision for their future:

> As we begin another century, let us not live in awe of the past but in hope for the future. Augustine in writing about the three theological virtues, faith, hope, and love, says that hope is the greatest, for faith only tells us that God is and love only tells us that God is good. But hope tells us that God will work his will! . . . Hope has two lovely daughters, anger and courage: anger, so that what must not be, may not be, and courage, so that what should be, can be! As we participate in a heritage that empowers, may the pieties of this period be anger and courage.[40]

Religious communities needed both of these virtues as they contended with tensions in the aftermath of the renewal period in the 1980s.

Candles on the altar of Saint John's Abbey Church representing the seven Benedictine monasteries of Region VI. (Pottery candleholders made by Sister Dennis Frandrup.)

Causes of Tension with Church Leadership

Many people were aware of the tensions between the hierarchy and religious communities that occurred in the period of renewal after Vatican II. What most people probably did not understand were some of the underlying causes for these tensions. True, struggles with the hierarchy were not new in the historical development of sisters' communities. The hierarchy often interfered with communities' internal affairs, such as election of superiors and acceptance of candidates. Tension concerning their decisions about apostolic work was understandable since the community's and the Church's mission are basically one. During the renewal period, however, the tension derived chiefly from the ambivalent messages given by Rome to religious communities.

On the one hand, the messages from Pope Pius XII in 1952 through 1954 had opened unexpected challenges for adaptations that even the sisters were hesitant to embrace. Vatican II in the 1960s had provided the context that made such changes acceptable culturally and religiously.[41] The Vatican II documents were forward-looking and trustful of the Spirit's work in and through the religious communities. They had simply, yet profoundly, described religious life as a way of following Christ, a way of living the Gospel. Though these documents were incomplete and somewhat disappointing in failing to connect Vatican II's fundamental insights of Church with the role of religious life, they did encourage religious to go back to their biblical roots and the spirit of their founder for inspiration in reading the signs of the times. Also reaffirming had been Pope Paul VI's apostolic letter in 1971, in which he appealed to religious to hear the cry of the poor and to respond to the need for social justice. For Pope Paul VI, "withdrawal from the world" did not have juridical overtones of enclosure; it was simply the human need to balance activity with recollection. So it seemed that religious were following Rome's directives in making changes to adapt to the contemporary Church and the world, knowing full well that periods of experimentation would sift out the true from the false ways of achieving it.

Two Post-Vatican II Documents with Pre-Vatican II Spirit[42]

On the other hand, the 1983 documents, the new edition of the *Code of Canon Law* and the *Essential Elements in the Church's Teaching on Religious Life*, all couched in pre-Vatican II language, once again left the sisters in limbo by seeming to go backwards from Vatican II. The *Essential Elements* merely served as a commentary on the new *Code of Canon Law*. The reason for the promulgation of these two documents was the Vatican's concern about the growing number and influence of secular institutes, especially in Europe, and the way renewal in religious life was moving, especially in America. It was feared that in time there would be confusion between these two categories. Secular institutes, such as Opus Dei, were organized lay groups who became actively involved in postconciliar renewal in the Church and in the political arena. Most had close ties with the Vatican.

In the two documents, *Code of Canon Law* and *Essential Elements*, authorities in Rome, reverting to the technique of definitions, defined religious life primarily as consecration to God, and defined the secular institutes as living this consecration in the midst of the world to distinguish between the two. But how and where were professed religious to live out their consecration? The new description, "consecrated life," not traditional in the Church and here used for both the secular and religious institutes, seemed to imply that the sisters were to live their religious life in the pre-Vatican II perspective of separation from the world by enclosure and traditional garb. In the documents, the theology and meaning of secular institutes were clear and inspiring, but religious life was described in juridic terminology with emphasis on externals. This treatment of religious life, so remarkably different from *Lumen Gentium* and *Perfectae Caritatis* of Vatican II, has left a scar of disunity in the sisters' experience of postconciliar renewal. Reverting to pre-Vatican II models of religious life caused confusion in the relationships between some religious communities and their local bishops and even among the sisters themselves. However, Pope John Paul II rescued the concept of consecrated life of the religious by giving it in his 1986 letter, *Vitam Consecratam*, the life-giving icon of the transfiguration of Jesus—of going up to the mountain with Jesus and coming down to live the mystery by working for justice and peace.

The Bishop's Visit

Knowing this background, the sisters at Saint Benedict's Monastery were apprehensive about the directive in these 1983 documents that communities dialogue with their bishop regarding renewal and the deepening of religious life. Bishop George Speltz, bishop of the Diocese of St. Cloud, came to Saint Benedict's Monastery for his official visit on March 19, 1984. The sisters were asked to reflect on the most valuable and positive results of their renewal program and their concerns about the future of religious life. Many sisters expressed their views, sharing their thoughts with the total gathering. Bishop Speltz listened and responded with a summary of what he had heard. This included a stress on prayer, a greater sense of responsibility for one's actions, and a broad support for renewal. However, he also responded with his own concern that the community was not accepting the Church's teaching role in defining religious life. For him, that raised the question of the place of the Holy Spirit in the collective as well as in the individual lives of sisters. He asked whether the counsel of obedience was still a part of the definition of religious life for them. Sister Katherine Howard, then prioress, responded with an emphatic, "Yes!" Bishop Speltz could not have missed the sincerity and the monastic heart that the dialogue had conveyed. His problematic question arose because some bishops still seemed to favor a strong hierarchical model of Church, whereas most religious institutions had moved toward the collegial form of governance. This meant, as Sister Katherine explained, "[They] had developed an understanding of obedience that is more internalized and takes seriously the manifestation of God's will through many channels in life."[43]

For the sisters, this particular dialogue was an historic moment and a far cry from some previous visits of their bishops in which there was no real listening or sharing and which the sisters endured in silence. In Bishop Speltz's visit, mutual respect and acceptance of differing understandings and perspectives of religious life predominated. His visit was warmly welcomed, as was the bond that developed between Bishop Speltz and the community.

Bishop George Speltz congratulating Sister Colman O'Connell at her inauguration as president of the College of Saint Benedict.

4
NEW REALITIES OF COMMUNITY

Demographics

An interesting human phenomenon is to enjoy a distinction that sets one apart, no matter how insignificantly. That the sisters at St. Benedict's enjoyed their distinction of being the largest Benedictine community in the world was well known. The community's membership reached the astounding number of 1,278 in 1946. European Benedictine communities gasped at such an anomaly and questioned how such numbers could possibly constitute a monastic community. Benedict had considered twelve as the ideal number. The sisters knew well the drawbacks of a large community—the isolation, the anonymity, and the gaps in communication—but they also enjoyed its many blessings including many gifted members, a large work force, and security in numbers.

In the late 1940s that membership was drastically reduced to 906 when Saint Benedict's Monastery divided itself into five independent monasteries in order to form the Congregation of St. Benedict (now known as the Federation of St. Benedict) to achieve pontifical autonomy. This meant that these monasteries were directly accountable to Rome rather than to the bishop of their respective dioceses. However, St. Benedict's paid a high price for this privilege by "losing" many younger sisters to the other four monasteries. Somehow, though, large numbers were on the side of St. Benedict's. By 1964 membership had again increased to 1,030. How, then, were they going to explain to themselves and to others the losses that brought down their membership to 741 by 1980 and to 393 as they entered the third millennium?

Four factors greatly affected the Community's membership and age-profile:

> 1. the transfer of 438 sisters of median age forty-two to the independent priories in Bismarck, North Dakota, Eau Claire, Wisconsin, St. Paul, Minnesota, and Olympia, Washington, (1947 to 1952)
> 2. the withdrawal of 130 sisters in perpetual vows of average age under thirty-nine, and 63 sisters in temporary vows—during the major period of departures, 1962 to 1988
> 3. the death of 477 sisters (1962 to 2000)
> 4. fewer admissions into perpetual vows
>   104 (1962 to 1969)
>   22 (1970 to 1979)
>   6 (1980 to 1988)
>   4 (1989 to 2000)
>
> (This profile was researched for Saint Benedict's Monastery by Sister Kathleen Kalinowski and did not include the Dependent Priories.)

Departures from Community

The exodus of sisters from religious life was the most excruciating cause of diminished numbers for American sisterhoods, and Saint Benedict's Monastery was no exception. So many factors interacted to bring about this exodus that it is difficult to distinguish between causes and effects. It was easy to place the responsibility on Vatican II because, at first, the departure of sisters occurred simultaneously with the Council. Actually, for most who left, the changes effected by Vatican II came too late. Perhaps closing schools and other institutions to which the sisters dedicated their lives in service to others caused the exodus, but the many departures also caused some of the closures. Some thought that the insecurity resulting from the community's questioning its practices, its works, and its very identity caused sisters to waver in their commitment. True, it was a time when some rethinking of their vocation surfaced as sisters realized that after Vatican II they could serve the Church and the world just as effectively as lay women. This may have been particularly difficult for those who entered at an early age and later realized that married life was more suitable for them.

Whatever the cause, the community grieved the loss of so many sisters and agonized over the reasons for these departures. However, they now view the exodus not as a blemish on community, but as one way in which the Holy Spirit worked to prepare some of its members for the work of the Church as active lay members imbued with the spirit of Vatican II and the spirit of Benedict.

It was Sister Mary Reuter, prioress from 1989 to 1995, who encouraged a reunion with these former members. The first such reunion was held in August 1993. Because at that time departures had been negotiated in private by the community and/or by the individuals, these sisters had left without closure to their experience as religious and consequently without a sense of freedom to associate with the community again. Likewise, members of the community were in need of reconciling the fractured bonds that had once been an important part of their lives. Sister Mary was in a good position to see this need for reconciliation. Because of her previous service as subprioress, she knew well the struggles of many of the sisters who left. The reunion was welcomed by former members and proved to be one of the most healing and reconciling events in the community's history. Sister Ephrem Hollermann shared her experience of that reunion:

I was overcome with bittersweet emotions. On the one hand, I remembered my own feelings of abandonment, as one by one twenty-three women who entered the postulancy [preparatory to novitiate] with me left between the years 1961 and 1974. I realized how much I still missed them and needed them. On the other hand, I was intensely inspired by their lives and the diverse ways in which each one's search for God was bearing fruit in prayer, work, and service to the people of God all over the country. . . . [Then] I knew with certainty that for those who have lived together in the heart of Christ and continue to cling to the desire to seek God, there is no separation, no permanent leave-taking.[44]

A second reunion in August 1998, with eighty-six former members attending, convinced the sisters of the need to continue these contacts. In a treasured response to these renewed relationships, twenty-two former members shared their experience of life in the community, their leaving, and their life after departure in *Forever Your Sister*, edited by Sister Janice Wedl and Eileen Maas Nalevanko.

The Vocation Question

Some questions regarding fewer admissions are similar to those raised concerning the departure of sisters from religious life: the evolving role of the lay women, the ambivalence in families and in society regarding a permanent commitment, the period of questioning and changes within religious life, the national trend toward smaller families, and fewer opportunities for youth to know religious. The sisters of St. Benedict's have continued to trust that the transformations they have experienced are part of the Holy Spirit's preparing them for a new generation of vocations. Moving from the vision of religious primarily as the work force of the Church, effective as that may have been in its time, to a Gospel-oriented life in its own right, is the work of God; it takes time and it is not easy. Vocations to this kind of vision may not be as numerous.

The sisters had gradually given up the mystique of large numbers and reminded themselves that it took only five sisters from Eichstätt to begin their first foundation in America. With the help of an energetic, Spirit-filled Vocation Committee, directed by Sister Marlene Meierhofer, the sisters of Saint Benedict's Monastery moved into the twenty-first century with new insights into the mystery of vocation—their own, as well as that of women today. Vocation awareness, awareness that God is doing something new, sparked the community with new life, commitment, and expectant joy as they entered the new millennium. Just as age did not stifle Abraham and Sarah's faith in God and hope in God's surprising promises, so too the community's age profile with a median age of seventy-six did not stifle the sisters' faith and hope in God's amazing fidelity. Rather, it challenged them to find new ways of sharing their gifts of wisdom, experience, compassion, and love learned in the school of life.

Sister Mary Reuter witnessing the signing of the document of final profession of Sister Mary Lou Carlson, a Native American from Red Lake, Minnesota.

The Longevity Factor

The community's decline in membership by death was thought to be quite predictable, but nature and science intervened and threw a surprising curve ball. Along with the nation's rising life expectancy, the sisters experienced the following dramatic change with challenging consequences:

Period	Number of Deaths	Average Age at Death
1920s	41	48
1930s	72	63
1940s	98	69
1950s	109	75
1960s	131	77
1970s	116	79
1980s	135	85
1990s	129	85

(In the year 1990 the average age at death was actually ninety.)

The challenging consequences identified by the community leadership in the early 1970s were:

continuing the Community's commitments of services to the People of God in the face of its growing obligations to its own elderly and infirm members;

providing retirement with dignity and adequate housing for retired sisters;

providing adequate nursing and skilled care for a much larger segment of sisters than originally planned.

The last two consequences brought the community headlong into a full-scale planning process for retirement.

Retirement

Benedict devoted a chapter of his *Rule* to the care of the sick, stating that it must rank above and before all else, so the care of the sick has always been a priority for the sisters of Saint Benedict's Monastery. Believing that the needs of their infirm members were met in an adequate manner in their own monastic infirmary, the sisters' immediate concern had shifted, in the late 1960s, to the increasing number of sisters who were moving into retirement due to the phenomenal shift in longevity. Providentially, St. Gertrude's Convent, the residence for sisters working at St. Cloud Hospital, gradually became available for retired sisters as the number of sisters working at the hospital decreased. It was a welcome though temporary solution. Its convenient location next to the hospital allowed the sisters to engage in energizing volunteer work, such as visiting patients.

In the community's self-study of 1971 through 1974, the task team of sisters working in the health-care apostolates recommended "that the Community seriously consider the use of either St. Raphael's or St. Joseph's Home for the Aged [in St. Cloud] for board and care and nursing care facilities for sisters if those homes should cease to operate as licensed homes for [lay people]."[45] This recommendation came to the community's rescue when a disastrous blow was dealt to its plan for the care of their sick and elderly. A fire inspector judged the newly renovated infirmary deficient in meeting the standards of the fire codes. The infirmary, fondly referred to as "Broadway," located on the second floor of the monastery's main building, was judged deficient as a health-care center. Although in 1972 the infirmary had undergone a complete renovation, in 1974 the fire inspector decided that its doorways were too narrow and that the lack of a fire sprinkler system gave sufficient reason to "condemn" the infirmary for the care of the sick. Immediate rectification of the deficiencies was demanded. Sister Evin Rademacher and the Council requested an extension of six months, promising a solution within that time frame.

Options were quickly explored. It did not seem wise to build an infirmary at the motherhouse large enough to meet the nursing care needs for the next fifty years because demographic studies at that time were showing that the community would be significantly smaller by then. Re-renovation of the infirmary was also ruled out, leaving one feasible but difficult solution: moving the infirmary to another location as recommended by the self-study task team. How possible was an immediate phasing out of the two licensed homes, St. Raphael's and St. Joseph's Homes in St. Cloud? They were continuously filled to capacity because there were no other Catholic nursing homes in St. Cloud. It was true that the community had received warnings of deficiencies in regard to these two homes but was given ample time to consider how those might be remedied. Both homes had at one time served as hospitals for St. Cloud and had been converted to serve as facilities for the elderly. Neither would easily be renovated to meet many more new specifications. The time was ripe to find a solution for both the retired sisters and for the residents in the two nursing homes.

St. Cloud Hospital Comes to the Rescue

The administrative staff of Saint Benedict's Monastery approached Bishop George Speltz to consider having the diocese build a new nursing home to take care of the lay residents who were currently at St. Raphael's and St. Joseph's Homes. Taken by surprise, Bishop Speltz declined to commit himself to such a project, but he did call a meeting of the administrators of the Diocese, Catholic Charities, and St. Cloud Hospital to consider the request. Father Richard Leisen, director of Catholic Charities in the Diocese of St. Cloud, offered to conduct a feasibility study to discern the advisability of building an alternative home for the elderly in St. Cloud. When the study revealed great interest in the project, Gene Bakke, the administrator of St. Cloud Hospital, expressed the willingness to build a replacement home large enough to accommodate the residents of both St. Raphael's and St. Joseph's nursing homes. Within a few years St. Benedict's Center (later named St. Benedict's Senior Community) was built and set up as a subsidiary corporation of St. Cloud Hospital. It was sponsored jointly by the Diocese and the Sisters of St. Benedict through the

St. Cloud Hospital Board of Trustees. Sister Rita Budig served as the administrator of the new center. Under her leadership, the center expanded so that in the year 2000 it was serving over 540 elderly, three times the capacities of St. Raphael's and St. Joseph's Homes combined.

The new center was a perfect solution, allowing for the transfer of the sisters from St. Benedict's infirmary and St. Gertrude's Convent to St. Raphael's and St. Joseph's Homes. It was determined to rename the latter, St. Scholastica's Convent (in honor of Scholastica, the twin of Benedict), and to designate it as the site of the community's skilled-care unit. St. Gertrude's Convent was then utilized for hospital expansion.

Recommended solutions, such as using the two nursing homes in St. Cloud as the community's retirement centers, were not as threatening on paper as in reality. The solution was difficult for the sisters because the presence and care of infirm sisters had been an important aspect of life for the motherhouse community. June 14, 1978, was a sad day at the monastery when the sisters gathered to sing their blessing song of departure as the cars bearing the sisters from the infirmary drove off to St. Scholastica's Convent. The hope that this solution was right for the elderly sisters was soon realized as a strong community life developed in these centers. They found freedom there to set up schedules that met their needs. They became involved in committee work to plan their liturgies and other community events. The sisters insisted on referring to the three places—the motherhouse, St. Raphael's, and St. Scholastica's—as "Centers" because they were considered to be of equal importance.

As demographic studies had predicted, the number of sisters requiring housing and care diminished, so that by 1999, St. Raphael's was discontinued. It was sold the following year to an agency that provides services to the poor and homeless. Thus, it continues to serve the St. Cloud community in a manner similar to the past one hundred years.

Sisters from the assisted-living and skilled-care units at St. Scholastica Convent praying the Liturgy of the Hours in their convent chapel.

Health Care Needs

National growing awareness of wellness and holistic health programs has also affected St. Benedict's. While there had always been a nursing staff to care for the sick, this service needed to be extended more generally within the community. In the early 1990s, the community began to provide an effective internal "health care system" to meet the needs of sisters in all of their living situations, thereby enabling the elderly to continue in their familiar home surroundings. The Health Resource Group (1991) and the Continuum of Care Task Team (1992) were established to coordinate all services available in community, to assess the needs of the sisters during their life phases of health, illness, diminishment, and death, and to implement programs and procedures accordingly. In 1993 Sister Juliana Lauer was appointed the Coordinator of Care to assist individual sisters in meeting their health needs and in making health-care decisions. The two committees were replaced in 1995 by the Task Team on Health Care Needs and Supportive Services. The concrete actions taken by this task team include nutritional care, infection control, alternative health care, profiling medications, preventive medical care, and education in the areas of theology of pain and death, ethical issues relative to health care, and basics of physical and psychological health care.

Sister Ephrem Hollermann, prioress, greeting friends on Donors Appreciation Day.

The philosophy and rationale of the internal health care system reflects the reverence for life that is found in Benedict's *Rule*. Certainly Archbishop Weakland's observation is true of Saint Benedict's Monastery: "The way in which religious, especially women, have taken care of their elderly sisters in the U.S.A. is a living witness to poverty and care of the weak. It is also a witness needed in our society at large."[46]

The sisters have been blessed in having had housing and financial flexibility in meeting the needs of their changing demographics without encumbering future members with "white elephant" structures or huge debts. This was made possible through the wise management of monastery funds and funding from other sources: the first Diocesan Opus Dei Drive, the National Religious Retirement Office, the St. Cloud Hospital, and donations received through the Development Office. The mainstay of Saint Benedict's Monastery has been the continuous generosity of the sisters' relatives, friends, and benefactors throughout the years of its existence.

Top: The back of the main monastery building in 1911, showing the west wing to which the new chapel was abutted. Seventy years later, this chapel acquired an entrance befitting its grandeur. Bottom: The new chapel in 1914 behind the main monastery building without a public entrance.

TOWARD A NEW MILLENNIUM

New and Renovated Sacred Spaces

The sisters of Saint Benedict's Monastery have an astounding history of risk-taking, notably:

> building Teresa Hall of the new college (1913), Sacred Heart Chapel (1914), and St. Cloud Hospital (1928), without funds on hand and with questionable security on America's economic scene
>
> starting a mission in China (1930) with no preparation or knowledge of that culture or political climate
>
> giving the community a free choice of membership in the process of re-establishing itself as a new autonomous Federation with four daughter monasteries (1948).
>
> divesting the community of all of its institutions of education and health care (1960s) and separately incorporating them as institutions of service in their own right.

It was time to take another risk in 1979. No doubt because of the challenge of the upcoming sesquimillennial celebration and the sisters' need to give visible and public expression to their growing new vision of their motherhouse as first and foremost a monastic center, the community decided to renovate and expand Sacred Heart Chapel.

It began one day at Evening Prayer. A huge slab of plaster loosened from the ceiling in the dome and fell with a thunderous explosion onto the altar. The sisters paused in their prayer, looked up to see what had happened and, without hesitation, continued praying. The warning was taken seriously, however. At first the Council suggested that the roof repair could begin that summer, followed by replastering and painting the interior, so that renovations would be completed by 1980 in time for the sesquimillennial celebrations. Community discussions changed those plans.

Sister Evin Rademacher reminded the sisters of Sister Grace McDonald's description of the plans for the chapel in 1911:

> The general preference [regarding location] was to extend the chapel east out from the east front of the main building toward Wisconsin Street [now known as College Avenue]. But because the distance was only ninety feet, such a plan would necessitate moving the street one half block east. The sisters sent a petition to the village council on March 28, 1911, requesting that Wisconsin Street follow the quarter section line from the parish cemetery due north and enter Minnesota Street through the block east of the old line. The village did not grant the request and the sisters were forced to place the chapel [to the west] of the main building.[47]

The west then opened up to the community's barn and farm area, so the 1911 plans had to abandon having a main chapel entrance. The chapel was simply connected to the west end of the corridor of the convent's main building. Celebratory and funeral processions had to make their way through a maze of monastery hallways. People would see the lovely dome from the highway, drive on campus to tour it, but find no public entrance to the chapel.

When the Council's conservative plan to repair the roof and to replaster and paint the chapel was presented to the

Chapter, discussion resulted in a more comprehensive plan. The Chapter suggested opening the west nave of the chapel for an entrance and adding other needed spaces—a welcoming gathering place, oratory, reconciliation rooms, music-rehearsal room, and an archives. By that time, the farm buildings had been moved and the west opened to other monastery buildings, to the college campus, and to Minnesota Street. Making a west entrance was not only feasible but a welcome feature unifying the monastery and college campuses and the village.

Despite their aging profile and need to set aside an adequate retirement fund, the sisters responded enthusiastically to the challenge of creating a "new chapel." Their motto at the Chapter meeting on October 25, 1980, in which the project received its final approval, was: "Go west, young woman, go west!" Had they known the disruption of community life and the grief of losing the familiar that would result from this project, they might have been more hesitant. Today almost no one regrets the boldness and wisdom of that decision. The community engaged Frank Kacmarcik, liturgical and design consultant, and Ted Butler and Dan Larson, associate architects with Hammel, Green, and Abrahamson of Minneapolis, to make this project a reality. They proved to be excellent choices in the way they worked with the sisters, especially with the project's manager, Sister Colleen Haggerty, to produce the architecturally excellent centerpiece of Saint Benedict's Monastery, the Sacred Heart Chapel and Gathering Place.

Meeting the Challenges of Reconstruction

In her characteristic spirit of faith, energy, and trust in God, Sister Katherine Howard, prioress (1981 to 1989), led the community through an exciting but challenging period of renewal, that of adapting to all the changes resulting from the chapel project. She welcomed this project as an important opportunity for theological renewal, especially of the Eucharist. In numerous presentations, Chapter meetings, and small group

Removal of west nave to create a Gathering Place and new west entrance to Sacred Heart Chapel.

discussions, the community explored the principles of theology enunciated by Vatican II, and in the American Bishops' Liturgy Committee statement, *Environment and Art in Catholic Worship* (USCC 1978). These principles undergirded the changes made. Noted theologians and liturgists, such as Father Nathan Mitchell, O.S.B., and Father Robert Hovda, were invited to speak to the Chapter, and Abbot Baldwin Dworschak, O.S.B., shared Saint John's Abbey's experience of building a new church. For the sisters this was a time of excitement, expectancy, and involvement, as step by step the developments of the project were shared and suggestions were solicited.

The chapel renovation project, of course, posed many challenges. Plans for living around the work of construction included: celebrating Eucharist, funerals, and other total-community times of worship in the auditorium of the Benedicta Arts Center of the College or in St. Joseph Parish Church; praying the Liturgy of the Hours in community subgroups; and eating in the College cafeteria because the motherhouse dining room was located directly below the chapel.

Especially poignant for the sisters were the funerals celebrated in the parish church instead of in the heart of their own community, the chapel. Praying in small groups was a new experience for many sisters at the motherhouse, and it gave them a new appreciation for the solemnity of community prayer when they could once again pray together in the new oratory, located below the Gathering Place. A remnant of that experience remains in the practice of praying Evening Prayer in the small community subgroups for their weekly community meetings. While it was a blessing to have the use of the college cafeteria's homey small dining rooms for meals, the sisters missed especially the celebratory meals in their community dining room on feast days.

In place of these kinds of community gatherings, the sisters gathered around the construction site watching the progress with great interest. Sister Verenice Ramler faithfully captured the daily developments with her camera. Moments of tension came with the removal of the west nave of the chapel—the dome did not topple!

The renovation was close to completion in 1983. At the September Chapter meeting, Sister Katherine reflected on the significance of the project:

> . . . we are now bringing this project to something of a conclusion. However, this conclusion is more truly a beginning than an ending. It's the beginning of a new day for us, a renewing life. . . . Our renovation and expansion of the chapel, the building that is the House in which our local church gathers, will not only support the changes we need to make, but it demands them.[48]

One of the highlights of the project's nearing completion was the celebration of the 1983 Christmas liturgies in the new space, though it was still somewhat in disarray. Father Kieran Nolan, O.S.B., from Saint John's Abbey, was the homilist for Christmas Day. He likened the experience to the conditions of the first Christmas and reminded the sisters that God delights in transforming such chaos with divine glory and light.

The simplicity of the inner spaces (above) incorporates the grandeur of the pipe organ (opposite).

Appreciating the Beauty and Meaning of the New Spaces

Surely the beautiful simplicity of the chapel space is a reflection of God's beauty. True, some people found the simplicity jolting, but Frank Kacmarcik explained the reason for simplicity: "The jewels of the space are the faces of the people in it. They are the community. The building is the container of that community. The building should be empty when the community is not there. It is complete only when the community is in it."[49]

A major addition to the chapel was a pipe organ. Sister Delores Dufner, one of the community liturgists who had taken a leading role in support of liturgical changes, reported on the needed acquisition of an organ at the September Chapter meeting in 1983. Linking the renovation experiences to traditional Benedictine values, she reminded the sisters of the community commitment to the renovation project:

> Our assumption from the beginning was that the building project really represents a new commitment on the part of the community to the monastic values of liturgy and hospitality . . . Both liturgy and hospitality require that the space be pleasing to the eye and welcoming to sound both musical and spoken.[50]

She reported that the new pipe organ was being built by Fritz Noack of Georgetown, Massachusetts, and would be installed in the summer of 1985. The design of the organ was a good example of the care taken for every detail of creating a beautiful space. Upon seeing the space, Noack abandoned his original traditional decorative design for an organ of exquisite simplicity that blended perfectly with the simplicity of the new space.

At the same Chapter meeting, Sister Mary Anthony Wagner gave a theological reflection on the renovated chapel and new areas, pointing to the link between sacred space and faith:

> The sacred spaces here within this Sacred Heart Chapel reflect our faith: the Gathering Place, our belief in being called together by God; the oratory, our faith in knowing,

that, when we chorally respond to each other in prayer, Jesus, our risen Lord and mediator, is in our midst praying with us; and the quiet, hallowed space of the Blessed Sacrament Chapel speaks of our kneeling in adoration to our eucharistic priest and victim. The spaces do not only reflect what we believe, but if we allow them to do so, they also shape us day by day into what we believe.[51]

Some sisters regretted the removal of the statues, the paintings, kneelers, and the stained-glass windows. Some also questioned a separate Blessed Sacrament chapel though the Bishops' Liturgy Committee's document, *Environment and Art in Catholic Worship*, recommended this. The community had another opportunity to reflect on the theological principle of Christ's presence, not only in the presider and in sacrament, but also in the assembly and in the word. Overall, the sisters were pleased with the results of the renovation-expansion project. Many observed that the

The new Gathering Place gave the renovated chapel a west entrance in 1984. The sisters treasure the story of Mother Benedicta Riepp's dream in which she saw a flowering fruit tree and knew in her heart that it represented her tiny American foundation budding forth into many branches and bearing fruit all over the continent. The blossoming apple trees in front of the Gathering Place remind the sisters every spring that her dream has indeed been fulfilled.

chapel now had a lightness and openness, with the color and life provided by the worshipers.

The sisters prayed in the oratory for the first time on May 7, 1983, and were overjoyed at the nearly perfect acoustics. Praying in the oratory was further enhanced in 1999 by the new pipe organ built for that space by Halbert Gober of the Gober Organ Company in Toronto, Canada. Sensitive to the sacred spaces and to the monastic choir, Gober produced a high quality organ of warm and beautiful tone "like silk velvet," as Sister Berno Flint described it.

With the renovation and construction completed, the community reclaimed its sacred space in which to re-commit itself to the Benedictine tradition of worship and hospitality and to experience day by day and Sunday by Sunday, a deeper solidarity with the wider community of sisters and brothers. Comments in the guest book by visitors who toured the new and renovated sacred spaces reveal a general delight with the new spaces. For example, Dame Gertrude Brown, O.S.B., from Stanbrook Abbey, England, remarked: "This is the most successful renovation of a church that I have seen in the United States."

Planning and Visioning

The "in" words for religious communities in the 1970s and 1980s were "planning" and "development." Workshops abounded nationwide to give assistance in setting up planning processes. As a number of sisters participated in these workshops, St. Benedict's Community gradually became involved in these processes and adept at envisioning its future. Sister Nora Luetmer guided the sisters through a study of priorities, and Sister Jacquelyn Dubay forged a path for a planning and public relations program. When it became clear in the late 1970s that the community needed an ongoing comprehensive planning program, Sister Firmin Escher, from the admininistrative staff of the college, was appointed coordinator of the Planning Committee. The committee was a mix of elected and appointed members who met monthly from 1980 to 1989. Sister Firmin saw her responsibilities as "a continuous process of making risk-taking decisions, the systematic organizing of efforts to carry out decisions, and measuring results of decisions made."[52] She and the committee served as a resource for the prioress and the Council, outlined a coherent general direction for community development, and set up task teams and unit groups to initiate and implement community goals and objectives. During those nine years, Sister Firmin trained many sisters in planning skills as they served on these task teams. She also trained the Chapter members as they listened and responded to her progress reports of the planning process. Sisters recall her delightful presentations when she placed them in a "space ship" imagining all manner of possibilities for the community's future.

Comprehensive Facilities Plan

The community continued its efforts of planning for its future during Sister Mary Reuter's term (1989 to 1995). Since Sister Mary had served as subprioress (1971 to 1977) during parts of both Mother Henrita Osendorf and Sister Evin Rademacher's terms, she had a sense of the continuity of the community's development. In 1978 she had continued her education and completed her doctorate in formative spirituality. Her special gift was her orientation to process, and she used it well in moving the community from planning by staff and committees to visioning by grassroots. Though not every sister was fond of "process," Sister Mary's approach achieved the desired goal of having the sisters talk freely about community goals, objectives, and action plans, and dream boldly about their future. To prepare for Chapter meetings, listening sessions were held at the three centers— St. Benedict's motherhouse, St. Raphael's, and St. Scholastica's Convents—to which sisters in outlying areas were also invited. The four main areas of interest that persistently surfaced at these meetings were community living, work, hospitality and outreach, and global community.

During the Renewal Week of June 1991, community living appeared as the primary focus. Through a leisurely pace of shared dialogue and relaxation, the sisters aimed at providing new models of community living to support the variety of lived expressions of the Benedictine value of community, and at exploring new models for the motherhouse in relation to the other two centers. Sisters remember the Renewal Week as the "community picnic of the century" replete with fun, games, treats, and obvious community bonding. There was energy. There was joy. The week ended with a Chapter meeting at which Sister Mary reminded the sisters: "We are challenged to think more broadly about where our power as a Chapter lies. It is not in casting a vote on issues. Perhaps more importantly, it lies in our coming together for prayer, listening to each other's stories . . . discussing and setting directions for the future."[53]

More effective than motivational lectures might have been, the sisters' active involvement with each other brought a clearer understanding of unresolved issues regarding community living and a greater acceptance of each other's diverse needs and perspectives. The sisters unanimously accepted the direction statements that emerged regarding community living, especially the interrelatedness and space needs of the three centers. They expressed their need to be engaged in short and long-range planning on a continual basis with regular reviews of goals and objectives by the Chapter.

With the appointment of Sister Mariterese Woida as planning coordinator to facilitate the visioning process that had begun, the sisters were ready to enlarge upon their hopes for the future at the March Chapter meeting in 1992. Anticipation and participation were at an all-time high as visioning proceeded concerning the space needs at the three centers. Sister Mary reminded the sisters: "In organic planning or discerning, one step grows out of another and is interrelated with other aspects even though a vision or direction has been chosen. The emphasis is on constant innovation . . . on creativity and evaluative feedback."[54]

These words aptly described what happened when the projected ideas of leadership groups to simply provide space for administration, small-group living, and the visual arts were gradually enlarged by the Chapter to require a Comprehensive Facilities Plan. The Chapter requested that the plan also include the construction of an addition to and a renovation of St. Scholastica's Convent; renovation of resident halls, Rosamond, Marmion, and St. Walburg's at the motherhouse; space for art and a museum; and further development of Evin Hall.

Visioning Consultants Assist Community

Overwhelmed by the needs they had articulated, the Chapter decided in June 1992 to hire the services of a consultant to develop an overall plan concentrating on the main monastery site—St. Benedict's. The firm of Yeater, Hemmings, Ruff, Schultz, Rokke and Welch from Moorhead, Minnesota, was chosen. In the February, March, and June Chapter meetings of 1993, these consultants led the sisters to envision what the future could and should hold. The sisters wanted the comprehensive study and plan to include the categories of: "who we are, our life together, our mission and ministries, our connections with others, and our support systems and resources."[55] The sisters agreed that all the categories were important and interrelated.

Sister Mary reflected on the question of the sisters' readiness to continue with the Comprehensive Facilities Plan: "Every reality is undergoing a paradigm shift. We live in an earthquake situation; we experience its tremors while trying to maintain our balance and walk forward. To feel fear is a normal reaction."[56] She named some dynamics of the sisters' experience in the visioning process: fear, grief, concern for the common good, valuing diversity, and respecting one another's visions and needs. It was a call to leadership, to transformation, and above all, to continued faith in God and in one another.

An important aspect of the discussions about the facilities project was the constant turning to the essentials of community life: the Benedictine values of hospitality, common prayer, and simplicity of life. This was the outcome Sister Mary had envisioned:

> [O]ur engagement in the planning process is an important dynamic in our conversion process, individually and as a community. . . . That is the cutting edge of growth, that we push our boundaries, . . . get new perspectives to think about and grapple with and bring into our lives in some way.[56]

Fears Mount

The consultants brought image boards for the February 1994 Chapter meeting. These boards laid out the space concepts and the square footage that the the consultants visualized from the sisters' discussions. The image boards sparked questions, and the discussions took on a sense of reality when the sisters began to put dollar figures on their plan. Concerns surfaced, especially that of traffic patterns that might necessitate a gatehouse at the entrance of the Monastery to serve as the reception area, and a separate chapter house for community meetings and for large-group hospitality events. There was also a concern for other prior-

The theme prayer of the renewal and visioning meetings of the early 1990s composed by Sisters Mara Faulkner and Christine Manderfeld.

ities such as a good sound system in the Sacred Heart Chapel. After an open-floor discussion, however, the sisters voted to accept the proposed Phase I of the Comprehensive Facilities Plan, and it was implemented in the spring of 1994 in the renovation of Rosamond and St. Walburg's residence halls.

Because the decision to proceed with Phase I caused some unrest, a special Chapter meeting was called in December 1994. The specific purpose of this meeting was "to give an opportunity to express and hear the hopes and expectations, fears, doubts, and concerns we are experiencing as we implement the first steps of the Comprehensive Facilities Plan."[57] Freewheeling discussion ensued as sisters spoke openly and honestly, expressing pros and cons about the facilities project. The question of decision-making power rose occasionally: some sisters questioned whether the Council had taken powers belonging to the Chapter; others suggested that the complexity of details made it infeasible material for Chapter agendas. In the end, support was strong to continue the project. The construction was another experience of re-adjustments for the motherhouse community so soon after the chapel renovations. Again, the end results proved the inconveniences worthwhile.

Because the visioning focused on facilities, it touched concrete concerns with which every sister could identify. Unlike many other community discussions on more abstract concerns, visioning regarding facilities created a high degree of involvement with greater attendant fears as Sister Mary had warned. However, Sister Mary's and the Council's respect for the process, trust in and sensitivity to the sisters' insights, and their willingness to risk a high degree of grassroots involvement brought the community to a new awareness of its decision-making responsibilities.

Direction Statements

All the time and energy spent on the Comprehensive Facilities Plan pointed the community to the need of setting clear, long-range directions for the future. In place of the previous cumbersome goals, objectives, and plans of action, Sister Mary and the Council developed a Chapter process for the community's articulation of the main themes and concerns that surfaced in the discussions regarding the Comprehensive Facilities Project. From these themes, the Chapter chose three direction statements in January 1995:

> to claim the monastic life as our common and primary work;
>
> to exercise effective leadership personally and communally;
>
> to address the social and environmental concerns of our times through prayer, action, and sharing of resources.

These directions proved helpful in the transition of leadership when Sister Ephrem Hollermann, was elected prioress in 1995, and they continued to follow the sisters into the new millennium.

Moving into the Next Phase

A major agenda item for Sister Ephrem and the Leadership Team was the 1994 Comprehensive Facilities Plan. It was put on hold until a similar community process of planning and decision-making would determine the next steps. Meanwhile, the long considered question of when to phase out St. Raphael's Convent required immediate attention. Two large centers for retirement were no longer needed, yet St. Scholastica's Convent could not accommodate all of the sisters living at St. Raphael's Convent. The Community wanted to ensure that the long-term health-care needs of the sisters would be met. That concern brought the Chapter in 1996 to decide on the next step in the Comprehensive Facilities Plan, the renovation and addition of residential units at St. Scholastica's Convent to prepare for the closing of St. Raphael's Convent. This project was completed in 1999 under the leadership of Sister Rita Budig, resulting in three additional resident wings for assisted care and a complete renovation of the buildings and the campus.

The transition from St. Raphael's Convent to St. Scholastica's Convent, which was completed in January 1999, needed to be planned in great detail. The telling of the story of that journey cannot adequately capture the care taken by the Leadership Team in planning the transition: the adjustment of the employment of the lay people, the careful work of St. Raphael's staff in effecting the move, the preparations of St. Scholastica's staff for the influx of twenty-five new residents and the motherhouse staff for ten, the loving assistance given to each sister-resident by sister-helpers, and the courageous spirit of the sisters whose acceptance of the move in faith transformed the transition into an experience of deepening love and unity of spirit.

Simultaneous with the project at St. Scholastica's Convent, the planning continued at the motherhouse with architects, Grooters, Leapaldt, and Tideman, for adequate space for the community artisans, a museum, small-group living areas, and the Spirituality Center. It resulted in a number of projects: the conversion of the former St. Joseph's Maintenance Center into a Monastic Artisans Studio; the construction of a new building for a museum, gift shop, and gallery; an addition to Evin Hall to house the Spirituality Center; and plans for a complete renovation of Lourdes Hall for living areas. The "new" Spirituality Center is the community's pledge to continue its outreach programs in spiritual ministry. The new Art and Heritage Place stands as a symbol of the community at the threshold of a new century and millennium. It is a place where the sisters honor the past and the present of St. Benedict's Monastery to inspire them to move into the future with the vision, faith, and courage of the sisters who have gone before them.

Transformative Vision for the Future

Many analyses of the postconciliar renewal period have been written both by members of religious communities and by interested onlookers. At Saint Benedict's Monastery, each prioress gave periodic "state of the union" reports to the Chapter, tracing the community's progress through its various stages and affirming the transformations of the community. It is interesting to note in these addresses that with the approach of the third millennium, the focus shifted. The sisters were letting go of that first phase of the renewal period that required many changes and were begin-

St. Scholastic's Convent with the three "angel" residences, Gabriel, Michael, and Raphael, added in 1998 and 1999.

ning to set their faces to a new age. They acknowledged that new members in the year 2000 have no lived experience of pre-Vatican II, nor did they struggle through the changes of the 1960s and 1970s, but they would desire to stand with the sisters at the edge of a new frontier. Forever grateful for the blessings of renewal, for the experience gained, and for the hope and courage with which it had inspired them, the sisters began to look forward, trusting in the continued guidance of the Spirit, for the next leap into the future.

Transformative Vision for a New Millennium

Standing at the edge of a new millennium was a challenging moment for Saint Benedict's Monastery. Paul Philibert, O.P., describes the challenge as follows:

> to bring about something new which is neither the resuscitation of pre-Vatican II radicalism nor the revival of the overly accommodating cultural Christianity of the 1970s and 1980s . . . but a witness to continuing transition [the transformative model] that has been called for by the theology and reforms of the council.[58]

The two poles are the tendency to shun the world or the tendency to embrace the world indiscriminately. The transformative vision, however, tends to put the Gospel and the world in dialogue. This "middle position" or transformative vision best describes the community's experience of renewal.

Father Philibert draws on H. Richard Niebuhr's *Christ and Culture* for his analysis of the transformative model as neither a gap nor a concordance between Gospel and culture but rather a critical engagement of culture by Gospel: "This model, is neither pessimistic nor optimistic but realistic. It recognizes the problems with an unconverted world, but also recognizes that the transformation of the world into a sacrament of the kingdom of God is the meaning of the Church."[59] Benedictine life and its monastic vow of conversion of life calls for this kind of transformative engagement, demanding an on-going and life-time renewal and search for God as individual monastics and as a community. Transformative engagement also demands listening to the Spirit, and cultivating an attitude of listening is the heart of the *Rule of St. Benedict.*

As the sisters stood on the threshold of a new millennium, they perceived a call to that radical monasticism, not the fearful radicalism that seeks refuge in the security of familiar perspectives, structures, and customs of pre-Vatican II, but a radical response to contemporary challenges. Pope John Paul II acknowledged the price of such efforts on the part of religious in an *ad limina* address in June 1998:

> . . . religious life in the United States has been characterized by change and adaptation as called for by the Second Vatican Council. . . . This has not been an easy time, since renewal of such complexity and far-reaching consequences involving so many people, could not take place without much effort and pain.[60]

Pope John Paul II affirmed the mandate and inspiration of Vatican II as the continuing criteria for faithful renewal and urged that it be applied to the new age. The sisters, then, revisited their monastic charism as the year 2000 approached. It was a two-pronged call for the community to continue inner transformation in the spirit of Benedict as well as to continue transformation of its evangelizing charism.

Re-examining the Call to Monastic Transformation

Sister Ephrem Hollermann, elected prioress in 1995, was well prepared by her experiences as a former formation director (1976 to 1983) and her doctoral studies in theology and Benedictine history to meet the challenges of the approaching millennium. She used the fruits of her background and her teaching skills in giving monthly conferences to continue building a firm foundation for monastic renewal upon sound principles of theology and spirituality. Copies of each conference were made available to all Community groups together with reflection guides for individual or group probing into each topic's foundations in scripture and in the *Rule of St. Benedict.*

Realizing the ongoing nature of renewal, Sister Ephrem did not hesitate "to draw out what is new and what is old" (RB 64, 9) from the treasury of knowledge of Benedictine tradition and, in particular, from the tradition of Saint Benedict's Monastery. She organized her conferences into a comprehensive treatment of the nature of Benedictine monastic vowed life, even though it had formed a large part of the agendas of the Chapters and renewal days throughout the postconciliar period. Knowing that new visions come slowly, Sister Ephrem hoped to bring previous renewal efforts to return to the sources of the Benedictine inspiration into a culminating expression as the community moved into the twenty-first century. The process of coming to a common vision is aptly described by Reinhold Niebuhr in his reflection on the three theological virtues, quoted by Sister Ephrem:

> Nothing that is worth doing can be achieved in a lifetime; therefore, we must be saved by hope. Nothing which is true or beautiful or good, makes complete sense in any immediate context of history; therefore, we must be saved by faith. Nothing we do, however, virtuous, can be accomplished alone; therefore we must be saved by love.[61]

An overview of the topics of her monthly conferences serves to highlight the basics of Benedictine monastic spirituality. Setting her approach in the universal call to holiness, Sister Ephrem described the various aspects of the monastic journey in a way that the sisters could find inspiration for their individual and communal way of life. In the context of celebration of creaturehood, she explored the community's "commonly held discipline of spirituality of prayer, humility, and monastic vowed living. The monastic instincts or habits of the hearts, such as awareness of God and the sacred, simplicity, and silence, that shape who we are as followers of Jesus [in] the way of Benedict," were the subject of her first conferences. One year her conferences reflected on the ways of relating to God, self, others, and material things in terms of Benedict's treatment of justice, forgiveness, discipline, service, and good zeal. Another year, she focused on monastic practices: "those things we regularly and routinely 'do' to express our spiritual ideals and lifelong commitment," such as *lectio divina*, work, the common life, hospitality, and silence. The unifying experience of giving expression to the community's vision of the meaning and relevance of monastic presence in the Church and in the world called for a renewed commitment of the community and offered hope for the next century and millennium.

Preparing for the New Millennium

During the last year of the second millennium, Sister Ephrem followed Pope John Paul II's call to prepare for a jubilee in the third millennium. Under the overarching theme of "For the Sake of the World: Proclaiming Jubilee in the Monastery," she chose the following topics for her conferences: keeping sabbath, living humanly, imaging peace, sanctifying time, embracing suffering, freeing the oppressed, and reverencing the earth. The overarching theme itself suggests the transformative vision of religious life, not as shunning the world or taking on its values indiscriminately, but reaching out from the heart of the Church to be Good News in the world. The shift in focus for the sisters of Saint Benedict's Monastery was the gradual claiming of their very way of monastic life as the message and the medium of the Gospel call: "Go out into the whole world and preach the Good News to all creatures (Mk 16:15).

Focusing Community's Evangelizing Charism

To assist the community in visioning the implications of the awareness that *its very way of life is its mission*, Sister Ephrem and the Council set up in March 1998 a Strategic Planning Committee, chaired by Sister Ingrid Anderson, to focus the community's evangelizing charism. This committee involved the sisters through questionnaires for small group discussions, workshops, and Chapter reports in the effort of making the community's mission statement concrete for the next three to five years. Three priority questions surfaced:

Should we have a major *focus* for our community and if so what is it?

How can each member be internally strengthened to be *committed* to the Benedictine monastic way of life (and the chosen focus)?

How do we nurture and increase community *membership*?

The sisters agreed to have a focus and that it should be concerned with committing themselves and their resources to enriching the spiritual lives of people, particularly women, both within the monastery and in the wider community. This focus sparked enthusiasm to partner with women in a way that would foster the mutual sharing of gifts: "the sisters contribut[ing] . . . wisdom, experience, commitment, knowledge of the Gospel, and how to live peacefully in community . . . our women partners [contributing] youthful energy, engagement in the modern world and a vital connection to the future."[62] The focus also pointed to a direction for the planning of community groups, such as the Lifelong Formation and the Vocation Committees and the Spiritual Ministries staff.

This focus was not new to the sisters who have a long Benedictine tradition of sensing the sacredness in the ordinary ways of interacting with others, especially in their ministry of hospitality and outreach programs. In the more intentional exercising of that ministry, the sisters had also come to recognize the mutual enrichment that occurs in the encounters with others: a wider vision of the world, a broader understanding of contemporary culture and spirituality, and a mutual encouragement in embracing the transformations that Gospel-living demands. The ways in which a monastic community is called to interrelate and bring its unique gifts to their contemporary *sitz im leben* is not static but must be discerned in every age. It cannot rest in the security of knowing that it has reached its goal, but it is called to a stance of continually seeking God.

Standing on the Brink of a New Millennium

The sisters entered the second half of the twentieth century by celebrating their centennial in 1957. With their
focus renewed and more clearly articulated, they ended the
1900s and walked into the new millennium with a different
kind of celebration, a New Year's Eve spent in vigil. Sister
Hélène Mercier, the most recently professed member of the
community, described this event in an article, published in
the community's newsletter:

> To alleviate pain, to reconcile the hatred in people's
> hearts, to prevent unexplained violence, it can appear
> that there is very little a monastic can do. Yet monastic
> men and women from around the globe were invited by
> AIM (Alliance for International Monasticism) and MID
> (Monastic Interreligious Dialogue) to spend the night of
> December 31, 1999/January 1, 2000 in prayer for rec-
> onciliation and healing, for hope and joy at the birth of
> the Divine Light. In solidarity with people of all faiths,
> monastics prayed for peace while owning their own fail-
> ures in peacemaking. . . . This night was different from
> anything we had ever experienced. We had come to pray
> in solidarity with people of all faiths around the world
> and we had found a new and deeper solidarity right here
> among ourselves.[63]

Lighting the millennium candle symbolized the sisters'
entry into the twenty-first century with lamps burning
anew.

The millennium candle lights the New Year's Vigil. (Sister Hélène Mercier is in the first pew.)

Summary of Part I

The prayer used at the community's visioning Chapter on March 27, 1993, gives voice to the fears, hopes, and aspirations of its renewal programs that characterized its history during the last fifty years of the twentieth century:

> *Gracious God, we pray to you as Benedictine women who cherish the memories that are ours, and who claim a common history as a sacred gift. Renew your grace in us that we may weave together the threads that unite us to one another, to the world in which we live, and to you. Break down any barriers that may separate us. Give us the courage to move into the future with hope as we co-create the vision to which you call us.*
> *We ask this through Jesus Christ. Amen.*
>
> Sister Kathryn Casper

Reflecting on the last half of the twentieth century, one can easily trace major renewal patterns of Saint Benedict's Monastery's evolution while it remained true to its core and its founding mothers. Change came steadily after 1960, sometimes like a whirlwind, but always the community found cohesion and commitment in a common faith, trust in one another, and in the leadership of the prioresses who never ceased calling the sisters to an awareness of their Benedictine heritage and vision. At times the community bent under the stress and strain of rapid change, but it never broke. Sister Mary Reuter articulated the confidence of the sisters when she said: "We are making a difference. We can continue the vision and mission of our Benedictine foremothers. . . . We can work in ways worthy of our foremothers as we bring the vision and mission of Christ's love to the world."[64] The varied apostolates, traditional and emerging, depicted in the following chapters witness to the vitality of this vision and mission.

Notes to Part I

(SBMA refers to Saint Benedict's Monastery Archives.)

CHAPTER 1: CHANGE ON THE HORIZON

1. Saint Benedict's Monastery, formerly known as St. Benedict's Convent, and the College of Saint Benedict were one corporation until 1961. Mary Hall Commons was the student center, built in 1956, to which the college later added residence wings.
2. SBMA: Motherhouse Special Events, Record Group (RG) 18-3-2c, f. 8.
3. Ibid, f. 3.
4. SBMA: Peters, Circular Letters, RG 5-9-2, f. 3.
5. SBMA: Peters, Correspondence, RG 5-9-9, f. 8.
6. SBMA: Minutes of Chapter Meetings, RG 3-1-2, f. 7.
7. Olivia Forster, O.S.B., *Ardent Women: the History of The Federation of St. Benedict* (Waite Park, Minnesota: Park Press, 1997), pp. 133-134.
8. SBMA: Minutes of Chapter Meetings, RG 3-1-3, f. 7.
9. Mary Ewens, O.P., "Women in the Convent," *American Catholic Women: A Historical Exploration,* Karen Kennelly, ed. (New York: Macmillian, 1989), p. 40.
10. Cardinal Leon-Joseph Suenens, *The Nun in the World: New Dimensions in the Modern Apostolate* (Westminster, Maryland: The Newman Press, 1963).
11. SBMA: Records of the Vocation/Formation Team, RG 7-3A-1, f. 7.
12. The sections on Vatican II are a summary of James Patrick Shannon, *Reluctant Dissenter* (New York: Crossroads, 1998), pp. 90-105.
13. Ibid., p. 91.
14. Ibid., p. 104.

CHAPTER 2: MOVEMENTS OF CHANGE WITHIN COMMUNITY

15. Grace McDonald, O.S.B., *With Lamps Burning* (St. Paul, Minnesota: North Central Publishing, 1957), p. 202.
16. SBMA: Osendorf, Correspondence on Divine Office, RG 5-10-9, f. 23.
17. SBMA: Records of the Office of Liturgy: Experimentation, 1968-70, RG 9-1-1, f. 2.

18. SBMA: Osendorf, Circular Letters, RG 5-10-2, f. 6.

19. Gaston Courtois, *The States of Perfection: Papal documents from Leo XII to Pius XII* (Westminster Newman Press, 1961), pp. 220-239.

20. SBMA: RG 25, 8-2-A2.

21. SBMA: Experimentation in Small-group Living, RG 8-2A-2c, Box 9.

22. SBMA: Minutes of Chapter Meetings, RG 3-1-2, f. 10.

23. Ibid.

24. SBMA: RG 3-3-8g, f. 14.

25. SBMA: Reuter, "Projects in Process," June 1995. (personal copy)

26. Archbishop Rembert Weakland, O.S.B., "Charism of Religious Life in the Church," presentation sponsored by CELAM and LCWR/CMSM in Santo Domingo, February 27, 1994, (personal copy).

27. Paul Philibert, O.P., "Toward a Transformative Model of Religious Life," *Origins*, 26 May 1999, p. 11.

28. Ibid.

29. SBMA: Osendorf, Circular Letters, RG 5-10-2, f. 8.

30. Ibid.

31. Ibid.

CHAPTER 3: MONASTIC SOURCES REVISTED

32. Ephrem Hollermann, O.S.B., *The Reshaping of a Tradition: American Benedictine Women 1852-1881* (Winona, Minnesota: St. Mary's Press, 1994).

33. Incarnata Girgen, O.S.B., *Behind the Beginnings* (St. Paul, Minnesota: North Central, 1981).

34. SBMA: Minutes of Chapter Meetings, RG 3-1-2, f. 15.

35. Ibid.

36. SBMA: Motherhouse, Special Events, RG 18-3-2e, f. 1.

37. Joan Chittister, O.S.B., "Benedictinism: A Heritage That Empowers," Keynote address at Region VI Benedictine Congress, June 1980 (audio-cassette).

38. Evin Rademacher,O.S.B., "Sesquimillennium," *The Crusader*, CHS, Vol. XXI, No. 6, 20, March 1980.

39. Chittister.

40. Ibid.

41. Philibert, p. 11.

42. Weakland.

43. SBMA: Minutes of Chapter Meetings, RG 3-1-2, f. 14.

CHAPTER 4: NEW REALITIES OF COMMUNITY

44. Janice Wedl, O.S.B. and Eileen Maas Nalevanko, eds. *Forever Your Sister* (St. Cloud, Minnesota: North Star Press, 1998), Introduction.
45. Nora Luetmer, O.S.B., *Priorities Study*, SBMA: Records of the Office of Planning and Research, 1974, 137.
46. Weakland.

CHAPTER 5: TOWARD A NEW MILLENNIUM

47. McDonald, 167-68.
48. SBMA: Minutes of Chapter Meetings, RG 3-1-2, f. 13.
49. Ibid.
50. Ibid.
51. Ibid.
52. SBMA: Records of the Coordinator of Community Planning, RG 11-5-2, f. 1.
53. SBMA: Minutes of Chapter Meetings, RG 3-1-2, f. 19.
54. SBMA: Minutes of Chapter Meetings, RG 3-1-2, f. 20.
55. SBMA: Minutes of Chapter Meetings, RG 3-1-2, f. 21.
56. SBMA: Minutes of Chapter Meetings, RG 3-1-2, f. 22.
57. SBMA: Reuter, Letters and Memos to Community, RG 5-13-2, f. 2.
58. Philibert, 12.
59. Ibid.
60. Ibid.
61. Ephrem Hollermann, O.S.B., Conference, "Dimensions of Hope in Benedictine Life," 3 May 1997.
62. SBMA: Strategic Planning Committee Progress Report, 3 December 1999 (working document).
63. *Benedictine Sisters and Friends*, Vol. 4, No. 2, Winter 2000.

SUMMARY OF PART I

64. SBMA: Minutes of Chapter Meetings, RG 3-1-2, f. 21.

One of Joseph O'Connell's sculptures depicting aspects of the life of the sisters (featured in the Gathering Place): Prayer—a sister at *lectio divina*.

PART II

TRANSFORMATIONS IN COMMUNITY MINISTRIES

by
Evin Rademacher, O.S.B.

One of Joseph O'Connell's sculptures depicting aspects of the life of the sisters (featured in the Gathering Place): Community—sisters praying with Mother Benedicta Riepp at her death shared their loss as a community.

INTRODUCTION

Part I reveals some of the conversions and transformations that occurred within the community life of the sisters of Saint Benedict's Monastery as they responded to the challenges of the last half of the twentieth century. Although it is hardly possible to separate the internal affairs of the community from its external involvements, **Part II** focuses on the transformations that occurred in the Community's services to the Church and the world. The insights gleaned from **Part I** will help give meaning to **Part II**.

Though the postconciliar changes within community and the transformations in the community's ministries happened simultaneously, the sisters experienced changes in these two areas of their lives differently. The internal community transformations had immediate rewards. The liturgical changes produced more meaningful worship. The changes in community life and governance resulted in personal growth, community bonding, and shared responsibilities. Revisiting monastic roots revitalized a sense of vocation and mission. However, the changes in the community's ministries were experiences of "being stripped" of familiar and vital service-commitments and relationships. The outcomes of the community's divesting itself of ownership of its institutions of service, challenging the far-away missions to become autonomous monasteries, and falling short in its staffing of diocesan institutions of service had to be accepted in faith. Hindsight provided the vision of growth and blessing resulting from these changes, but the actual experience of these transformations were the hard work of moving into uncharted waters in hope—hope in the mission of the lay apostolate and hope in the future of monastic life.

Sister Nora Luetmer, architect of the Community Self-Study, 1971 to 1974.

6

MANAGING CHANGES IN MINISTRY

Priorities Study

> After decades of a relatively stable period of contin-
> uous extension of services, the Sisters of Saint
> Benedict in St. Joseph, Minnesota, find themselves
> in an unfamiliar position calling for a changed ap-
> proach to the conduct of the works of the Com-
> munity. Numerous and complex factors, internal
> and external to the Community, are responsible for
> this. The most immediate and pressing one is the
> changing [age] profile of the Community while re-
> newal and adaptation according to the directives of
> the Second Vatican Council are the occasion for a
> deepened search for life's meaning and direction. If
> the Community has to alter its expression of serv-
> ice, what procedure is to be followed? Is there some
> way of determining priorities?[1]

With these words, Sister Nora Luetmer introduced the most
comprehensive research and self-study that the community
had ever undertaken. Sister Nora, serving as the Assistant
Superintendent of Education of the Diocese of St. Cloud,
had first-hand information and experience of the problems

facing one area of the apostolates: Catholic education. The rapid growth in the Catholic parochial school population in the 1960s and the decline in sister-personnel placed a great strain on the religious community and on the people whom it served. In the fall of 1971, therefore, Mother Henrita Osendorf asked Sister Nora to project the needs of the apostolates and the needs of the community to find ways by which the community might shape its future involvements rather than be shaped by circumstances it did not foresee or plan. The project included all areas of the community's apostolates: elementary and higher education, religious and music education, health care in hospitals and nursing homes, social services, practical arts and homemaking, and outreach services in distant places, such as Utah and New Hampshire, as well as foreign countries.

The self-study was a huge undertaking involving over 150 sisters who worked in task teams representing each of the apostolates in making assessments, projections, and recommendations for the project. The self-study was carefully structured to consider its research in the context of the Vatican II understandings of Church, religious life, and the needs of the contemporary world. Earlier community studies, particularly the W. I. Christopher Associates survey, *Profile of a Priory*, in which 569 members of the community had participated in 1971, served as important reference points.

Voicing Concerns

The *Priorities Study* dealt with many other community-related issues that surfaced as the task teams discussed sisters' concerns in the various apostolic works. Because of the increasing needs in ministry and the community's declining and aging membership, some sisters felt that undue emphasis was being placed on performing work rather than on living monastic life. Overwork, under-preparation for work, or incompatible work led some sisters to the decision to leave the community. The *Priorities Study* offered one avenue to suggest alternative solutions.

As a result of the sisters' stated priorities, the task teams first studied aspects of Benedictine life, such as prayer, leisure, work, silence, solitude, and hospitality. The concern was the balance of work, prayer, and leisure. This was the first time that leisure was articulated as a value by the community. There was also a concern for sisters whose work commitment necessitated living outside a community setting. The varied general recommendations certainly raised community awareness and led to further action when a Community Synod became active in the mid-1970s. Other work-related concerns were raised, such as providing clear job descriptions and evaluations so that recognition of growth potential might give the sisters a sense of achievement and pride in their work and in their community. Above all, the sisters requested involvement in decisions regarding their work placement.

Sisters' retirement was also given prime consideration in the *Priorities Study*. Because of their work ethic, some sisters were reluctant to consider retirement as a necessary and a possibly rewarding time of their lives. Task teams studied the need for pre-retirement education, housing, financial planning, and personnel to provide care and management of a retirement program. Significantly, the task team's recommendations to provide a call-bell system, additional and private bathroom facilities, an elevator, and an enclosed stairway for the monastery infirmary were immediately heeded in the 1972 renovations of the main building.

Projections of future needs resulted in some reorganization of community administrative work, such as committees to follow up on the *Priorities Study* recommendations, especially regarding retirement, health care, and finances. The study was also replete with suggestions from the grassroots for the Lifelong Formation Committee's plans for community programs. The *Priorities Study* actually provided a long-range plan, much of which was still apropos in the year 2000.

Sister Nora organized the 284-page research report into three parts: assumptions and objectives, information and statistical data, and programs with alternatives to achieve the goals. The *Priorities Study* was ready for implementation by 1973. Mother Henrita used its findings in making personnel placements already for 1972-1973. Sister Nora's untimely death in 1974 at the age of fifty-three, no doubt robbed the project of some of its potential, but the administrators used it as a kind of "bible" as they faced a deluge of decisions regarding the community's apostolates in the 1970s.

In reality, the *Priorities Study* did not come too soon. Changes were already taking place in the apostolates. Personnel shortages had closed eighteen elementary schools in the 1960s; St. Benedict's community had shifted from ownership to a sponsoring relationship with its hospitals and the college. These changes caused unrest within the community and some concerns and misunderstandings on the part of the diocese and the people whom the sisters served. The *Priorities Study* gathered the facts underlying the changes that were happening so that people could understand that they occurred because of the sheer impact of forces beyond anyone's control. This study also helped the community project its course into the future in such a way as to keep the community viable and to engage other agencies to take responsibility for continuing apostolic works.

Sharing the Burden

A difficulty was to find forums in which the sisters might engage diocesan authorities, clergy, and lay people in finding solutions. The first forum came from a request of Abbot Jerome Theisen, O.S.B., from Saint John's Abbey, to Sister Evin Rademacher, prioress, to speak to the Abbey Chapter. He felt it would enhance the relationship between the two monasteries. Furthermore, since some of the monks were pastors of parishes, they could help inform the diocesan clergy. The next opportunity came when Sister Evin was asked to address and dialogue with the clergy at Diocesan Clergy Day. However, there was little opportunity to address the laity directly; it was hoped that the understandings gained by the pastors would filter to the parishioners. For the most part, sharing the demographics of the community and demonstrating the community's need for retirement funding convinced people of the sisters' need for increased stipends, for withdrawing from some of the current apostolates, and for finding new ways of serving the Church and the world.

The primary forum of communication was the community itself. In every Chapter meeting, administrators made efforts to inform, listen to, and involve the sisters in the inescapable changes. The *Priorities Study* was made available to each local mission so that every sister could acquaint herself with the research and the recommendations the task teams had made regarding each area of ministry. These formed the basis of many formal and informal Community discussions and of public information. The sisters could inform, mediate, and serve as messengers of peace and good will. Despite these efforts to inform and involve the sisters and the people concerned, the fact remained that the actual closing of a school or withdrawal of sisters from a nursing home was heart wrenching. The sisters grieved these decisions and kept fond memories of their days, years, or a lifetime of service to and with the people whom they had come to love.

Benedictine Community and Work

"While no one type of work is essentially Benedictine, 'to work' is. Monastic work springs from and enriches monastic life. It is an integral part of monastic observance, not something super-added to it, and still less opposed to it."[2] The Benedictine Order has been well known for its motto, *ora et labora*, pray and work. Paradoxically, while the *Rule of St. Benedict* organized the life of the monastics to the service of God and not directly to service of humankind, Benedictine monasticism has had a profound influence on civilization throughout its 1,500 years. Its history is one of adapting to the situations in which it finds itself. For Saint Benedict's Monastery, the great challenge of the last half of the twentieth century was adapting its apostolates to the changing circumstances within community, in the Church, and in the world. For a living organism to adapt to its surroundings is not an abdication of its identity but a claiming of the vitality that is truly its own. That principle can certainly be applied to the way in which the sisters experienced changes in their ministries. Because no particular work or ministry constitutes the *raison d'être* of a Benedictine community, the sisters found in the transformations that occurred in their apostolic work the challenge to claim their being a monastic community as the true source of their vitality. It was a long passage of facing harsh realities, of letting go, and of articulating ideals. The sisters' suggestions to the Priorities Study task teams indicated a community direction that served well in the midst of the confusions, transitions, and adjustments of the next decade.

To understand the dynamics of the changes in the community's ministries, it is helpful to note the three different arenas of responsibility in which the sisters worked:

> managing and staffing Community-owned institutions
> other than the Monastery;
> staffing institutions owned by dioceses and other agencies;
> managing the Monastery, its internal services, and its
> outreach programs.

Before the 1960s over eighty percent of the sisters lived and worked outside the motherhouse, the first two of these arenas. After the 1960s, that ratio shifted to the third arena. The shift happened gradually but steadily because of a mixture of both unforeseen and planned circumstances as Part II reveals. The story of the first one hundred years of the community had been one of almost continuous expansion in membership and apostolic works. The next fifty was a period of pruning, collaborating, divesting and handing over to others, and of shaping a monastic identity for the twenty-first century.

Overview of the Changing Ministry Profile

From the beginning, even in its Bavarian roots, the work that came naturally to the sisters was education within their monastic setting. Wherever the sisters went—St. Marys, Pennsylvania, and St. Cloud and St. Joseph, Minnesota—they immediately set up schools on their monastery grounds, which records show were well-attended. Already in the late ninteenth century the sisters' work-horizons expanded. Saint John's Abbey requested help with their Indian missions in northern Minnesota. Mother Scholastica Kerst, a transferee to St. Benedict's when the Benedictine community in Shakopee, Minnesota, was closed, realized her dreams of social services. Her sound business acumen enabled her, during the nine years she served as prioress (1880 to 1889), to open a select boarding academy at the motherhouse in St. Joseph, to build and staff hospitals in Bismarck, North Dakota, and in St. Cloud and Duluth, Minnesota, and to launch the community into a full-scale involvement in elementary education by staffing seventeen schools. Pastors continued their requests for sisters to staff their parish schools, as it seemed to become Bishop Peter Bartholome's dream in the 1950s to have a parochial school in every parish of the Diocese of St. Cloud.

These apostolic works increased the visibility of Saint Benedict's Community and resulted in a steady flow of new candidates entering the monastery. It reached its peak membership of 1,278 and its peak performance in ministries in 1946. In *With Lamps Burning*, Sister Grace McDonald listed eighty-three schools and institutions served by the sisters at that time. For some candidates the interest in joining the sisters was sparked by the community's apostolic works; for others the main interest was the monastic community and its orientation to prayer. The two seemingly different yet complementary vocation-orientations have provided a healthy tension throughout Benedictine history.

Taking on apostolates in huge numbers made Saint Benedict's seem to be an apostolic order, but the sisters never lost their monastic orientation. No matter where they worked among the people, the sisters lived in convents known as local missions. As much as possible, they followed the same monastic schedule as the motherhouse. St. Benedict's at its highest point of membership and performance seemed a departure from the ideal small monastic community; nonetheless, its peak was a glorious moment of its monastic history. In actuality, most of the sisters lived in "little monasteries" located in eighty-three rural and urban communities, chiefly in central Minnesota. These little monasteries were focal points where evangelization took place in ordinary ways when: children came to the back door for cookies, piano students trekked in and out of the convent to practice, neighbors exchanged recipes, homeless travelers came for a meal, people just came to visit or to ask for prayers. The sister-cooks and housekeepers were at the

Life on the local missions, "little monasteries" (above and opposite).

heart, not only of the local mission, but of the wider community as well. In *They Came To Teach*,[3] Sister Ann Marie Biermaier listed 1,650 sisters of Saint Benedict's Monastery who lived and worked in these local missions or convents in parishes at some time between 1857 and 1990. During that same period 300 sisters lived in the little monasteries connected with the hospitals and 334 with nursing homes to

serve untold numbers who came for healing and compassion and to find meaning in their last years.

Saint Benedict's Monastery was always "a monastery without walls" for the sisters with so many of them living and working away from the motherhouse. In fact, the motherhouse residences could house only a small fraction of the membership of the Monastery. The only times a large number of sisters assembled at the motherhouse was for retreats and certain Chapter meetings which were held in the summer so that the sisters could use the college residence halls. The "little monasteries" served as "home" for the majority of the sisters. The network of community bonds created there is still evident at the present time.

Given the sisters' huge involvement in the Church's work up to the 1960s, it is easy to understand the fear and panic that people felt when the services were no longer forthcoming in the usual manner. Parishes and health care institutions had to find more costly but less stable staffing alternatives. The curtailing of ministries caused similar panic for the sisters as they experienced the diminishment of their outreach services, which gave them life-giving purpose. New paths needed to be forged by the sisters and by their constituencies.

The community's changing membership profile became the most controlling cause of changes in its ministries. By 1957, the community's centennial year, its membership had dropped to 967. That first decline happened when Saint Benedict's Monastery divided into five monasteries with the view of developing an autonomous Federation of St. Benedict in 1948 through 1952. This division did not interrupt the various apostolates because the new monasteries were set up in the areas where they could continue to staff the schools and other institutions that had been served by St. Benedict's. Since these areas—southern Minnesota, Wisconsin, North Dakota, and Washington—were more distant from the motherhouse, the division served to consolidate St. Benedict's apostolates more closely in central Minnesota. It did, however, adversely affect St. Benedict's personnel because several hundred of its younger members at the average age of forty-two, opted for the venture of beginning new monasteries. By the time the Priorities Study Team did its research in 1971-1972, the membership had dropped to 857. This decline was caused by fewer admissions into the community and more departures from the community. The 1971-1972 statistics used in the *Priorities Study* represent about seventy percent of the services Saint Benedict's Monastery's provided at its peak performance:

1971 to 1972

Areas of Ministry	Number of sisters
elementary education:	187 (130 were full-time teachers, 31 principals)
secondary schools:	40
college	54
music education:	56 (full-time teachers)
religious education	26 (full-time teachers but an extracurricular for others)
hospitals	61
nursing homes	53
internal Community services	132 (44 at motherhouse, 88 on local missions)
foreign missions	74
Utah, New Hampshire	29
prayer apostolate	138 (the retired and infirm)

By the year 1999-2000, the community-profile of apostolic services had changed quite drastically in number (membership having declined to 393) and had shifted in types of services:

1999-2000

elementary education	16
secondary schools	3
college	29
parish ministries	23
nursing homes	10
hospitals	13

diocesan and Federation
    positions   14
internal Community
    services and programs   152
volunteer work   27
new ministries   19
prayer apostolate   87 (the retired and
                                                     infirm)

How the community's works of ministry were transformed
and how these changes transformed the community during
the last half of the twentieth century, more especially in the
last thirty years, is the focus of the remainder of **Part II**.

7
CHANGES IN COMMUNITY-OWNED INSTITUTIONS

From Ownership to Sponsorship

The greatest financial commitment of Saint Benedict's Monastery in the 1960s was in its community-owned institutions of ministry:

St. Benedict's Academy
(High School) . . . founded in 1880, St. Joseph, Minnesota
St. Cloud Hospital . . . . founded in 1886, St. Cloud, Minnesota
St. Joseph's Home . . . . founded in 1900, St. Cloud
College of Saint Benedict . . founded in 1913, St. Joseph
St. Raphael's Home . . . . . . founded in 1928, St. Cloud
St. Benedict's Hospital . . . . . founded in 1946, Ogden, Utah
Queen of Peace Hospital . . . . acquired in 1952, New Prague, Minnesota

Foreign missions . . . (convents and places of ministry— acquired 1930-1970)

These ministries were the first to experience a significant transformation when the community moved from ownership to sponsorship of these institutions. In 1961 Mother Henrita

Osendorf, prioress, reported to the community Chapter that at national meetings religious communities were urged to separately incorporate all hospitals, nursing homes, and institutions of higher learning. This change meant that the religious would relinquish ownership and management, but they could choose to retain certain rights, such as the appointments of the Boards of Directors and the chief executive officers. The continuing "sponsoring" relationship of communities with these institutions would need to be defined to clarify the ways in which the religious would continue to exert leadership and influence. Four main reasons were given for making this change from ownership to sponsorship:

> to limit liability exposure when making loans for expansion of these institutions   and when facing possible law suits;
>
> to lessen the community's involvement in the growing complexities of management;
>
> to deflect from the religious communities the increasing accountability to state and federal government;
>
> to increase the possibilities of obtaining outside funding, especially federal funding.[4]

For Mother Henrita, three other fundamentally more important reasons for separate incorporation of all the monastery-owned institutions of ministry were: to insure the future of these ministries when the community could no longer assume leadership, to encourage the lay apostolate, and to free the community to develop and express more directly its Benedictine monastic life and charism as its primary mission.

Mother Henrita never questioned the validity of the arguments for separate incorporation and moved the community into the process in 1961, merely informing the Chapter members of the Council's decision to do so. The College of Saint Benedict was the first institution to be incorporated separately because it needed a government loan to build a dormitory. Since little seemed to change, the sisters did not question the new relationship. Sponsorship seemed to be just a new term for the community's relationship to its institutions.

Growing Fears Force Clarifications

When the St. Cloud Hospital was separately incorporated the following year, some sisters became uneasy. Mother Henrita invited legal counsel Kevin Hughes to explain the new concept of sponsorship to the Chapter. The community trusted the legal firm since Fred Hughes and his sons, Kevin and Keith, had loyally supported it through many years of various legal concerns. Nonetheless, the topic aroused a lively discussion of pros and cons for sponsorship versus ownership. The meeting cleared some of the confusions and the process of separate incorporation moved ahead. By 1966 the community had relinquished ownership and management of the college and all of its health-care institutions.

"[Mother Henrita Osendorf] . . . believed that increased involvement of the laity was a blessing for the Church." Sister Barbara chatted with Fred Hughes at a Chapter meeting.

Hindsight has proved the decision of separate incorporation of the monastery-owned institutions to be providential. Most sisters were relieved that they no longer had special Chapter meetings for their approval every time the hospital or college needed a new piece of equipment. The community's administration was relieved of one of its most burdensome tasks, managing the growth and expansion of these institutions in the face of growing complexities and legal implications, although members of the community's leadership continued to serve on the corporate boards of these institutions.

Still, some uneasiness about the lack of a Chapter vote on sponsorship surfaced sporadically during the ensuing years. Each succeeding Leadership Team of the Monastery needed to deal with clarifications and modifications of the concept of sponsorship to tailor it to each institution's needs. Corporate minutes in 1967 of Saint Benedict's Monastery contain a full report by Mother Henrita explaining once again the rationale for separate incorporation:

> This places those institutions under laws of the state, from which they receive their charter, and makes of them a civil entity. Their purpose is one of service; they are non-profit organizations. . . . Any excess income [the institution] may have over and above expenses must be returned to the institution for improvements in construction or equipment necessary for [its purpose]. . . . Our Catholic institutions of higher education and public health are institutions of *public trust*. Their task is primarily one of service to the general public.[5]

To answer the question about the right of the community to divest itself of these properties, Mother Henrita explained that canon law regarding ecclesiastical property did not apply here since our institutions had been incorporated under civil law. These were difficult questions because not even canonists agreed on the interpretations given to the concept of sponsorship. Mother Henrita acknowledged that it was the hard work and earnings of the sisters that brought the St. Cloud Hospital into existence and maintained it in the difficult years of the Depression. She explained that the only repayment the community could realize was payment of the monies borrowed from community funds and income accrued from the sisters' salaries. These payments had already been made.

Of all the renewal changes, this one cost Mother Henrita the most anxiety and pain. Despite the misunderstandings of some sisters, clergy, lay co-workers, and the public, she kept to her course because she was convinced that it would eventually be a blessing for the monastic community. She also believed that increased involvement of the laity was a blessing for the Church.

In 1974 Sister Evin Rademacher and the Council created a new position on the administrative staff, a second vice-president of external affairs, to be the community's liaison to other institutions, especially those sponsored or staffed by the sisters. This freed the other members of the staff for the internal work of the community. Sister Kathleen Kalinowski served in this position and worked with every separately incorporated institution to create the sponsoring relationship uniquely for each one. Her annual reports to the Chapter sharing the evolving nature of sponsorship gave the sisters opportunities to raise their concerns.

The community's prized achievement in the entire process of separate incorporation was realized in 1975 when the diocesan authorities joined the sisters in co-sponsoring the St. Cloud Hospital to strengthen the hospital's mission. Sister Mary Reuter and the administrative team of the monastery agreed with the diocesan authorities to go one step further in 1995 and arranged to have the diocese take the full responsibility of sponsoring the St. Cloud Hospital to give the hospital the influence it needed on complex ethical issues.

While deliberating this transfer of sponsorship entirely to the Diocese of St. Cloud, the question of alienation of ecclesiastical property surfaced again. This time Bishop Jerome Hanus, O.S.B., determined to settle the issue of the validity of the actions of separate incorporation. He requested an investigation of the problem of canonical ownership by a renowned canonist, Father Robert T. Kennedy from the Department of Canon Law of The Catholic University of America. Sister Kathleen Kalinowski provided the documents, *History of Saint Cloud Hospital Corporation*, and *Sponsorship of Benedictine Institutions by the Sisters of the Order of Saint Benedict, St. Joseph, Minnesota.* The corporation officers of the monastery and of the Diocese of St. Cloud, together with members of the Board of Directors of the St. Cloud Hospital, met with Father Kennedy. He acknowledged the conflicting advice that religious communities were given by canonists, but after a careful review of Canon and Minnesota Law and the community's history of incorporation transactions, he concluded:

> According to the law of the Church, ownership of the physical assets of The Saint Cloud Hospital has passed by virtue of prescription from the Sisters of the Order of St. Benedict to the civil law corporation known as the St. Cloud Hospital, Inc. . . . It is not necessary for a religious community to own, or be otherwise financially invested in, a health-care institution in order to influence it or be its continuing source of inspiration.[6]

Bringing Ownership of Institutions of Ministry to Closure

The other two hospitals, Queen of Peace, New Prague, Minnesota, and St. Benedict's Hospital, Ogden, Utah, were separately incorporated in 1965. The two nursing homes, St. Raphael's and St. Joseph's Homes, St. Cloud, Minnesota, were separately incorporated in 1966. These two facilities were merged back into the Saint Benedict's Monastery corporation when they were discontinued as licensed homes and served instead as the community's retirement centers. The sisters in the foreign missions and Utah separately incorporated their properties of apostolic work at the time they achieved the status as autonomous monasteries as described in a later section.

The basic concern for most sisters was the perceived diminishment of the community's ability to influence the separately incorporated institutions. They questioned how its influence would be exercised if no sisters were available to serve on the boards of the sponsored institutions. Even if it would happen that no sisters would be interested in serving in that capacity, Mother Henrita assured the community that the institutions it had founded would continue to carry out their mission: "Incorporation makes [these institutions] the property of the members of the corporation, and it is incidental [for the carrying out of their mission] that, in our case, all members of the corporation are religious."[7]

The development of the community-owned institutions into separate but community-sponsored institutions enabled the sisters to realize one of the important visions of Vatican II, a collaboration in mission between religious and laity. To meet the American culture of the twenty-first century, Vatican II had advised calling on the dedication and gifts of lay people and involving them in the commitment to preserve and promote the tradition and value of the Church's mission. In the forefront of involving the laity, religious communities released to the laity the ministry commitments the laity could now more fittingly keep viable.

St. Benedict's Academy/High School/College[8]

St. Benedict's Academy/High School, a community-owned school, had a unique place in the history of Saint Benedict's Monastery. Its forerunner was St. Agnes Academy, a boarding school for girls that was housed in an old log church and school in St. Cloud. It had opened September 4, 1878, but was discontinued two years later when the sisters opened a boarding academy in St. Joseph. The sisters rented the old Haarman building across the street from the convent to serve as St. Joseph's Academy. Two years later this school moved into a new building, a combination of convent and academy. The school and the convent were renamed from St. Joseph's Convent and Academy to St. Benedict's Convent and Academy. Thus began a close relationship between the sisters and their students. The academy was incorporated with the Sisters of the Order of St. Benedict in 1887. As one of the oldest secondary schools in Minnesota, it was one of the few Catholic "finishing" schools for girls in the 1880s. It drew students from the central states west to the Rocky Mountains, east to Indiana, and south to Iowa. In 1940 the academy's name was changed to St. Benedict's High School which it retained until its closing in 1973.

St. Gertrude's tower (right), the landmark of St. Benedict's Academy and college. St. Gertrude's Hall (below), the addition to the convent-academy quarters built in 1899.

At first the academy educated girls on both the elementary and high school level. In 1897 it opened a department for boys but in a separate building known as St. Benedict's Boys School. By 1912, when the Academy had become exclusively a secondary school, the boys' school was operated as a separate institution remaining on St. Benedict's campus until 1938 when it was moved to Altoona, Wisconsin. There, ten years later, the newly established monastery in Eau Claire assumed the boys' school in Altoona as one of its apostolates.

The relationship between Monastery and Academy was indeed close. The students followed the same schedule as the sisters. Students were expected to be at morning Mass with the sisters and to retire at 9:00 P.M. as did the sisters. While the students had their own dormitories (fifteen students per dorm), some sisters slept in those dormitories as "prefects." Often the sisters and students prayed the night prayer, Compline, together in the dormitories and the prefects blessed each student while checking the "private" curtained cubicles. Some sisters ate their meals with the students, an excellent opportunity for teaching table etiquette. They played ball or skated together, went on picnics to the

Students serving Mother Richarda Peters and Lydia Rosa Ortiz at a tea.

woods, and formed bonds of friendship that often lasted a lifetime. The sisters chaperoned the students to and from their homes until the enrollment was large enough to charter buses to central points.

The Academy Sprouts a College

Meanwhile, because the academy's enrollment increased steadily, St. Gertrude's Hall was added to the convent-academy quarters in 1899. Some sisters began to dream of extending the academy to include a college. This gradually became a reality when, as early as 1905, the community plans included preparing sisters to serve as a college faculty. Some collegiate courses were being offered in 1912, and a state inspection placed the academy on the list of accredited high schools. A two-year college program was in place by 1913 under the same administration as the academy

Sister Remberta Westkaemper sharing her love of nature with biology students.

until 1927. At that time Sister Inez Hilger, directress of both schools, separated the administration and became the first dean of the college. Already in 1913, the community had to build Teresa Hall, an addition to Gertrude Hall, for the expanding college. Basically the academy and college shared the same buildings: the library, classrooms, gym, cafe,

Faculty and students cheering the basketball team: Sisters Romaine Theisen, Elizabeth (Zachary) Roufs, Linda Kulzer, Felicia (Gwen) Stende, and Shaun O'Meara at the drum.

store, laundry, and dining rooms. In the college's growth, St. Benedict's Academy had only to gain. It shared the collegiate environment, its excellent teachers, the companionship of the college students, the enriching programs at the college convocations, its theater productions, its extracurriculars, its health care center, and a joint alumnae association. The 1915 catalogue listed the following departments: collegiate, academic, normal, music, art, expression, home economics, commercial, primary, and preparatory.

The academy and college continued this twin existence, though each maintained its separate curriculum and began to develop separate extracurriculars. By the late 1930s, this close relationship waned as the college had an increased enrollment that required more space, while the make-up of the academy's student body began to include more prospective candidates for the community. The 1931 to 1958 academy records show that fifty percent or more of the students were aspirants, candidates for the community. At that time the community had encouraged candidates to enter the community after completing grade school, with the hope that their vocations would be nurtured in their high school days at St. Benedict's. The unfortunate regulation that the candidates were not to associate with the other high school boarders or day students did not create a strong class or school spirit. Through the years, as the number of candidates had increased, less effort had been made to recruit high school boarding students. The profound change in the tenor of the student body did not augur well for the future of the academy. The Council decided to discontinue the academy as a boarding school in September 1938 and to continue it only for day students and candidates for the community.

Efforts to Rescue the Academy/High School

Hope for the high school did not die easily. By special request, the community opened the old Knapp farm house to high school boarders between 1943 and 1947. Between

1947 and 1956, there were no high school boarders, but then, because of continued requests, the community's former building for candidates, the Scholasticate, was converted into a boarding high school. This move effected the separation of the twin schools. The academy lost the wind in its sails by moving from its familiar environment in deference to the expanding college to which it had given birth. Moreover, as the college campus began extending southward in the late 1950s, the high school felt the separation even more keenly.

As one more effort to save what had once been an important and intimate part of the monastery, the Council voted to build a new high school next to the college on the south campus; it opened for the school year of 1960-1961. Mother Richarda Peters did not hesitate to ask Bishop Peter Bartholome for financial assistance. Her letters to him often evoked a rebuke, this time for not keeping him informed about the plans for the high school. She responded with a gracious explanation in great detail and in the end rejoiced at the generous donation of $400,000 from the Diocese of St. Cloud for this new venture. The community was eager to give the high school another chance, having invested many resources, human and financial, in this educational apostolate over the years. Two hundred twenty sisters had been in this ministry— some for almost half a century—from its beginning in 1878 to its closing in 1973. The enrollment was never intended to be larger than two hundred because the sisters believed that their approach to education as shared life in community could be realized only in a small group where students could feel at home. The highest recorded enrollment was 170 in 1961-1962. Even as the new high school was being planned and the question of adding a third floor was raised, Mother Richarda declined because she wanted the high school to be a small, intimate, learning community.[9] Though an enrollment of two hundred was envisioned, she assured Bishop Bartholome that a third floor could be added in the future to accommodate three hundred students should his anticipation of a larger enrollment ever be realized.

For a short time, St. Benedict's High School thrived in its new location, but it was difficult to develop a new spirit and tradition separate now from both the monastery and the college. After ninety-five years of service to the young, the high school closed in 1973. While the sisters still wanted to support its secondary education apostolate, the enrollment did not warrant continuing its operation. Minnesota's consolidation of public schools and the effects of the cultural revolution of the 1960s and 1970s resulting in the youth's decreased interest in organized religion, made it difficult to maintain Church boarding schools. Saint John's Abbey was experiencing the same problem of enrollment with their high school whose history was similar to that of the academy. With the closing of St. Benedict's High school, St. John's Preparatory School accepted young women as well as young men.

After many years of leasing arrangements, Saint Benedict's Monastery deeded the high school buildings, now appropriately named Henrita Academic Building and Richarda Hall, to the College of Saint Benedict. Some of the clergy questioned that action because of the diocesan financial contribution to the high school. However, the sisters felt that using the building for a like purpose for which the moneys were donated was a logical and just solution. Richarda Hall reverted to its original purpose in the 1990s when the college devoted it as residence for the young women attending St. John's Preparatory School and added a faculty-office wing.

Academic building and residence hall, the new St. Benedict's High School, 1960.

Monastery and College Each Claim Their Own Respective Vitality

The gradual evolution of both the academy and the college effected a major change in life at the motherhouse. While the sisters had freely shared their spaces—retaining a minimum of monastic privacy for sleeping quarters, dining room, and novitiate, they enjoyed the youthful life-giving energy of the young women in their midst. The close relationship with the students was also a fruitful source of vocations since the young women experienced first-hand the life of prayer and dedication of the community. The physical separation of the schools from the monastery as they moved to the south campus for more space gave the sisters the freedom to claim their monastic life, privacy, and surroundings in a new way. They came to realize themselves as a monastic center and a center of hospitality for a different set of people, adults with whom they now shared their Benedictine heritage. Many certainly were former students. While making the monastic life the primary ministry at the motherhouse has been a significant change, the sisters continue to prize their connections with the college. They take pride in its growth, excellence, and continuance of the monastery's commitment to the education of women. A detailed description of the evolving monastery-college relationship is given in **Part III**.

From Missions to Dependent Priories to Autonomous Monasteries

Missionary work has always been part of the Benedictine tradition. *With Lamps Burning* recounts how Saint Benedict's Monastery responded generously to serve the people of God in other parts of the world, first in China, from there to Taiwan and Japan, and later in Puerto Rico and the Bahamas. However, Saint Benedict's Monastery was not oriented to the foreign mission apostolate. Some adventuresome sisters were interested and willing to give themselves to these evangelizing projects, but the community did not always realize the importance of preparing them for the cultural understandings that effective missionary work demanded. After many years of frustrating efforts, the sisters realized the importance of allowing those missions to be indigenous to their cultures.

Already in 1958, Mother Richarda Peters had the foresight to petition for canonical novitiates to be set up in Taiwan and Japan so that their candidates would not be confused by formation in another country. Also, in the early 1970s, Mother Henrita Osendorf had appointed sisters native to their respective cultures as superiors of these missions. These actions were taken at the request of American sisters serving in these missions. The insights of Vatican II affirmed their own experience that the way missionaries were present to foreign cultures needed to change. Missionary work was becoming more and more a challenge of collaboration as the Priorities Study Task Team described it in its assumptions: "Mission is going out in faith to share and to develop together; this is a [change] from the confident viewpoint that the mission-sending [group] has all the answers and only needs funds and personnel to execute its purpose."[10]

By 1970 the number of sisters interested in missionary work waned. The W. I. Christopher study, *Profile of a Priory*, 1971, revealed that only 1.4 percent of St. Benedict's sisters felt called to work in the foreign missions, yet, the *Priorities Study* also indicated that the communities that St. Benedict's had founded in foreign countries gave evidence of real strengths upon which to build a future:

> the sisters were committed to the Benedictine way of life;
>
> their apostolic works were recognized as good;
>
> the native communities were attracting vocations;
>
> there was evidence that they had the potential to become self-supporting.

The main weaknesses that the Priorities Study Task Team cited were the linguistic and cultural barriers that inhibited the formation of true community and the isolation resulting from the great distance that separated the missions from the founding community. What would the next step be?

Taking Steps toward Autonomy

When Sister Evin Rademacher became prioress in 1973, she kept in close consultation with Sister Nora Luetmer, who had directed the *Priorities Study*, to insure a follow-up of the concerns and recommendations of its various task teams. The future of the foreign missions was one of these concerns. Sister Evin had an opportunity, while attending a conference of Benedictine prioresses in 1973, to confer with Abbot Primate Rembert Weakland, O.S.B., about St. Benedict's foreign missions. He was well acquainted with all of the Benedictine communities in the world and remembered his visits to St. Benedict's missions. He affirmed Sister Evin's plan of approaching them to consider changing their mission status to dependent priory status as a step eventually to becoming autonomous monasteries. He viewed that step as the best gift Saint Benedict's Community could give them, and added that truly indigenous monasteries are a great gift to the Church in those countries as well. With the encouragement of the Council, Sister Evin made her first visits to the foreign missions in 1974 with the intention of suggesting to them that they consider becoming dependent priories. The first to be visited were Japan and Taiwan. The sisters there responded with mixed feelings of surprise, excitement, and fear, but they were assured that they could take time to consider a decision before Sister Evin's visit the following year.

That same year Sister Evin visited the Bahamas. While that mission community had personnel and sound finances, the sisters resisted the suggestion of autonomy because just twelve years earlier, they had experienced the trauma of being absorbed by Saint Benedict's Monastery as described in **Part III**. The suggestion to move to autonomy evoked some feeling of rejection by the community with whom they had cast their lot in 1962. However, they were also attracted to the idea of being the only indigenous religious community in the Bahama Islands.

Finally, Puerto Rico was approached with the proposal of becoming a dependent priory. Because Puerto Rico was close to Minnesota in comparison to the missions in the Far East, the sisters there had developed strong ties with St. Benedict's. Most had experienced their initial formation at the motherhouse, and personal relationships with the sisters had developed. Moreover, more sisters from Minnesota had served there; some years as many as eight sisters were part of the Puerto Rican community. It was difficult to think of breaking these ties. On the other hand, political unrest in Puerto Rico had awakened and strengthened the pride of the Puerto Ricans in their heritage and culture. Hence, the sisters were open to exploring the idea of autonomy as a possible future.

While in the Bahamas, Sister Evin received a letter from the sisters on mission in Manchester, New Hampshire, requesting her to stop there on her way back to the motherhouse to discuss with them their possibility of becoming a dependent priory. This had not been part of the original plan, but Sister Evin encouraged them to discern that option. She then offered the same option to the sisters in Utah.

So 1974-1975 became the year of opportunity for the distant missions to take their futures into their own hands. Before Sister Evin's next visits a year later, the sisters in Japan, Taiwan, Bahamas, and Puerto Rico had all consulted with their local bishops about becoming dependent priories. They were ready to sign the documents of request to be taken to the Chapter of Saint Benedict's Monastery for approval on February 8, 1975. The Manchester mission followed in June 1975. The sisters in Utah waited until the sesquimillennial year,1980, to request and celebrate their status as a Dependent Priory.

What followed was a life-giving collaboration between the motherhouse and its distant missions. Programs were set up in each priory to assist them in making preparations to elect their regional superiors, establish their own financial systems, and create their own legal documents. Workshops were held at the motherhouse to help them in drawing up their own formation programs. The workshops were especially helpful because the members of these different priories came to know one another, and their sharing with each other helped sift out the cultural elements unique to each priory. The superiors of these dependent priories were invited to audit the Chapter meetings of the Federation of St. Benedict, providing another opportunity to share progress, hopes, fears, problems, and programs. It was a time of strengthening relationships necessary for the next step of requesting status as autonomous monasteries and a time to come to appreciate more deeply their Benedictine roots. In July 1983, the Heritage Day boat trip on the Mississippi River, re-enacting the historic last lap of the pioneer sisters' journey in 1857, was reserved for sisters from the dependent priories. Each of these priories would have a pioneering future in store for them and courageous women of the past to inspire them for this venture.

As each dependent priory approached the final step toward achieving autonomy, Sister Kathleen Kalinowski worked with the priory's leadership and its legal counsel to set up the priory as a separate corporation and to clarify issues regarding its properties. The final approval of the Saint Benedict's Monastery Chapter and the formal acceptance into the Federation of St. Benedict by its Chapter happened as each priory felt ready:

> St. Benedict's Monastery, Japan, 1985;
> St. Benedict Monastery, Taiwan, 1988;
> Mount Benedict Priory, Utah, 1994;
> St. Martin Monastery, Bahama Islands, 1994;
> Monasterio Santa Escolastica, Puerto Rico, 2000.

Further detail in regard to each priory's development is given in **Part III**. Because of lack of members, the priory in Manchester, New Hampshire, returned to mission status in 1989.

Since these distant missions and their institutions of apostolic works were community-owned, the process of separately incorporating them as autonomous monasteries marked the last stages of St. Benedict's divesting itself of properties acquired for its ministries. However, it will never relinquish the evangelizing impact that the involvement with the intercultural communities had on the sisters. The new foundations stand as a witness, not only to the missionary work of Saint Benedict's Community, but, most of all, to the Spirit working in and through the trials of cultural misunderstandings to bring to birth new monastic communities to nurture God's reign in the world today. As Sister Grace suggested in the conclusion of *With Lamps Burning*: "With that work accomplished [building up the missions to enable them to become priories] the American Benedictines will have repaid Europe for transplanting Benedictines on American soil."[11] Just as their European foremothers heard the cry of America in 1852, so, too, the sisters of Saint Benedict's Monastery passed on monastic life when they heard the call from other cultures. Seeds sown in Minnesota soil a century earlier bore rich fruit in foreign soil; seeds of foreign cultures continue to enrich and diversify the community at St. Benedict's.

Manchester Priory

Establishing a mission in Manchester, New Hampshire, deserves special mention. It was another response of the community to assist in the education of young women. The mission seemed to have the promise of growth toward establishing it as an autonomous priory, but that may have been a premature decision. The experience of Saint Benedict's Monastery in setting up autonomous monasteries has been that it takes an average of forty years of presence as a mission to mature into autonomous status. It takes time to arrive at a common vision, to set down roots for a stable community, and to become an integral part of the Church and the people in the locality. It was believed that the acclimation of a mission in the United States would take less time. The Manchester mission had existed only sixteen years when it requested dependent priory status. In the work of establishing new monasteries, there is no success or failure; it is simply the attempt to respond to the needs of the People of God in whatever way circumstances allow. The story of Manchester Priory is one of courageous commitment of sisters to give such a response in New Hampshire.

An invitation from Abbot Gerald McCarthy, O.S.B., from St. Anselm Abbey in Manchester, brought the sisters from St. Joseph, Minnesota, to Manchester in the fall of 1968. Abbot Gerald wanted the presence of Benedictine sisters to assist the monks in their educational apostolate, especially for the women student nurses. Sister Mary Grell, president of the College of Saint Benedict, along with Sister Patrick Joseph Flynn, personnel director of Saint Benedict's Monastery, visited the campus and abbey in April 1968. They recommended accepting Abbot Gerald's invitation. Both later became a vital part of this Manchester venture.

Father Placidus H. Riley, O.S.B., president of St. Anselm College, encouraged Mother Henrita to send at least three or four sisters so they could experience community and the support of one another in their work. Three sisters accepted the invitation, arriving in Manchester in August 1968: Sisters Nivelle Berning (biology), Gonzaga Plantenberg (physics), and Carmen Mulcahy (nursing). Sister Job (Norma) Zimmerman joined them as a full-time nursing student. They lived with the Sisters of St. Jeanne d'Arc, domestic workers for the abbey-college complex, until they could move into a women's dormitory on campus. In the 1970s Sisters Christopher Weber (education), Patrick Joseph (Admissions Office), and Etienne Flaherty (French) joined them. At the same time, young women from the area were expressing interest in Benedictine life. By 1975 the sisters felt ready to request dependent priory status. Sister Nivelle was elected superior. A new residence hall, St. Mary Hall, opened in the fall of 1976 with the sisters occupying the first two floors while women students lived on the third floor. In 1980 Saint Benedict's Monastery purchased St. Mary Hall, and it was named Manchester Priory.

Between 1976 and 1985, five more professed sisters joined the priory, among them Sister Mary Grell, who was elected superior in 1979. She also served in the dean's office of St. Anselm College, which by that time had become a fully co-educational institution of approximately 1,300 students. Several women had joined Manchester Priory, but none professed final vows. In a few years, the priory's membership dwindled. Some left for health reasons; Sister Mary Grell died of cancer in 1981. Some sensed a lack of common vision. The original purpose of assisting in the educational apostolate of St. Anselm College did not serve as a compelling focus for forming an autonomous monastery for the those who joined later or were not prepared for a collegiate ministry.

Manchester Priory returned to its mission status in 1989. Sisters Nivelle and Christopher are continuing their ministry there, Sister Nivelle working at Scholastica House and Center for Volunteers, both housed at St. Anselm College, and Sister Christopher teaching at St. Anselm College. The sisters who participated in the Manchester venture speak of it as a growthful experience and always remember the gracious hospitality of the monks of St. Anselm Abbey.

St. Cloud Diocesan Elementary Teachers' Meeting (c. 1955). Education in parish elementary schools was the primary ministry of St. Benedict's Community. In 1960, there were 314 sisters teaching in fifty-one grade schools.

Sister Clare Shadeg and her First Communion Class (top) in Melrose, Minnesota. Sister Ruth Anne Schneider shares in a secret (bottom). Sister Suzanne Slominski (opposite), principal of Meire Grove-Greenwald parish schools, providing latest technology for her students.

8
CHANGES IN STAFFING DIOCESAN SCHOOLS

Diocesan Elementary Schools

The elementary education apostolate had the largest share of sister-personnel in the monastery's ministries. Since 1857 in Minnesota alone, the Benedictine sisters

taught, for varying periods of time, in over one hundred schools. Such expansion could not be maintained; the decline began in the 1950s and continued relentlessly for the next thirty years. Sister Nora Luetmer clearly articulated in the *Priorities Study* the trends and issues that Catholic education faced, especially after Vatican II. She cautioned that the new self-understanding of the Church and its lay apostolate; the growing complexities of contemporary religious, theological, and ethical issues; and the manner of exercising authority in the Church, families, and schools would be problematic for unprepared clergy, religious, and laity. The influence of mass media and new educational theories of learning and styles of teaching would pose challenges.[12]

Preparing for the inevitable changes in staffing the diocesan schools was more complex for the sisters than was the change in their community-owned institutions. For example, negotiating personnel changes in diocesan schools involved going through several layers of accountability: the diocesan superintendent of education, the bishop, pastors, parish councils, and school boards. Not only did the community need to ascertain the availability, competence, and need for training of sister-personnel, but it also needed to apprise the parishes and school boards of the trends and issues that would challenge the schools. The most immediate concern, however, was the growing shortage of sister-personnel.

Informing the Diocese of St. Cloud about the shortage of sister-personnel began as early as the 1950s. Letters exchanged between Mother Richarda Peters and Bishop Peter Bartholome portray two strong individuals committed to education: the one protecting the sisters, the other supporting the diocese. Although they struck hard bargains with each other, a mutual respect characterized their relationship. Mother Richarda suggested a plan in a letter February 1, 1955: "If ten schools in the diocese would each employ one lay teacher for three years, we would be in a position to furnish well-prepared teachers after that."[13] Mother Richarda had wanted to place more potential secondary and college teachers into graduate degree programs, but increased pressure from the clergy and their parishioners for more sister-personnel had prevented her plan. In that letter outlining a three-year plan that might alleviate both the community's and the parishes' dilemma, she suggested withdrawing five teachers from the schools in St. Martin and Duelm and replacing them with lay teachers. Her suggestion drew an immediate rebuke from Bishop Bartholome:

> I feel you should give definite assurance to Father Cyril at St. Martin for sisters this coming Fall. Your delay in making a decision is hampering the purchase of the public school. Father tells me that he will be satisfied with three teachers and that he is willing to hire a lay teacher in addition. . . . An opportunity of establishing a Catholic school at St. Martin presents itself perhaps once in thirty years and should not be passed lightly.[14]

Several months later, however, he did respond favorably to the general plan that Mother Richarda had outlined, especially in regard to hiring more lay teachers, but not without another rebuke: "I wish also to state very frankly that in the past quite a few of the pastors have felt that you have been quite adamant in your position and did not give enough consideration to the problems in the parish . . . kind consideration must always go with firmness of position."[15] Within a week, Mother Richarda invited Bishop Bartholome for the laying of the cornerstone for the new college residence, Mary Hall, and she added a personal note to the invitation which evoked his immediate acceptance as follows:

> Your little personal note was very much appreciated and I assure you that the displeasures are soon forgotten by the priests. I can say without reservation that you have ruled well during your six years and have accomplished a good deal for your community and the Church. It is impossible to satisfy everyone so do not be unhappy because of my criticism.[16]

With the expansion of Cathdral High School, Bishop Bartholome once again challenged Mother Richarda to find more sisters, now for the secondary level. Mother Richarda again described her distress about teacher-preparation: "This fall we are sending sixteen inexperienced and inadequately prepared sisters to teach in our grade schools. Most of these sisters have less than two years of college work."[17] To send more sisters to Cathedral High School, it was necessary to withdraw them from elementary schools and these sisters needed a few years for teacher-preparation. Mother Richarda's persistence about hiring lay teachers was rewarded by an increase in the number of lay teachers from thirty-four (eleven percent) in the mid 1950s to seventy-six (fifteen percent) by 1963, though the national average by then was thirty-two percent. Mother Richarda thanked Bishop Bartholome for his efforts, but she continued to remind him that the day of the lay apostolate had arrived, and that there was a definite place for Catholic lay teachers in the diocesan schools; in this she anticipated Vatican II by fifteen years. The bishop's reluctance to hire lay teachers caused difficulties, not only for the sisters in making necessary withdrawals from teaching, but also for the parishes' plans to keep their parochial schools viable.

The trend toward new educational theories also influenced the competence of sister-personnel. Sister Nora noted that contemporary education was becoming more aware of the need to stimulate students to self-involvement, creativity, and experimentation. These new styles required new approaches and adaptation to teaching, such as discussion-discovery learning, seminar methodology, cross-disciplinary dialogue, and even the physical arrangement and equipment of the classroom. How would the sisters be prepared and re-trained to meet these new challenges already facing them? Once again the community relied on the College of Saint Benedict. The education department offered special summer sessions for sisters to update their education credits. The college also offered late afternoon classes at centers in St. Cloud, Pierz, and Melrose to enable the sisters to complete their college education more quickly. Some sisters chose to withdraw from teaching and take up another type of service for which they felt more qualified, such as parish ministry. Some retired to a much-earned respite from teaching after dedicating thirty, forty, fifty, and even sixty years of their lives to that ministry. And some left religious life. Every year the community found itself having to reduce its personnel in ministry to elementary schools.

The Financial Implications of Changes

In the 1970s, administrators of Saint Benedict's Monastery met with pastors, parish councils, and school boards on a one-to-one basis to discuss ways in which they might keep their schools open or regroup schools regionally. The ministry of the laity was beginning to develop, but it took time for parishes to trust their own competence and commitment and to build up a financial budget to support hiring lay teachers. This was the experience nationwide. Despite efforts to stem the tide, by 1990 there was a sixty percent decrease in the total number of parochial schools in Minnesota. In the schools remaining open, the percentage of sisters and lay teachers had reversed itself. The percentage of sisters in the parochial schools in 1990 was eleven percent.

Finances were an important cause of the closing of schools. The sisters explained that, given their growing retirement needs, they could no longer give their services for a low stipend that did not include their professional update costs and retirement benefits. One particularly sensitive issue was the use of convents that had been built for the sisters in lieu of full salaries. Again, the administrators of St. Benedict's met with pastors and parish councils well in advance of withdrawing from these convents to give parishes ample time to find other uses for these buildings.

The need for the sisters to withdraw from teaching was often misunderstood and judged as a lessening in the community's commitment to education. Nothing could be further from the truth. To teach had been the very purpose for which the sisters originally came to the United States. The changes were uncontrollable and just as difficult for the sisters as they were for the parishes. The days were gone when a person could step into the classroom and be considered qualified just because she was a religious. Gone too were the days when the sisters could continue their extracurricular activities such as choir work, training and supervision of altar boys, sacristy work, and teaching religion classes on weekends. By the year 2000, five sisters remained in elementary schools as principals, and eight sisters continued as teachers.

Obviously, the work of the parishes had to become the work of the laity. In this shift, the laity gradually reclaimed their rightful responsibility for the faith formation of their parish community. Thus, laity and sisters had come full circle to their beginnings in central Minnesota. Some parishes had sought to retain the lay teachers they had before the sisters came to their area; however, pastors had insisted that sisters staff the schools. Was it again the work of the Holy Spirit that these transitions served as stepping stones for both laity and religious to realize their true mission in the Church and in the world?

Diocesan Secondary Schools

Besides their own St. Benedict's High School, the sisters staffed several diocesan secondary schools in Minnesota: Cathedral High School, St. Cloud; Father Pierz Memorial High School, Pierz; and St. Boniface, Cold Spring. A few sisters served on the faculties of schools in the Twin Cities and at Judge Memorial Catholic High School, Salt Lake City, Utah.

Eighty-five sisters were teaching on the secondary level in 1963. By 1968 both Pierz Memorial and St. Boniface high schools were closed because these two rural parishes were no longer able to support both public and private elementary and secondary schools. By 1972 only two diocesan secondary schools served by the sisters from St. Benedict's remained open: Judge Memorial Catholic High School in Salt Lake City, and Cathedral High School in St. Cloud. The faculty of Cathedral High School included twenty-five sisters. These sisters also needed to update their education, especially in re-orienting to new educational trends and skills. It was a time for the sisters to rededicate themselves to youth education, to transfer to other ministries, or to retire. By the year 2000, only Sister Clare Witzman was on the faculty of Cathedral High School/John XXIII in St. Cloud, and Sister Jean Marie Vanderlinde on the faculty of Benilde/St. Margaret in St. Louis Park, Minnesota.

Both the sisters and the laity involved in these ministries have treasured the memories of the invigorating times when the energy and spirit of adolescents transformed their days into excitement, worry, and commitment. Thousands of graduates from Cathedral High School and hundreds of graduates from St. Boniface High School and Pierz Memorial High School have formed a broad base of friendship and support for the sisters of Saint Benedict's Monastery. The youthful spirit of these students demanded a response of dedication and helped shape the sisters' stance of mission in the contemporary scene of the Church and society of the postconciliar era.

Sister Merle Nolde, active in community and national social justice roles, participating in a rally at the United Nations headquarters.

9

READING THE SIGNS OF THE TIMES

Recognizing Contemporary Concerns

Awareness of the needs around them seemed to be a natural part of the life of the sisters of Saint Benedict's Monastery. They were no sooner settled in their new environment in St. Joseph, Minnesota, when they opened their home to orphans (as many as sixty-three a year), providing them care and an education. They offered a home and education for Native American girls in St. Benedict's Industrial School (1884 to 1896) in St. Joseph, and conducted boarding schools and pastoral ministry on Ojibwa reservations. They opened St. Benedict's Boys School, first known as Bethlehem Boarding School for Little Boys (1897 to 1948) on their motherhouse campus. Long before any women's movement in the United States, the sisters championed the cause of education for women in St. Benedict's Academy and College (1878 to the present time). The sisters also responded to the health care needs of the sick and elderly in their area from 1885 to the present time, even though it was at first considered as an inappropriate ministry for monastics. Even in the early 1900s, this was the reason given for the refusal to accept St. Benedict's Monastery into other Benedictine Congregations that were being formed.

The sisters were more hesitant and cautious about non-traditional, contemporary needs. Mother Henrita Osendorf urged them to expand their concern to the contemporary scene of the 1960s and 1970s, which was experiencing national anxiety over Vietnam, the Civil Rights Movement, and the plight of the poor in general. She wrote to the sisters in 1964:

> For a long time I have planned to say something in an official letter about the cause of civil rights. It seems to me that religious especially, totally committed as they must be to Christ in all his members, cannot be indifferent to the sufferings of the [African-] American and other minority groups. It is a matter in which all of us must be interested! We may not keep aloof from it on the pretext that [religious] have no place in human relations work. To love Christ is to love his members. This calls in the first place for our prayers and deliberate sacrifices so that the cause of justice and charity will be furthered. We have a duty to keep ourselves informed and interested; we have a duty to help others, especially those entrusted to our care, to understand the basic principle of the [solidarity of all people]. . . . We must teach and encourage our students to become involved in bettering human relations in their communities. It is our responsibility to oppose the forces of hatred and injustice to the best of our ability. . . . If we are indifferent or unconcerned about this serious evil in American society, our love of Christ is purely theoretical.[18]

Still there was hesitation. An informal 1967 community survey revealed that forty percent of the sisters still felt that their obligation to social justice was to be fulfilled by prayer alone. The 1971 W. I. Christopher study, *Profile of a Priory*, indicated that many sisters expressed a desire for greater involvement in the civic community and a greater concern for the poor. Only four percent, however, indicated a readiness to make a decision to move into social services other than the traditional ones of education and health care. The community's heavy investment in the educational and health-care apostolates also precluded branching out into other works of social justice.

For the sisters, new readings "of the signs of the times" came so gradually and in such small bursts of insight along the way that it is difficult to trace its development. Certainly one important value was the community's engagement with the College of Saint Benedict where educational opportunities broadened vision and awareness of responsibilities to be for the world. These opportunities included exposure to the social encyclicals, to African-American students already in the 1940s and 1950s, and to social activists like Catherine de Hueck, Peter Maurin, and Dorothy Day. Stirrings within the community of an awareness of the injustices of structures, systems, and wars, and of a growing desire to become involved with these issues became more evident in the late 1960s. These stirrings resulted in some changes in sisters' ministries and in movements toward action within the community. Providentially, sisters gifted with a call to justice and peace took initiative in helping the community take social responsibilities seriously, although a disturbing aftermath of sisters' involvement in a "protest" of the Vietnam War at St. Mary's Cathedral in St. Cloud in 1967 may have dampened the spirit of some in regard to taking social action.

The Symbolic Action at St. Mary's Cathedral

Some persons are called to be prophetic and to challenge the malaise of apathy that can paralyze a community, a church, or a nation in the face of overwhelming injustice, prejudice, ruthless violence, oppression, and poverty. One test of the authenticity of such a vocation is the sense of spiritual urgency in spite of the burden it places on the ones so called. Whether the attempt to draw attention to the atrocities of the Vietnam War at a Eucharistic Celebration in St. Mary's Cathedral in the fall of 1967 could be described as prophetic may be questioned. It was a sincere attempt on the part of some faculty at Cathedral High School (seven of them Benedictine sisters) to make a difference in the Church's and the nation's stance on the issue. It takes wisdom, experience, humility, and courage to voice a minority and opposing opinion of the status quo. It takes integrity and honesty to discern when following the dictates of conscience takes precedence over the dictates of acceptable behavior. The lessons learned on this occasion were many and far-reaching.

In the first place, the plans for the protest were in the hands of experienced activists who were engaged in civil disobedience protesting the war. What the group from Cathedral High School did not realize was that in order for such a protest to have the desired impact, arrangements would be made to have the media present and to plant hecklers to make the incident more dramatic. What was intended to be a simple reading of a petition at the time of the Prayers of the Faithful, a petition that the United States bishops speak out against the Vietnam War, turned into chaos. Some persons began shouting, "Sacrilege! Sit down!" The disruption is what the media chose to emphasize in its reporting. Members of the group felt "used" in what turned out to be a staged event. One member tried to explain the group's intention over the microphone, but the microphone was immediately turned off. It was true that a representative of the group had asked the celebrant of the Eucharistic Liturgy to use the microphone for this petition so that people would hear it. When the celebrant informed him that he would not call him to the pulpit, the group decided to read their petition from the pews at the usual time petitions were made. This was construed as an act of inexcusable disobedience.

Needless to say, the resulting confusion over what really did happen was painful for all concerned: St. Benedict's Community, the bishop and clergy of the diocese, Cathedral High School staff and board, and the local community at large. Unfortunately, the group never had an opportunity to speak for themselves, to explain what they had done and why. However, Mother Henrita called the sisters involved in the public witness to her office. Sister Katherine Kraft, who described the incident many years later wrote:

> Given the disapproval of many of the sisters, I fully expected to be reprimanded, or at least chided. What I will never forget is that instead of a scolding for causing the community public embarrassment, she simply said, "I know you were all sincere in what you did because I know you are good persons and I love you." She must have understood that we were feeling like community "pariahs" and she wanted to effect some healing in the community. All I know is that I left her office feeling affirmed, embraced by love and acceptance and able to go on with life.[19]

For the community, there has always been a mixture of pride for the courage of this group, confusion over the validity of such exteme action, and appreciation for the wisdom of Mother Henrita's acceptance that brought healing to the community on such occasions.

Community Supporting New Ministries

Despite the Cathedral incident, sisters began in 1969 to organize in various groups to study social concerns, to communicate them to the community, and to encourage the engagement of the community in responding to the concerns. The Political Affairs Group led to the establishment of the Social Concerns/Justice Committee, which in turn was later organized as one of the Planning Committee's working teams and given the title Operations Awareness Task Team (OATT). Members of these groups were inspired by their attendance at social concerns workshops, like the 1974 "Call to Justice" sponsored by the National Assembly of Women Religious (NAWR), and brought conviction and energy to the community's committees. Their energy, courage, and persistence in keeping the community informed and involved, significantly raised community awareness and action on social issues.

All along, the community had given of its human and financial resources in support of the needs around them, no doubt asking themselves, as did the disciples of Jesus, "But what is this in the face of so many needs?" The sisters subsidized their ministries in poor parishes, in their Native American missions, and in their foreign missions. In the last fifty years they sought to expand their corporate response to new social concerns, especially by supporting organizations which promoted peace and justice, such as:

> releasing Sister Merle Nolde to serve as co-director of the National Assembly of Women Religious (NAWR);
> giving direct aid to causes like the Civil Rights Movement, Bread for the World, and Global Education Associates;
> offering scholarships for African-American students;
> sending sisters to Mississippi to register voters;
> becoming a corporate sponsor of Pax Christi USA;
> supporting the sister-coordinator of Partners Across Borders, an organization linking St. Cloud, Minnesota, and Tenancingo, El Salvador, as sister-cities
> dedicating the Sunday collections to causes and programs to help the poor and oppressed locally and globally;
> participating in the Monastic Interreligious Dialogue.

Sister Sheila Rausch signing postcards for the Bread for the World.

Sisters adopting a highway: Sister Thomasette, Kathy Ryan, and Sisters Owen Lindblad and Elaine Schroeder.

Sister Phyllis Plantenberg planting in the children's plot of Common Ground, an organic gardening project.

A significant breakthrough for the sisters' social awareness had been the entrance of the community's first African-
American candidate, Sister Joyce Williams. She had gradu-
ated from the College of Saint Benedict in 1948 and entered
the novitiate in 1950. Her teaching career in high schools
provided the first exposure to African-Americans for most
students and their families in Stearns County and she won
their hearts. Her presence prepared the area schools for the
influx of the Bahamian sister-teachers who came to central
Minnesota in the 1960s when the sisters of the Blessed
Martin de Porres Community in Nassau, Bahamas, transferred to St. Benedict's Monastery (see Part III: Bahamas). In
the 1960s Sister Joyce became involved nationally and
internationally in programs concerned with racial harmony.
She served as coordinator for Project Bridge, a National
Catholic Conference for Interracial Justice (NCCFIJ) enter-
prise, and as national director of educational services for
NCCFIJ. She attended social justice meetings connected
with the Bishops' Synod in Rome and served on the Steering
Committee of the National Black Sisters Conference. From
1973 to 1993, she taught at Harlan Community Academy, a
Chicago public school, where she also tutored students with
learning disabilities. Sister Joyce defended on state and
national television her firm belief that integration is the key
to racial harmony. In 1988 the College of Saint Benedict
acknowledged her work in behalf of racial concerns by
establishing the Joyce Williams Scholarship for minority
students.

Along with a growing awareness of social justice concerns, the Benedictine tradition of reverence for all of creation also nurtures a sensitivity to environmental concerns.
The sisters have been vigilant about recycling, preserving
and planting trees, and conserving nature's gifts. Since
1970 they have annually celebrated Earth Day in gratitude
and recommitment to care for the earth. In the 1990s they
nurtured an organic gardening project known as Common
Ground under the leadership of Sister Phyllis Plantenberg.

Community administration established a Land and Natural Resources Task Team to study the best use of community properties and resources. Awareness of good stewardship and reverence for all material goods hearkens back to Benedict's injunction to the cellarer, the distributor of the goods of the community: "[The cellarer] will regard all utensils and goods of the monastery as sacred vessels of the altar" (RB 55:10). Benedict's warning to monastics about human nature's susceptibility to greed and wasteful extravagance with material goods is still appropriate for all earth-dwellers of the twenty-first century.

Individual sisters taking initiatives in responding to new social concerns and discussions of the Community Synod in the 1970s sparked the desire to make public statements on social justice issues, but it took some time to develop a process to insure community involvement in making effective responses.

Community Taking a Stand

The community took its first public stance in 1973. A pro-life statement, drafted by the Social Justice Committee at the request of the Council, was released to the press on March 5, 1973. The concern for peace led the community to take its second position, a stand for nuclear disarmament in 1981. When a host of other concerns clamored for corporate responses, Sister Katherine Howard and the Council developed a Community Stance Policy to guide the process. During Sister Katherine's leadership, the community took three additional public stances. Facilitated by the OATT, the Community Chapter came to the decision of declaring the monastery a Nuclear Free Zone in 1984. An overwhelming majority of the Chapter saw this as a public way of awakening and revitalizing the community stance on peace. Previously in the 1970s, the community had developed an active chapter of Benedictines for Peace, a call to actions of peace initiated by the Benedictine sisters of Erie, Pennsylvania.

In 1986 the OATT called the community's attention to

another issue, the Sanctuary Movement for refugees, as a contemporary response to the monastic tradition of granting asylum. The majority of sisters expressed approval of the concept of sanctuary and in 1988 took the final step in "declaring our Benedictine monastery a public sanctuary."[20] The first refugees came the following year, and over the next two years, five received asylum. The number of Central American refugees declined in the 1990s with the lessening of United States' intervention in Central America's domestic affairs. For the sisters as well as for refugees, sanctuary was another experience of evangelization.

The community's desire to be committed to bringing Christ to the world was evident in the individual sister's choices in working with and for people in new and varied ministries, in the community's outreach programs, and in its growing awareness of its mission as a monastic community. The work of "reading the signs of the times" continues to challenge the sisters as they discern how God is calling them to work for justice and peace as monastics in the twenty-first century.

Individual Charisms/New Ministries

After Vatican II, the sisters were given more voice in assessing their capabilities and interests in the decisions regarding their work placement. By 1970, in a spirit of collegiality, the sisters freely discerned which work of ministry would foster the use of their skills and potential on behalf of the Church, their community, and their own development. Interviews with sisters who took on some new type of service revealed a desire to be with and among the people. Some sisters preferred working with adults. A significant number of sisters sought further education in pastoral theology and chose forms of parish ministry. Some sought the work of pastoral care and patient-visiting in hospitals and nursing homes.

Other sisters branched out into new ministries as the community recognized and nourished signs of individual charisms of mission. Examples of ministries in which sisters served in the year 2000 reveal a broad spectrum:

pastoral associates

directors of parish programs, particularly in rural and
inner-city areas

coordinators of programs for minority groups

family nurse practitioners

volunteers for programs for the needy and shelters for
abused women and children

counselors and spiritual directors

prison ministers

directors of Catholic Charities services and volunteer
programs.

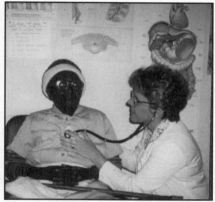

For Sister Ellen Cotone (left) in Recife, Brazil, there is no language barrier. Sister
Patricia Ann Sniezek (right), nurse practioner in Alabama.

Pastoral Ministry Team providing assistance to parishes' pastoral programs.
Present are: Sisters Mary Weidner, Joyce Iten, and Marlene Meierhofer.

Some individual apostolic works had the potential to point the community in the direction of making it a corporate work. An example of this developed from Sister Madonna Kuebelbeck's missionary work in Recife, Brazil. Invited by missionaries already serving there, Sister Madonna went to Brazil in 1978. Later, for varying intervals of time, other sisters followed to form a community of Benedictine presence in Brazil and to work with Basic Christian Community leadership programs, parish administration, and religious education. Sister Madonna returned to St. Benedict's for health reasons. Sisters Ellen Cotone, Kerry O'Reilly, and Mary Schumer continue to the present time. In their service to the poorest of the poor, the sisters have heeded the caution of Recife-Olinda's former bishop, Dom Helder Camara's, "Work with, don't do for, the people." The moving story of their presence and simple way of life among displaced families in Jordão is captured in sensitive photographs and poetic prose by Sisters Annette Brophy and Mara Faulkner in *Born of Common Hungers: Benedictine Women in Search of Connections*. Of this "tiny community clinging to the edge of a Brazilian slum," Sister Mara writes: "It may survive and grow, or it may be gone within a few years. For now, the women there are doing what Benedictines have done throughout history—putting down tentative roots in a place that seems to need their presence."[21]

Another example of an individual's sister mission becoming the community's work is Sister Patricia Ann (Grace) Sniezek's service in Alabama as nurse practioner. Her venture has lured other sisters to join her, presently Sisters Dorothea Lenz, and Luanne Lenz.

With the growing needs of immigrants in the United States, it is not necessary to look across the sea for mission work. Saint Benedict's Monastery is situated near several Hispanic communities that beckon its involvement. In 1998 with the help of Sister Janet Thielges, volunteer grant writer, Sister Renee Domeier organized, and presently coordinates, Casa Guadalupe Center for the Hispanic community in Cold Spring, twelve miles from St. Joseph. It serves as a kind of clearinghouse, consisting of Anglos and Latinos, to meet the needs of the immigrants, to assist adjustment to each other's cultures, and to facilitate the acceptance of Latinos in the area. Sister Renee is hopeful that the project's potential of replication by other local communities will be realized.

Sister Renee Domeier with a family from the Hispanic community in Cold Spring, Minnesota.

Since community is made up of individual sisters, a community charism, whether it be hospitality, evangelization, or praying for others, is possible only when nourished by the way individual sisters exercise their gifts for others. Marie Hickey, O.S.B., abbess of St. Scholastica's Abbey, Drinklage, Germany, described the interplay of individual and community charism as follows:

> There may be [monastics] called to preach or do pastoral work inside or outside the monastery. The more these missionary charisms grow and flourish in individuals and are accepted and integrated into the community, the more the community as a whole will radiate Good News and develop an antenna for the movement of the spirit of God touching them to respond in concrete situations where evangelization is needed.[22]

The interplay of individual sisters' gifts strengthened the community charism of Saint Benedict's Monastery, giving it vision and energy to continue sharing its charisms in ways given it by long tradition, and creating new ways of sharing the Good News of love and freedom.

10
COMMUNITY CHARISM AND OUTREACH MINISTRY

Monastic Community as a Primary Work

How is the monastic way of life itself the community's ministry? What charism is at the heart of a monastic community? Benedict's vision of monastic life was simple and practical. In his *Rule* he described a down-to-earth, everyday spirituality rooted in Christ. For Benedict, simply living a life of prayer in loving communion with others and open to all who came to the monastery was the monastic way. Benedict highlighted the basic Christian virtues: reverence for God, for one another in community, and for all the goods of the monastery as though they were the vessels of the altar; humility, the recognition and acceptance of the limitations of creaturehood; zeal that fosters fervent love; mutual obedience, the way by which monastics go to God; dispossession to be possessed by God. The models for Benedict were not the martyrs or giants of asceticism, but rather the following: an abbot/prioress who is a shepherd winning others with mercy, kitchen workers who serve the community with love, a porter/receptionist who provides a prompt answer with the warmth of love, and a cellarer who knows how to meet the needs of the community with a kind word. Striving

167

to live the monastic life with faith in God's presence in everyone and in everything is one way, among many others, to further the reign of God in the world today.

Gradually the sisters became more intentional about the monastic way as their primary work. The community changed from its initial focus of serving the urgent needs of a pioneer American culture to becoming a spiritual center to nurture society's spiritual longings. In doing so, the sisters were returning to their roots while breaking new ground. In fact, to ritualize the reclaiming of its distinctive monastic heritage and tradition, in 1996 the community changed its title from St. Benedict's Convent to Saint Benedict's Monastery. The sisters believed that the title "monastery" more accurately conveyed the permanance of their commitment to one another, to prayer, and to hospitality.

Instead of describing the transition process as "coming into a new age," Sister Ephrem Hollermann, prioress, called it "coming of age." The *St. Cloud Times* summarized an interview with Sister Ephrem as follows:

> Shrinking in size, increasing in years, but definitely coming into its own, [Saint Benedict's Monastery] has found new gifts in its feminine spirituality, revitalized its artistic roots, and embraced new technology to globalize its outreach.
>
> Outreach—providing Benedictine values to areas of society that need them most—is one of the cornerstones of Benedictine life. When it comes to matters of the soul, the sisters are ahead of the curve. They have established a unique concept called "Studium," which allows monastery members furthering their studies to share office space and ideas. They [have created spaces] dedicated specifically to the arts. Their Spirituality Center offers an increasingly popular site for [persons] looking for spiritual retreats, special instruction, and spiritual mentoring.[23]

In the last thirty years, the sisters developed various programs through which every member of the community has the opportunity to devote herself, in some way, to the traditional intellectual, spiritual, and artistic concerns that have been the domain of monastics through the ages. Above all, every sister is involved in the work of hospitality, the heart of monastic ministry.

Sister Agatha Zwilling (center) welcomes Pamela Planche and Roberta Bondi, a Studium scholar-in-residence.

Sister Lisa Kittock and hospitality bell ringers welcome worshippers.

The Benedictine Charism of Hospitality and Outreach

In the *Priorities Study*, Sister Nora Luetmer challenged the sisters to view hospitality as a part of their apostolate or ministry. She asked: "What makes hospitality chacteristically Benedictine? Is it just a myth, or is it an ideal that has been cultivated and nurtured throughout the centuries?"

> Benedictine hospitality cannot be defined by listing a catalog of components because it is a blend of intangible qualities which defy simple description. It is a spiritual quality quietly present in genuine interest in human values . . . [with] a new dimension added, the conviction that [we] are receiving Christ. In his *Rule*, Benedict had great concern for the guests: he stressed the qualities necessary for the porter; has the guest seated at the [prioress'] table; permits the [prioress] to break the fast in honor of the guest; and provides a guest house as part of the monastic complex.[24]

For the sisters at the motherhouse, hospitality intensified with the opening of the new sacred spaces in 1983. As Sister Katherine Howard remarked when asked about people's response to the new spaces, "People just came!" They found their way into the heart of the community. The new spaces, particularly the Gathering Place, offered a welcoming place for the sisters to greet the various community guests: employees of the Sisters of St. Benedict; the college community; families, relatives and friends; invited and unannounced guests; the needy; those looking for spiritual guidance and companionship; or those looking for tours through the sacred spaces or for a place of peace and quiet. In particular, the Gathering Place has welcomed college students to join a community of worship on Sundays and special occasions, to seek a blessing on their works of Christian service, or to find a community of friendship. The new sacred spaces and dining room have become places that hold in reverence the sorrow of loss and the celebration of new life at wakes and funerals of sisters and the celebrations of jubilees and other important community events with relatives and friends. The tasks of coordinating events and serving as receptionists and hostesses have been a daily ministry of many sisters in carrying out Benedict's injunction, "All guests who present themselves [monasteries are never without them] are to be welcomed as Christ" (RB, 53:1).

Monastery Programs

Sisters have created various ways of sharing themselves and their monastic traditions and values within the monastery's environment of community support and prayer. In recent years the Leadership Team has coordinated these services under the direction of Sister Dolores Super to provide collaboration, mutual support, and a common mission of ministry and hospitality. They are Spiritual Ministries, Arts and Heritage, Studium, and Monastic Enterprises.

Spiritual Ministries

Beginning with Mother Louisa Walz in 1920, the community has a long history of being involved with spiritual ministry by providing retreats for women. In summer the community housed large numbers of retreatants in the college's residence halls. As the college began using its residence halls for summer programs, the sisters planned small-group retreats in other areas on the monastery campus. For several years, a house on campus served as a retreat center, and in 1978 the sisters opened a year-round retreat center on the second floor of the main monastery building.

A spiritual ministry program was organized in 1984 in a separate building named the Monastic Resource Center. The center was advertised as a place providing programs, facilities, and human resources for individuals and groups of all faiths in an environment of Benedictine hospitality, worship, and community. The staff of the center sought to expand the program to include all elements of a holistic program—spiritual, social, intellectual, physical, and aesthetic—and invited a broad range of people. In the 1990s, the center, now called Spirituality Center, developed an even broader outreach program by offering workshops and retreats in parishes, schools, and retirement centers. Both sisters and lay people give spiritual direction and provide workshops of initial and ongoing formation in the art of spiritual direction.

The center was moved in the year 2000 to a more secluded area at the west end of Evin Hall, to which a new addition and entrance were added to accommodate the Spirituality Center and its faith-formation programs. With the help of Regent Communications and the Kendrick Foundation, the Spirituality Ministries Team launched a radio project to provide "Meditations from the Monastery." The center has also become a popular site for monastery-college

Sister Kathryn Casper reads the daily reflection of sisters on WWJO.

student activities, such as "Busy Persons' Retreats" and the "Benedictine Friends" program.

The Community claimed its spirituality programs as a priority ministry in 1999 when it focused on "enriching the spiritual life in central Minnesota," with an emphasis on partnering with women in a mutual sharing of gifts.

Studium

Along with longevity came a longer productive retirement. Sister Mary Reuter wanted to provide an environment within the community where the sisters in retirement could continue working in their areas of expertise in a new way. Consultants, researchers, and creative writers needed a place to work in a community environment. A brainstorming session with twenty-two sisters in 1992 gave birth to the new ministry program called Studium, which was given space in Evin Hall. Its goal was to support and challenge each participant in her work and to offer collaborative support to programs, sponsored by the monastery, college, or community-at-large, that encourage individual talent.

Studium further identified its mission to promote its members' research and experience through informal dialogue, lectures, conferences, and publications in an environment that is interdisciplinary, intergenerational, interfaith, and intercultural. An important part of Studium is its Scholars-in-Residence Program. These scholars participate in Studium as they work on their projects and join the community for prayer and meals. During the first five years of Studium's existence, forty scholars were participants for varying lengths of time. Studium provides office space for both sister and lay faculty members from the College of Saint Benedict while they are on sabbatical. Monthly meetings devoted to discussions of a work-in-progress, a recent publication, or a presentation form an important part of its program. The resident scholars also give presentations of their work to the community. Books published under the aegis of Studium include:

Born of Common Hungers: Benedictine Women in Search of Connections, photographs by Annette Brophy, O.S.B., and essays by Mara Faulkner, O.S.B.

Divine Favor: The Art of Joseph O'Connell, edited by Colman O'Connell, O.S.B.

Forever Your Sister, co-edited by Janice Wedl, O.S.B., and Eileen Maas Nalevanko.

Full of Fair Hope: A History of St. Mary's Mission at Redlake, by Owen Lindblad, O.S.B.

Histories of parishes in the Diocese of St. Cloud by Janice Wedl, O.S.B.:

> *As Living Stones: The History of St. Michael's Parish, Motley, Minnesota*
>
> *The First 75 Years: The History of St. Anthony Parish, St. Cloud, Minnesota*
>
> *Padua, God's Country: History of St. Anthony of Padua Parish, Padua, Minnesota*
>
> *Sacred Heart Church, A Parish on Track, Staples, Minnesota*

The Literature of Spiritual Values and Catholic Fiction: Mariella Gable, O.S.B., edited (and Introduction) by Nancy Hynes, O.S.B.,

Medieval Women Monastics, by Miram Schmitt, O.S.B. and Linda Kulzer, O.S.B.

The Reshaping of a Tradition, by Ephrem Hollermann, O.S.B.

Sing a New Church, by Delores Dufner, O.S.B.

They Came to Teach, by Annabelle Raiche, C.S.J., and Ann Marie Biermaier, O.S.B.

Threads from Our Tapestry, by Imogene Blatz, O.S.B., and Alard Zimmer, O.S.B.

A number of the scholars-in-residence have also found Studium an environment conducive to writing their books.

The Studium lobby art piece of the Benedictine women monastics, Lioba (d. c 781), Scholastica (480 to 543), and Hildegard (1098 to 1179) inspires love for truth and beauty. The original batik designed and crafted by Judith Goetemann was commissioned by St. Paul's Monastery.

Art and Heritage

> In the Benedictine tradition, we respond to the hungers
> of the human spirit by fostering, preserving and sharing
> the art and heritage of our monastic culture.[25]

The basic hunger of the human spirit is for goodness, truth, and beauty, or, more simply, it is hunger for God. The long tradition of Benedictines in their search for God has not overlooked the yearning for beauty and the gift of creativity. Benedict's simple yet profound observation—"if there are artisans in the monastery, they are to practice their craft with all humility" (RB, 57:1)—showed a sensitivity to creative talents that has characterized monastic life for more than 1,500 years. Because St. Benedict's Community has been blessed with gifted artists in music, painting, sculpture, pottery, creative writing, photography, and fiber and graphic arts, the sisters consider it important to foster and

Sister Thomasette Scheeler, paper making.

Sister Dennis Frandrup at the potter's wheel.

share this giftedness. The community renovated the former maintenance center as a Monastic Artisan Studio in 1997. With the help of grants and the support of private donors and under the leadership of Sister Ingrid Anderson, a new Art and Heritage Place to house the Haehn Museum, Whitby Gift Shop, and gallery was completed in the year 2000. These buildings stand at the entrance of the monastery as concrete expressions of the sisters' support of the arts and pride in the Community's heritage.

Sister Margaret VanKempen weaving.

The new museum provides space to preserve individual artifacts and to tell the story of the community. Curator, Sister Ruth Nierengarten, prepares exhibits of Benedictine tradition and monastic values by which the sisters lived and worked among the people in central Minnesota and in various areas of the world. For example, the museum's collection of the hand-embroidered vestments embodies the community's cultivation of the beautiful and the sacred. Vestment-making was an important ministry of the sisters during the mid-twentieth century. The Minneapolis Institute of Arts prized this collection, calling it "world-class" in its 1992 exhibit. The Stearns History Museum also featured the vestment collection in 1985.

The spaces of Saint Benedict's Monastery speak of the sisters' intentional cultivation of aesthetic values and the

Curator, Sister Ruth Nierengarten, displaying a set of embroidered vestments.

artistic talents of persons. The sisters have come to appreciate beauty as a two-fold gift. While they shaped their monastery's environment through its architecture, the presence of art pieces in its spaces, and the artistry of its landscaping, these in turn have quietly shaped the community and affected its ministry of hospitality. Welcoming and beautiful spaces create a monastic atmosphere of peace, contemplation, and openness to God, Source of all beauty.

Monastic Enterprises

Making handcrafted articles has also been recognized and organized in a community program called Monastic Enterprises. About eighty-five sisters were involved in this program in the year 2000. Skilled in various crafts, the sisters create a great variety of products for area sales and for the gift shops at the motherhouse and at St. Scholastica's Convent. These handmade articles are products of weaving,

Chinese Paper-Cutting Exhibit commemorating the seventieth anniversary of the sisters' mission to China—Sister Baulu Kuan, curator, fall 2000.

Sister Elaine Schindler making candles for chapel services and for the gift shops.

candle-making, calligraphy, card-making, quilling, needlework, and other skills. The handcrafted articles also attest to the sisters' sensitivity to the use of natural, homemade, home-grown, and recycled materials.

Renovation of the former maintenance center gave the sisters a workshop, the Monastic Artisan Studio, in which to explore their talents and form a community of mutual encouragement and support as they share in the work of supporting the community and its ministries. It is part of the Benedictine tradition to hand down the inspiration, materials, and know-how of creativity, recognizing in that community experience a share in the creativity of God.

Sister Marold Kornovich quilling.

Many sisters help supply the gift shop with creative needlework.

Community Outreach Networks

Through old and new programs, the sisters reach out to invite others to join in their mission and life commitment. The long-standing programs are the Vocation, Oblate and Communications Programs; the relatively new one is the Development Program.

Oblates of Saint Benedict's Monastery

An Oblate Program became a new venture of hospitality for the sisters in the last half of the twentieth century. It invites hundreds of people, men and women, to develop a close relationship with the sisters in order to deepen their spirituality. Oblates formally associate themselves with a Benedictine monastery to experience a mutual bonding with that community and to share in the prayers and good works of that monastery.

Prior to 1961, Saint Benedict's Monastery could not receive oblates because that was considered a prerogative of male monasteries. Reception of oblate candidates took place at Saint John's Abbey. The sisters appealed to the Sacred Congregation of Religious in Rome for the privilege of direct reception of oblates at their monastery. When the permission was granted, some of the oblates transferred their membership from Saint John's Abbey to Saint Benedict's Monastery. Sister Joanne Muggli directed the oblates from 1961 to 1972. The program expanded considerably in the 1970s under the leadership of Sister Mary Anthony Wagner.

In an interview, Sister Mary Anthony Wagner described her methods of connecting oblates with the monastery and with each other: regular mailings, annual renewal days, regional group meetings, and community celebrations. The letters to the oblates constitute the major part of formation of oblate spirituality by suggesting Scripture readings for lectio or prayerful reading. The letters also publish news about the community and oblates. By 1999 seven annual letters were being sent to 700 committed oblates and 170 oblate candidates. Asked how the community benefits by having oblates, Sister Mary Anthony responded:

> Oblates are the 'lay arm' of a Benedictine community, reaching out into areas of life, seeking to share with others what they themselves gain as disciples of Benedict. They strive . . . to bring the Benedictine ideals of prayer and service into the world where they live and work.[26]

In their discernment on the focus of community for the new millennium, the sisters indicated an eagerness to explore alternatives to membership in community and new approaches to the oblate program—especially for the college students. Noting the eagerness of people today to connect with a community to deepen their spirituality, the sisters wish to respond in ways that meet contemporary needs.

Vocation Program

Some programs, such as the vocation ministry, focusing on recruiting candidates for the Monastery, had long been part of the community. The Vocation Team was given a much broader task in the 1990s: to involve all community members in encouraging and discerning vocations, to publicize the choice of religious life in terms of contemporary understandings, to give opportunities to young people to experience life in community, and to guide women in making vocation choices, whether for religious life or for other areas of Christian service. Increasing membership was established as one of the community's priorities in the strategic planning process of 1999 and 2000. In doing this, the sisters claimed their responsibility to vocation ministry by collaboration and support of the vocation staff.

Sisters and visitors enjoying a common search. Sister Marlene, Vocation Director, sits third from the right.

Development and Communications

Some programs, such as Development, were new to the community. In the 1980s the Lilly Foundation determined that the best way to aid religious communities was to help them help themselves by implementing their own planning and development programs. Over a period of years, the Lilly Foundation funded training workshops to assist religious communities in setting up development programs tailored to their mission and goals. The foundation stressed the importance of giving others opportunities to participate in the community's ministries by financial contributions. In the early 1990s the administration set up a Development Program, which became, under the able leadership of Sister Gen Maiers, the arm of community reaching out to the friends of the community and meeting new friends. For example, the staff arranged for reunions of the community with its former members. They invited former St. Benedict's high school students to reunions and arranged to have them participate in the College of Saint Benedict's alumnae communications and gatherings. The Development/Communications staff publishes regular community newsletters, one for community news and one, *Benedictine Sisters and Friends*, for the thousands of friends and benefactors who have kept in touch with the community. Grants have made possible various monastery projects. Above all, the Development and Communications staff views its work as a ministry of collaborating with the community's friends and benefactors to answer the needs of contemporary Church and society.

Internal Services of the Monastery

Considering the monastic life as the primary mission of the Sisters of St. Benedict places the internal services of the monastery in a privileged position. It requires skilled and dedicated personnel to keep the monastery's functions

Service with a smile. Top: Sisters Jane and Marcella Weber, Esther Reischl, Sisters Sylvia Flicker, Modesta Arceneau, and Dorothy Heinen. The secretarial and postal services, below: Sisters Francella Janson, Myrtle Schmitz, Dorothy Noll, Mary Schneider, and Malachy Hurley.

Sisters Ruth Boedigheimer and Imogene Blatz, present and past archivists.

effective for community living and for the community's hospitality programs. Benedict did not value these services for their efficiency but for their supportive role in creating a monastic community of love and service to one another and to all guests of the monastery. His intentional placement of ordinary daily tasks within the monastery as part of its mission defies the society's tendency to stratify work for the sake of status. Everyone in the community is important, regardless of age, talent, or status upon entrance. Everyone faces the same challenge to be Christ for others, and to find Christ in one another and in all guests.

Those who think of monastics only at prayer or with a book in hand for holy reading, miss the other side of the same monastic coin: the seamstresses, cooks, servers, secretaries, librarians, housekeepers, liturgists, gardeners, sacristans, drivers, nurses, beauticians, archivists, receptionists, and those who work in the business office and post office. Benedict stressed the monastic manner of work as much as the manner of prayer. He valued the everyday work of monastery upkeep as the ordinary way of extraordinary love, an antidote to work used to climb the social ladder of power and wealth. The sisters have also found that they need the help and expertise of lay people in performing the community's internal service, especially in nursing care, maintenance, financial management, and hospitality. This collaboration creates a bond between the sisters and the surrounding community—lifetime bonds which in many cases result from twenty to forty years of employment.

Sister Paula Revier discussing a maintenance project with Roger Zimmer (employed thirty-seven years).

The hidden apostolate lies in the heart of the monastery: the prayer and suffering of the retired and infirm sisters. Most often it is a ministry of sheer faith. These sisters are a powerhouse of prayer for the needs of the world, a consolation to those who seek their prayers, a source of inspiration to their sisters in community, and a witness to the ultimate meaning of life. In turn, the community's care for the elderly and infirm supports them in their diminishment, pain, depression, or loneliness.

Praying, suffering, and serving within the monastery create extraordinary community bonds. Being monastics for a lifetime is possible only in the solidarity of community. In that communion of love created by God's call and sustained by God's faithfulness, monastics strive to live in fidelity to prayer, continuing conversion, stability, mutual obedience, forgiveness, and the sharing of love wherever they live and work.

Sisters Laurent Trombley and Ardella Kvamme honoring Winnie Dehler, receptionist for twenty-nine years.

Lyndis Cully, thirteen years of nursing care at St. Scholastica's Convent.

Summary of Part II

Part II has described the transformations of Saint Benedict's Monastery's ministries and how these transformations have affected the community of sisters and the community-at-large. Two important outcomes highlight the changes that have taken place. The apostolate of the laity was enhanced, and the apostolate of the sisters, that of being a monastic community, was strengthened.

The Apostolate of the Laity

The Vatican II documents, *The Church in the Modern World* and the *Decree on the Apostolate of the Laity*, clearly called for an emergence of the laity to help the Church fulfill its mission, seeking the heavenly city while working to reshape the earthly one. The Church had relied heavily upon its religious to lead in addressing social needs and concerns. Vatican II invited all to participate, and in many cases the laity were better prepared than ever before to assume leadership in bringing the Gospel to bear on society individually and collectively.

While religious may have taken the initiative in pre-Vatican II times to perform works of mercy, such as healing, teaching, and counseling, they have since encouraged laity to work alongside them and, in some cases, to replace them in these works. Hence, the services given by religious since Vatican II have been more likely done in cooperation with or by the laity in the firm belief that it is everyone's vocation to be Christ for others.

The Apostolate of the Monastery, being a Monastic Community

As the renewal after Vatican II focused more on religious life as a charism within the Church rather than as a "work force," sisters began to realize that "who they are" was more important than "what they do." As the community divested itself of the ownership and management of its institutions, the sisters could concentrate more fully on who they were as a monastic community. Gradually, living a monastic life became the focus of their ministry, whether they lived and worked at one of the community centers or were called elsewhere to perform corporal works of mercy and earn a compensation in support of the community, whether they were young and active, or were retired or infirm. The sisters appreciated anew the evangelizing aspect of monasticism: it is more about living than about teaching. A monastic community is both the message "God is"; and the medium, "living a God-centered way of prayer, community, and mission."

Within the last decades of the twentieth century, Saint Benedict's Monastery has given its "message and medium" architectural expression in three major thrusts of monastic ministries:

> the spiritual—enhanced Sacred Spaces and Spirituality
>   Center
> the intellectual—Studium
> the artistic—the Art and Heritage Place.

The new Art and Heritage Place stands at the Chapel Lane entrance, a symbol of the community's appreciation of its heritage and love of beauty.

For the first one hundred years, the sisters experienced their way of life as highly esteemed; their roles were clear, and the fruitfulness of their apostolic works immediately obvious. Through the renewal and transformations of the last fifty years of the twentieth century they lived in the hope that the time of crisis and transition would bear its own fruit. The transformations traced throughout **Part I** and **Part II** reveal that fruit as a consistent deepening of the community's vocation to be a monastic presence always in search of God in the here and now. The future is in the hands of God, who continues to promise:

> I will put my spirit in you that you may live, and I will settle you upon your land; thus you shall know that I am [God]. I have promised and I will do it (Ezekiel 37: 13-14).

The community's traditions are passed on. Sister Enid Smith delights Novice Denese Rigby with her stories.

Notes to Part II

Chapter 6: Managing Changes in Ministry

1. Luetmer, *Priorities Study*, 1974, p. 1.
2. Ibid., p. 74.
3. Annabelle Raiche, C.S.J., and Ann Marie Biermaier, O.S.B., *They Came to Teach* (St. Cloud, Minnesota: North Star Press, 1994), pp. 203-215.

Chapter 7: Changes in Community-owned Institutions

4. Kathleen Kalinowski, O.S.B., "Sponsorship of Benedictine Institutions by the Sisters of St. Benedict," 29 April 1993 (personal copy).
5. SBMA: Corporation Minutes, RG 3-1-2, f. 9..
6. SBMA: Council Minutes, RG 3-3-1, f. 33.
7. SBMA: Corporation Minutes, RG 3-1-2, f. 9.
8. SBMA: Introduction RG 19, Imogene Blatz, O.S.B., Victorine Houde, O.S.B. (attended St. Benedict's Academy, 1929 to 1931), Personal Interview, May 2000.
9. SBMA: Minutes of Meeting of Board Members, 2 April 1960.
10. Luetmer, *Priorities Study*, p. 263.
11. McDonald, 286.

Chapter 8: Changes in Staffing Diocesan Schools

12. Luetmer, p. 143.
13. SMBA, Peters, Correspondence, RG 5-9-9, f. 8.
14. Ibid.
15. Ibid.
16. Ibid.
17. Ibid.

Chapter 9: Reading the Signs of the Times

18. SBMA: Osendorf, Circular Letters, 1964, RG 5-10-2, f. 5.
19. Katherine Kraft, O.S.B., "My Recollection of the Events Surrounding the Symbolic Action in St. Mary's Cathedral, St. Cloud, Minnesota, Asking the Bishops of the United States to Speak Out Against the Vietnam War," 18 June 2000 (Personal Interview).
20. Minutes of Chapter Meetings, RG 11-5-3c, f.
21. *Born of Common Hungers: Benedictine Women in Search of Connections*, photographs by Annette Brophy, O.S.B.; essays by Mara Faulkner, O.S.B. (Notre Dame and London: University of Notre Dame Press, 1997), p. 5.

22. Marie Hickey, O.S.B., "Evangelization and Monasticism," *Tjurunga* 44, May 1993, p. 18.
23. *St. Cloud Times*, 30 March 1997.

CHAPTER 10: COMMUNITY CHARISM AND OUTREACH MINISTRY

24. Luetmer, pp. 99-100.
25. "Art and Heritage Mission Statement," 30 October 1996.
26. *Sisters of Saint Benedict*, Spring/Summer, 1988.
27. Mary Anthony Wagner, O.S.B., interviewed by Carol Berg, O.S.B., April 2000.

One of Joseph O'Connell's sculptures depicting aspects of the life of the sisters (featured in the Gathering Place): The apostolate—a sister protecting a child from the winter storms.

PART III

HISTORICAL MINISTRIES OF THE COMMUNITY

by
Emmanuel Renner, O.S.B.
Olivia Forster, O.S.B.
Carol Berg, O.S.B.

Saint Benedict's Monastery and the College of Saint Benedict (c. 1995). The monastery expanded westward (center and lower right) and the college expanded southward (upper half). The southeast campus: the East apartments, Haehn Campus Center, Henrita Academic Building and Richarda Hall are not shown in this view. See page 198.

INTRODUCTION

A sequel to the history of the first one hundred years of Saint Benedict's Monastery spans the last half of the twentieth century. That history would be incomplete without a companion **Part III** describing, from their vantage point, the ministries that grew out of and developed alongside St. Benedict's Community. Some ministries have been discontinued, and new ones have been called forth as recounted in **Part II**; some have taken on a life of their own, and others continue to be an integral part of the life of the monastery. Rather than cover all the bases of the community's ministries, aspects of the long-standing ones of education, health care, and missionary activity have been chosen to illustrate the transformations that continue to take place in these services.

While the College of Saint Benedict deserves its own history, it has been chosen here as the representative of the education ministry in relation to the community because it has been an integral part of Saint Benedict's Monastery for almost a century. The hospitals and nursing homes represent a large investment of human resources on the part of the community, as well as a large financial investment, especially when the St. Cloud Hospital was built in the late 1920s when the nation's economy slumped. The missions to the Native Americans and to foreign countries have pointed St. Benedict's Community to the contemporary need of sensitivity to minority groups and to the broader horizons of a global community. The development of these ministries fleshes out the energy, spirit, and commitment that underlies the community's history.

Southeast view of a portion of the campus of the College of Saint Benedict. The Haehn Campus Center (Student and Sports Center)—lower center.

11
TO HOLD IN TRUST: THE EVOLUTION OF THE RELATIONSHIP BETWEEN THE MONASTERY AND COLLEGE

Emmanuel Renner, O.S.B.

The full history of the College of Saint Benedict (CSB) remains to be written. In the meantime, the focus of this chapter is the evolving relationship between the founding Benedictine monastic community and the college. This relationship reveals the significant contribution by the Benedictine sisters as the sponsoring body and as faculty, staff, administrators, and trustees in the college since its founding in 1913. While this chapter records a great deal of the history of the college, that history is necessary to clarify the sisters' contribution and to describe the gradual evolution of the relationship between the monastic community and the college. The early stage of the evolution is characterized by near-familial ties between the monastic community and the college until the 1960s. That stage is followed by a gradual distancing of the two institutions, as the college grew dramatically in size while the number of sisters engaged as faculty, staff, and trustees decreased significantly. As that change developed, it became clear to the monastery and the college that the original sponsorship model would no longer serve the interests of the two institutions. By the 1980s, the monastery and college undertook the difficult task of creating a more intentional collaborative relationship between

199

the monastic community and a college that by then had a majority of lay persons serving as faculty, administrators, and members of the Board of Trustees.

American Context for Catholic Colleges for Women

For Saint Benedict's Monastery to establish a college in the second decade of the twentieth century was to situate the college amidst a critically important debate among Catholics. The history of that early national debate about Catholic women attending college gives us a context for understanding a few of the issues facing religious communities of women as they pondered the desirability of founding colleges. At the end of the nineteenth century, many of the Catholic hierarchy objected to Catholic women attending college, fearing that education might inspire women graduates to seek professional careers and then either not marry or marry later in life and bear only a few children. In the midst of this debate the School Sisters of Notre Dame, in 1895, opened the first Catholic women's college in the United States, the College of Notre Dame of Maryland, as an extension of their girls' academy. The courage and foresight of these Notre Dame Sisters contributed to the education of Catholic women in that state and inspired other religious communities of women to consider providing collegiate level education for women.

By 1900 many of the bishops began to understand that Catholic women would be attending private women's colleges or public state colleges if no Catholic colleges were available to them. Several bishops believed attendance at such institutions might be damaging to the faith of Catholic students. Furthermore, some bishops believed that the liberal arts curriculum taught in the eastern private women's colleges would foster professional career ambitions and competitiveness among the graduates, thereby weakening their quality of traditional femininity. Moreover, the bishops could not but feel responsible for the several Catholic women who had been refused acceptance into The Catholic University of America, a college the bishops had founded for men.[1] For these reasons, some of the bishops began to favor the establishment of Catholic women's colleges sponsored by women's religious communities.

Some bishops and clergy wanted Catholic women's colleges to offer only vocational courses. However, Trinity College in Washington, D.C., founded in 1900, was fortunate in having the support of Bishop John Spalding and Cardinal James Gibbons in its commitment to a liberal arts curriculum modeled upon that of such a prestigious Eastern women's college as Mount Holyoke College. From the beginning, Trinity emphasized critical thinking and supported a view of women's role in life that was broader than that of traditional wife and mother.

In the introduction to her book, *Higher Education for Catholic Women*, Mary Oates uses Trinity College as a model for evaluating other Catholic women's colleges that began to proliferate after 1910.[2] She claims that most of those colleges did not achieve the caliber of excellence set by Trinity College. This failure on the part of many Catholic women's colleges was partially due to the bishops who pressured, or even ordered, religious communities in their dioceses to open a local Catholic women's college specializing in vocational courses. The bishops hoped by this means to discourage Catholic girls from attending public colleges. In many cases, these communities of women were neither strongly motivated to establish a college nor likely to have been educationally prepared to do so.

Those religious communities of women who did establish colleges often began by expanding their academies to include college level courses. Gradually these offerings evolved into a complete college program. Many of the academies that gave birth to colleges, however, were themselves no more than finishing schools for girls. They stressed vocational courses rather than a classical education and social graces more than substantive academic work. Thus, Oates claims that the quality of the faculty and the curriculum in such finishing schools did not provide the necessary foundation upon which to provide a quality liberal arts collegiate level curriculum.

Foundation and Early History of the College of Saint Benedict, 1905 to 1940

Given this national context, it is interesting to examine the origins of the College of Saint Benedict. Unlike Trinity College, Saint Benedict's grew out of an academy that was founded in 1880. St. Benedict's Academy attracted many Minnesota students but also enrolled students from Indiana to Idaho and Utah.[3] While the academy had boasted being a "finishing school," it appears that the faculty's understanding of such a school was that students should take a course in etiquette, behave with gracious manners, and practice the Christian virtues of faith, hope, and charity, but unlike typical finishing schools, the majority of students at Saint Benedict's pursued a rigorous classical course of studies. They were required to take such courses as English, Latin, mathematics, history, biology, chemistry, and physics.[4] Clearly, St. Benedict's Academy provided a strong foundation on which the college could build its liberal arts curriculum, in contrast to so many other academies founded by religious communities.[5]

There is no evidence that the bishop of the Diocese of St. Cloud pressured the Benedictines to found a college or that the Benedictine sisters even asked for the bishop's permission to establish a college.[6] The common story told by members of the monastic community has been that the request to found a college originated in 1905 with two teachers in the academy. Sisters Adelgundis Bergmann and Dominica Borgerding asked Mother Cecelia Kapsner and her Council to approve the establishment of a college. Supposedly, Mother Cecelia consulted with her Council and approved the founding of a residential Catholic women's college, but written evidence, which would ordinarily be found in the

Council minutes, is not available because publication of Council minutes began only in 1930. It seems likely that a few sisters who taught in the academy understood the value of a college for women and urged the founding of a college. There is no doubt about the fact that the college officially opened in 1913.

The College of Saint Benedict became the thirteenth Catholic women's college in the United States. It began as a junior college with six faculty members: Sisters Dominica Borgerding, Adelgundis Bergmann, Irma Schumacher, Grace McDonald, Jeanette Roesch, and Father Henry Borgerding from Saint John's Abbey. The beginnings were humble, with only six lay students in 1913-1914 and with most faculty not yet having completed their graduate degrees. Sister Jeanette Roesch received her Ph.D. in philosophy in 1918; the other sister-faculty members completed their M.A. degrees in 1915 or 1916.

The 1913-1914 Bulletin states: "The purpose of St. Benedict's College is the higher education of women. In order to attain this end, the work has been outlined for two years of college work, in conformity with the best educational standards." The Bulletin lists the following specific requirements for freshmen students: either English or American literature, rhetoric and composition, Latin, and either French or German, history, philosophy, solid geometry, and either chemistry or physics. Sophomores continued courses in the same fields but substituted psychology for philosophy, trigonometry for solid geometry, and biology for chemistry or physics. From the beginning the college has emphasized the fine arts and supplemented course work with student productions, gallery shows, and vocal and instrumental concerts by students and by professional artists.[7] A few domestic science courses were offered as electives in dietetics, textiles, and food and cookery.[8] Since courses in theology were not at first given credit, they were not listed specifically in this Bulletin, but they have been consistently a part of the curriculum.

In the first five decades, Saint Benedict's assumed that women's principal role was that of Catholic wife and mother, but the faculty also expected its graduates to serve the Church and the broader society. By 1934 the Bulletin spelled out the ideal qualities of a graduate of St. Benedict's:

> She has a reasonable faith—that is, she knows Bible history, Church history, philosophy, and ethics well enough to make her religious practice intelligent. She has a strong moral fiber. She has the intellectual culture that comes with the best that a liberal arts college can offer. She has the savoir-faire of a perfect lady. As a social leader she contributes to the happiness and advance of the community in which she lives. Christian home-building is to her not only a most desirable vocation but also an art deserving the fullest attention of a cultured woman. To it she brings intelligent planning, clear sighted appreciation of its beauty and difficulties, enthusiasm, and a gracious spirit. She is sensitive to the refinements of the arts. Her inmost life is fine and beautiful. Yet her intellect is vigorous, awake to the varied aspects of modern life. . . . Her philosophy of life is based upon the blessedness of giving and helping.

St. Benedict's and other Catholic colleges for women based their student life system on the conventual life of the founding religious communities. Indeed, life at St. Benedict's in the monastery as well as in the college was hardly distinguishable for its regularity, simplicity, and earnestness of purpose. Daily life for the lay students at St. Benedict's consisted of a routine schedule of classes, study, and prayer, with some recreational time for physical and social activities. Several of the sister-faculty also lived as prefects in dormitory rooms that often housed as many as fifteen students. A degree of privacy was maintained by curtains drawn around each student's cubicle that contained a single bed, dresser, and chair. There were also several single and double rooms for students who could afford them. Students gathered for the evening prayer of Compline in their dormitory rooms at 10:00 P.M., after which the prefects turned off the lights and imposed the rule of silence for the night. Such dormitories were used until 1956 when Mary Commons and Aurora Hall were built with two students to a room. This daily routine sounds rigid by comparison with contemporary college disciplinary standards, but the majority of alumnae from those years remember their life at Saint Benedict's with a great deal of nostalgia, albeit with some humor about their ability to circumvent house rules.[9]

Catholic University approved affiliation of Saint Benedict's junior college in 1916, and the University of Minnesota accredited it in 1917. By 1916-1917, the college began to offer courses in the upper division, making the Bachelor of Arts degree available to students. Since the University of Minnesota had changed its policy of accrediting a college as a whole to that of accrediting department by department, Saint Benedict's received the accreditation of all its major departments by 1926.

Sister Adelgundis Bergmann, the academic dean from 1928 to 1932, applied to the North Central Association (NCA) for official recognition as a senior college. Because of the minimal amount of endowment, Sister Adelgundis listed all of the assets of the religious community in her NCA application. She adds:

> The College of St. Benedict may, therefore, be assumed to have an unquestionably solid financial basis since in case of need the entire holdings of these sisters can be put at the disposal of the College. . . . While the College does not have an endowment in the technical sense of the word, the results of such endowment are more than equivalently supplied by the fact that the resources and income of the entire Order safeguard the integrity and the stability of this institution in addition to the fact that the Sisters who are teaching in and administering the College are contributing their services free without any remuneration except their board, lodging, and educational expenses.

Mother Louisa Walz, the prioress of the monastic community, appended a statement saying:

> With the full consent of her advisors, (the resources of the Sisters of the Order of Saint Benedict of St. Joseph, Minnesota, will be placed at the disposal of the College

of Saint Benedict), if at any time an emergency arises which may threaten the integrity and continuance of the College.[10]

After a visitation by Father Alphonse Schwitalla, the NCA declined the accreditation in 1932. The report acknowledged that the college's:

Development and maintenance of educational standards of scholarship, standards of collegiate spirit, of an atmosphere of culture and refinement, of college discipline, of administration, conscientiousness and of complete sincerity in school administration places the College of St. Benedict in a position considerably above mediocrity when compared with other institutions of similar ambitions and character.[11]

Nevertheless, the NCA recommended several changes to address certain deficiencies.

Sister Claire Lynch, who became academic dean in 1932, took strong measures to meet the recommendations of the NCA. She ensured that the Bulletin announced the restriction of upper division courses to juniors and seniors and the reduction of the number of courses offered. She also specified the year each course would be taught. She reduced the number of faculty from forty to twenty-five and arranged that the faculty teach full time in the college rather than teach part time in both the academy and the college. She defined the policies regarding admission, promotion, and graduation. And she insisted that sisters be given sufficient opportunity to complete their graduate degrees.

As a result of these changes, the NCA accredited the college in 1933. In the 1935 NCA inspection report, the examiner representing NCA noted, "There were many evidences . . . which indicated a high degree of educational idealism and competent administrative practice." He noted, for example, the thorough revision of records, the improved quality of students, the increased enrollment, the appointment of a lay advisory committee, and the development of a good accounting system. Reconfirmation of accreditation by the NCA was given in April 1935.[12]

Sister Claire's years as academic dean, from 1932 to 1940, marked several significant improvements in the quality of the faculty, the curriculum, and the bulletins. In addition, she was one of the founders of Delta Epsilon Sigma, a national honor society for students of Catholic colleges, at a time when Phi Beta Kappa excluded Catholic colleges from membership. In 1940 Saint Benedict's established the charter Omega chapter of Delta Epsilon Sigma and has continued to enroll several students annually to recognize their outstanding academic performance and their intention to use their intellectual gifts in service of the Church and society.

In 1935 the college produced its first annual Pageant, "So Let Your Light Shine," to initiate first-year students into the spiritual and cultural heritage of fourteen centuries of Benedictine history. This ritual celebration—presented through choral reading, song, and interpretive dance—culminated in the new students receiving the flaming torches of learning and thereby accepting their responsibility to pass on the learning to others in the future. The pageant depicted the historic role of Benedictines in the civilization of Europe. The event played a formative role in students' lives by insuring their understanding of the Benedictine heritage and inspiring them to value learning and culture.[13]

Sister Claire also ensured that extracurricular activities would supplement the educational experiences for the students. Students participated in one or more clubs such as the Minnesota League of Women Voters, the International Relations Club, Art Club, Glee Club, Orchestra, Ardeleons Drama Club, Women's Athletics, and Scribes and Critics. The latter club's publications often won the All-American rating from the National Scholastic Press Association.[14] In addition, the college regularly provided a series of concerts and lectures as required convocations to challenge students and faculty intellectually and, at the same time, encouraged the development of personal commitment to social justice causes. The 1935-1936 Annual Report notes four concerts and fifteen lectures, including those by Mortimer Adler, Carl Sandberg, Peter Maurin, Helen C. White, and Christopher

Hollis. In 1937-1938 there were six concerts and twenty-three public lectures.

Through the influence of Dorothy Day and Baroness Catherine de Hueck, two of the frequent lecturers at convocations, a number of students volunteered their services during the summer at Friendship House in Harlem and in Chicago and at the Catholic Worker in New York. As a result of such enriching experiences, in 1938 two students, Betty Schneider and Josephine Zehnle, working under Baroness de Hueck at Friendship House, recruited Kathleen Yanes and Gertrude Danavall, the first two African-American students to matriculate at Saint Benedict's. Shortly after that, Sister Claire Lynch received a letter from the St. Paul chapter of the alumnae association protesting the acceptance of these two women as students. In her usual forthright manner, Sister Claire responded by saying, "as a Catholic college it is our policy to accept students of any race. . . ." She pointed out that as early as 1908 St. Benedict's Academy had accepted an African-American student; in addition, several Chinese and Native American students had enrolled in the college in the 1930s. Sister Claire added:

> St. Benedict's professes to be a Catholic college. As such it tries to inculcate and live the teachings of the Church, which condemn racial discrimination as unjust, immoral, and unChristian. . . . We would be failing utterly to abide by Catholic principles were we to reject these young women who are living members of the Mystical Body of Christ. . . . In conclusion, I can only say that we are even more eager than our alumnae that our College retain its present prestige, but we are certain that our status as a Catholic college will be but improved by an act which is, after all, only outward evidence of our belief in Christian—not to say Catholic principles.[15]

Sister Claire Lynch is a strong example of the many sisters who established a solid foundation for Saint Benedict's as a Catholic undergraduate liberal arts college for women. Others would follow and continue to shape the college in the Catholic university tradition.

Mother Rosamond Pratschner, president, and Sister Claire Lynch, academic dean, meeting with lay advisors.

World War II and the Mid-Years, 1941 to 1960

Because Saint Benedict's was a college for women, the effects of World War II on the college were different from effects on men's or coeducational colleges. Students did not personally have to face the draft, although obviously they faced the anxiety of having their fathers, brothers, and boyfriends inducted. Student enrollment, 271 in 1940, declined to 164 in 1943-1944, with some students taking time off for wartime jobs or helping in their family businesses.

By 1942 many of the customary activities were dropped for the duration of the war. The sister faculty members established a War Committee, the first Minnesota college to create such a college unit. Sister Grace McDonald was in charge of all war work at the college, and Sister Alfreda Zierden assumed charge for the Surgical Dressing Station in St. Joseph.[16] They centralized all war activity, inaugurated new activities, and acted as liaison between the college and the local and district war boards. As part of their work, the faculty and students sold war bonds and stamps, regularly contributed blood to the Red Cross, knitted thousands of garments for the armed forces, and took classes in home nursing and first aid. Toward the end of the war, they also sent large boxes of clothing to war victims in Europe. Such activities strengthened the students' sense of commitment to serve others.

Saint Benedict's remained fortunate in having sister faculty members who continued to exercise leadership in the classroom and in administration of the college after World War II. They ensured the carrying out of the mission of the college and, as faculty, they insisted on high academic standards for their students. Alumnae from the class of 1948, who returned for their fiftieth reunion in 1998, spoke lovingly of the influence these sisters and their liberal education had on their lives. One alumna summed it up by saying, "Coming to CSB opened up the whole world to me, and I thought I could save the world." Another said she learned to appreciate CSB even more when she was in graduate school because "I didn't realize until I got to graduate school how much I had learned at CSB because I knew so much more than the other graduate students." All the participants in the interview spoke in terms of learning to think and to appreciate the beauty and goodness of life. The alumnae also spoke positively about the value of a residential college as part of their educational experience, integrating the emotional, social, and spiritual aspects of their lives with their intellectual growth. They spoke, too, of the value of developing lifelong friendships with other women, including their mentors and their classmates.

Several of these alumnae named specific sisters who were their teachers and who taught them so much about the liberal arts and about life. One praised Sister Remberta Westkaemper, her biology teacher, who taught her how to study and how to approach learning, including a sense of awe at the beauty of nature. Another claimed that Sister Linnea Welter's love of literature and poetry turned her life around. Another stated, "Linnea saw something in me I didn't know I had; she was my mentor." Several named Sister Patrick Joseph Flynn, a sociology teacher, as their most beloved friend. One said, "I loved her—she was pure delight." All who had Sister Mariella Gable as an English teacher agreed that they learned to think, to write clearly, and to illustrate with concrete examples. In addition, they admired Sister Mariella's vast scholarship, her creative writing ability, and her enthusiasm for learning.[17]

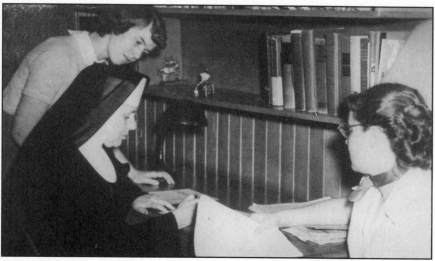

English students consulting with Sister Mariella Gable.

While the faculty in general were well qualified and good teachers, Sister Mariella Gable attained national, and even international recognition for helping to shape the artistic standards for Catholic fiction. For example, John Harriott applauded her editing of anthologies of short stories as superb collections.[18] In his review of Sister Mariella's anthology, *Many Colored Fleece*, John Cogley stated that Sister Mariella "had probably done more than anyone else to show people what decent Catholic fiction looks like and to hint at what it might be."[19] Irish writer Bryan MacMahon praised her addition of Irish short stories into her anthologies, making many Irish writers known to Americans and British readers.[20]

Sister Colman O'Connell, president, with sister staff members Sisters Miriam Ardolf (finances), Ingrid Anderson (student development), and Dolores Super (academic affairs).

These specific sisters are representative of the numerous sisters who have contributed as administrators, faculty, and staff who have witnessed to the fact that women were indeed capable of leading and staffing a strong institution long before the women's movement of the 1960s. The graduates frequently mention the mentorship of these strong women when they reflect on their own understanding and appreciation of the role women can play in society.

In 1957 Mother Richarda Peters, the prioress of the monastery, resigned her position as president of the college, a position that had been held by the prioress since its founding. Mother Richarda believed that her responsibilities in the college, added to her duties as prioress, were making it impossible for her to accomplish her goals in either position. Thus, on July 27, 1957, she appointed Sister Remberta Westkaemper (1957 to 1961) as the first full-time president. This important change enabled the president to concentrate efforts not only on the major issues of the college but also to develop fundraising activities, and to build significant relationships with the public through such institutions as the Minnesota Private College Association, and the Association of Catholic Colleges and Universities. After Sister Remberta's term of office, the following Benedictines served as president: Sister Linnea Welter (1961 to 1963); Sister Mary Grell (1963 to 1968); Sister Emmanuel Renner (1979 to 1986); and Sister Colman O'Connell (1986 to 1996). Strong academic leadership was also provided in the crucial role of the vice president for Academic Affairs: Sister Johanna Becker (1957 to 1961); Sister Firmin Escher (1961 to 1972); Sister Mary David Olheiser (1972 to 1974); Sister Katherine Howard (1974 to 1977); and Sister Linda Kulzer (1977 to 1985).

Incorporation and Involvement of the Laity, 1961 to 1968

During her term as prioress, Mother Henrita Osendorf and her Council separately incorporated the college and the monastery's major health-care institutions.[21] The primary reasons for this action included a desire to limit liability exposure, to manage more effectively the increasingly complex institutions, to respond better to the state and federal governments' increasing demands for accountability, to lessen the financial drain on the monastic community, and to make possible the college's obtaining government funding.[22]

Mother Henrita Osendorf officiating at the laying of the cornerstone for the Benedicta Arts Center in 1963.

Mother Henrita referred only to the latter reason when she spoke to the Chapter on October 13, 1961, about incorporating the college. She explained that the college was planning to build Regina residence hall as part of the Mary Hall complex. Therefore, she said, "College incorporation is imperative now in order to obtain a government loan for the new dormitory." Within a year, plans were also made to build the Benedicta Arts Center. Since there were questions about the legality of federal loans being given to church-related institutions, separate incorporation seemed a sensible precaution.

Separate incorporation did not change the working relationship between the monastic community and the college for several years.[23] In the Annual Report of 1962-1963, Sister Linnea Welter, president 1962 to 1964, stated that the Board of Directors' monthly meetings continued to shape the college as a separate legal entity, "while both consciously and subconsciously attempting to set practical precedents for the day-by-day relations between two legal bodies . . . which will continue to be bound intimately to each other both spiritually and physically." She noted that fifty percent of the sisters' salaries were to be given to the college and fifty percent to the monastery.[24]

Despite separate incorporation, the Monastic Council and Chapter continued to approve expenditure of major funds for the college. The Board of Directors, later renamed Board of Trustees, continued to be composed solely of sisters, including the prioress and her administrative team as well as the administrators of the college. In 1966, Fred Hughes, as legal counsel, wrote that he would be derelict in his duty if he did not state very strongly that "the times and events with which we live indicate that it is prudent and expedient that some lay people be on the Board."[25] Hughes thought that some of the sisters seemed reluctant to "give up this degree of authority," but Mother Henrita believed the reason for the reluctance was their ignorance of what lay members could do on the Board.[26] By April 30, 1968, however, the Board voted to invite T. Richard Anderson and Alan

Ruvelson to be the first lay Board members, and the sisters soon came to understand the significant contribution the lay Board members could make to the college.[27]

It took time for the administrators and faculty of the college to assume more and more independence in their decision-making process, another important step in the evolution of legal separation. It is clear that the full implications of the act of separate incorporation were not at first completely understood. However, it became evident that the separate incorporation of the college and of the health-care institutions was a wise decision. It was the beginning, albeit small at first, of partnership with the laity in administering these institutions, and it freed the administrators of the monastery to concentrate on the mission and major issues of their large monastic community.

Cooperation with Saint John's University, Another Milestone[28]

While cooperation between the monastery and college was evolving, a second opportunity to form a partnership was identified. The importance of the gradual development of cooperation between the College of Saint Benedict and Saint John's University can hardly be exaggerated, and it is one more example of the value of cooperation between institutions with a similar mission. It has, in its own way, helped administrators and faculty of both institutions to hone collaborative skills of interdependence. In spring of 1963, the administrators of the two colleges and the two monasteries met to study the possibilities of a more formal expanded program of cooperation between the two colleges.

Since the beginning of the College of Saint Benedict, there had been some degree of cooperative activities. For example, because women were not yet admitted to graduate schools of theology, the college relied on St. John's for theology teachers as well as for chaplains. In addition, the two colleges often shared national speakers for their convocations, and students from both campuses met occasionally for club meetings. In the 1950s two teachers from each campus taught courses at the other campus. In 1954, for the first time, students from CSB and SJU participated together in plays. But such cooperation was very limited in comparison to what was to come.

Beginning in 1963-1964, a few small classes were opened to seniors from both campuses regardless of where the courses were taught. By 1969, the number of students who participated had increased to the point where it was necessary to establish the registrar's office as a joint office. By the mid-1970s, students were free to attend classes and select majors on either campus. In the 1980s, most academic departments and some administrative areas, like the library, were joined. In the 1990s, there were three types of cooperative arrangements: unification of several administrative offices, coordinate programs in the areas of Student Development and Development, and cooperative programs in the residential life programs.

No one could have imagined the journey that was to be taken between these two colleges in the process of developing a unique relationship of coordination. Together the colleges have aimed to serve all students and to enrich the environment in which they study and live. They conserve fiscal resources by avoiding unnecessary duplication of facilities, library materials, and equipment. They hire faculty to provide breadth and depth in each discipline. Because of cooperation, each department can offer introductory courses for the general students and courses of greater specialization for majors than could be offered by a faculty of only one school. The success of that coordination would not have been possible without the leadership of the presidents, the academic vice presidents, and the faculty since 1964. But it also required the cooperation of the other vice presidents and the energy and enthusiasm of the students. In the first two decades of formal cooperation, the leadership and commitment of Mother Henrita Osendorf, the prioress at Saint Benedict's Monastery, and Abbot Baldwin Dworschak of Saint John's Abbey, along with the other members of the two Boards, was crucial. Presently the two Boards meet regularly together and have a standing committee on cooperation.

Dr. Stanley Idzerda, First Lay President, 1968 to 1974

In 1968 the search for a new president extended beyond the monastic community because the Board believed there was no sister ready to assume that position. In July 1968, Dr. Stanley Idzerda was appointed as the first lay president. His vision and personal commitment would be an extraordinary force in shaping the future of the college. He brought a fresh perspective and helped instill a strong sense of confidence about the quality of the college. He challenged the faculty and students to share his love of scholarship. He applauded the college's emphasis on personal attention to the individual development of students. He began an aggressive attempt to increase enrollment, even to the point of temporarily adding a "trailor park" to provide residences for these students. In addition, he worked diligently to ensure that a solid foundation was being built for the cooperative relationship with St. John's University.

In 1974 Dr. Idzerda resigned in order to accept a special assignment at Cornell Uni-

Dr. Stanley Idzerda, first lay president.

versity as editor-in-chief of the publication of the Marquis de Lafayette papers. During his six years, the college had flourished. Enrollment more than doubled. Several new programs were developed, including East Asian Studies, Continuing Education, and Nursing. With his strong support, Sister Firmin Escher, director of Planning, initiated a planning process in 1970 at a time when few small colleges engaged in systematic planning. As the chair of the Board said, "Dr. Idzerda's leadership in the past six years has been highly effective and inspiring. His love and respect for the Benedictine tradition, his unflagging and unflinching dedication to his work, his ability to unleash the leadership potential in others around him has been very evident.[29] His term had assured the monastic community that a lay president could exercise leadership in promoting the mission of the college. He was followed by another lay president, Dr. Beverly Miller.[30]

Evolution of the Monastery-College Relationship, 1913 to the Mid-1970s

Throughout the years, from the foundation of the college in 1913 until the late 1960s, sister faculty members made up an average of eighty-five percent of the faculty. For example, in 1955, out of a total of forty-nine faculty, eighty-four percent were sisters. By 1970-1971, sisters comprised seventy percent of the faculty. Because of this downward trend in the ratio of sisters to lay faculty, the monastic community and the college undertook a serious study. Leaders of the two institutions pondered the potential consequences of this decline of sisters. The college examined its purposes and goals, structure and programs, and concluded that in order to retain its Benedictine tradition, a considerable number on the faculty and staff would have to be Benedictine sisters.[31]

By 1972-1973, only fifty per cent of the faculty were sisters. This trend of decreasing percentage of Benedictine faculty has continued. The reasons for this trend had as much to do with the college's dramatic increase in student enrollment since the 1970s as with changes in the monastic community. In 1970-1971 the college had 710 full-time students. By 1980-1981 there were 1,713 full-time students, an increase of 141 percent over that ten-year period. In that same time period, the number of faculty increased from sixty-seven to 133. Because of the need to hire a large number of lay faculty, the percentage of sisters had dropped to twenty-three percent of the faculty by 1980-1981.

Besides the college's increased enrollment, there were several complex changes in the monastic community that help explain why there were no longer sufficient numbers of sisters prepared to teach in the college. By 1946 the monastic community had grown to 1,285 sisters, and many of these sisters had been students at the college when they entered the monastic community. In 1947 the sisters began a several-year process which separated this large community into five independent Benedictine communities. Between 1947 and 1952, 438 sisters transferred their membership to new priories, founded originally by Saint Benedict's Monastery, in Minnesota, North Dakota, Wisconsin, and Washington. Seventy-one percent of these transferees were under the age of fifty. Of the sister faculty members who moved to these new communities, five were department heads at the college, and others had also been employed as faculty and staff.[32]

In addition to the significant number of sisters who moved to establish new foundations, one hundred four sisters in perpetual vows withdrew from the monastic community between 1968 and 1987. This loss was prompted both by the changes in the Church following Vatican Council II, and by the paradigm shift in thinking about the role of women prompted by the Women's Movement. The average age of these women who withdrew from the monastery was 38.8. The loss of a significant number of younger sisters raised the median age of sisters who remained at St. Benedict's Monastery. The monastery's decrease in size also influenced the number of sisters available for graduate studies, for teaching in college, and for the other ministries of the community.

Finally, since the 1960s the number of men and women who choose to live in religious communities in the United States has decreased dramatically. The college, along with all other ministries, has shared the consequences of this change.

These trends prompted the monastic community in 1973 to undertake a self-study of its priorities. Their study dealt with the implications of changing demography and other external factors that called for a new approach to conducting the community's ministries.

> Numerous and complex factors, internal and external to the Community, are responsible for this. The most immediate and pressing one is the changing age profile of the Community while renewal and adaptation according to the directive of the Second Vatican Council are the occasion for a deepened search for life's meaning and direction. The Study articulates a key question raised as a result of these dynamics: What effects do the changing trends in our religious community and the community attitudes have on the ability of the Church to continue apostolic activity that is dependent upon the contributed services of the religious?[33]

The study acknowledges that the current crisis in available personnel for placement in existing institutional ministries had been mounting in elementary education since the early 1960s, due to the rapid growth in Catholic parochial school population. Later, this crisis affected the availability for sisters to work in other areas such as the college and health-care ministries. While the sisters could not guarantee any increase in the number of sisters teaching in the college, the study reiterates a commitment to the college as a ministry which is eminently suitable for sisters' involvement.[34]

Ironically, this commitment was considerably weakened that year when five sisters with doctorates retired from the faculty at a time when no sisters with the necessary qualifications were available to replace them. The monastic community had been unable to prepare a sufficient number of sisters for these replacements.

As a result of the interrelated changes taking place in the college, the monastery, and the broader world, it became impossible to meet the stated goal of both the college and the monastery: "the Benedictine sister must be visible in the College, out in front, in leadership situations, showing the Benedictine ideal through a simple life of faith, love, generosity, and stability."[35]

Such changes made it impossible for the monastic community to continue to sponsor the college in the same manner it had been doing. While other religious communities who sponsored Catholic colleges might have experienced their own type of changes, they too experienced the need to review their mode of sponsorship. As Alice Gallen, executive director of the Association of Catholic Colleges and Universities (ACCU), described it, sponsorship had meant that the founding religious community provided administrators, faculty, and the financial resources in the founding years and for generations to come.

> Those religious communities that founded colleges contributed their services by receiving minimal salaries. They were committed to the goal of Catholic higher education and received, in turn, a high sense of purpose in the mission of their college. Sponsorship of Catholic colleges provided significant religious meaning, and it implied a control by the religious community that made the goals realizable.[36]

Restructuring the Relationship between the Monastery and College, 1970s to the Present

Circumstances in the 1960s and 1970s led to a realignment of power and responsibility within the colleges founded by these communities of women religious. The faculty and administrators shifted from a majority of sisters to a majority of lay women and men. Separate incorporation of these colleges also led to some unnecessary conflicts between the religious founding group and their college. For example, transfers of property made at the time by the religious community to their college have led to some complicated situations today. Gallin cites an example of cases where the land belongs to the religious community, and the buildings erected with government funds belong to the college.[37]

Because of such conflicting situations, the ACCU dedicated one of the issues of their journal in 1984 to explore options in regard to the authority held by the religious founding group and that held by the college it founded. As part of the context for such an exploration, Gallin acknowledged the timeliness of the topic since many religious communities were rethinking their relationship to institutional apostolates. Because many religious communities had more retired sisters and fewer active members, they were seeking new ways to relate to their schools, colleges, and hospitals and to invite the laity to assist them in ensuring the mission of their institutions. Gallin's report to ACCU concludes with a positive message:

> Today we have a far better ecclesiology concerning the essential role of lay persons in our church. By and large, they will be the ones to carry out the work of our colleges and universities in the 21st century. We speak, therefore, not so much of sponsors and lay trustees as distinct entities but rather as partners in the work of holding these institutions in trust for coming generations.[38]

This national dialogue on Catholic colleges and religious communities helps to give context for the evolutionary changes taking place in the relationship between the Benedictine Monastic Community and the College of Saint Benedict, especially since the 1960s and 1970s.

Because of the continuing decrease of the numbers of sisters involved in the college, the monastic community sought new ways to ensure the continuance of the college mission as a Benedictine institution. Due to the emphasis of the Second Vatican Council on the essential role of the laity as partners in carrying out the mission of the Church, the monastic community was encouraged to welcome the involvement of the laity in their ministries. It took some time, however, to recognize this transition to be not so much an abdication of the sisters' responsibility as a coming of age of the Catholic laity.

There has been a gradual evolution of the role of the monastic community in the college. The monastic community shared responsibility for the college as members of the Board of Trustees. Because members of the monastic community no longer were the majority on the Board, the monastery sought to ensure that the mission as a Catholic college could not be changed without the permission of the founders. In addition, since the college and monastery shared buildings as well as a campus, it was essential that the monastic community be involved in any possible decisions on merger or sale of land.

Another factor that resulted in the change in governance structure was the fact that the state of Minnesota required not-for-profit organizations to have a dual governance structure. Thus for these several reasons, the Board of Trustees changed the Articles and By-Laws in 1976 to include a dual governance structure of a corporation membership and a board of trustees whose functions are distinct. The membership of the Corporation of the College of Saint Benedict, consisting of the officers of the Sisters of the Order of Saint Benedict, retained the following reserved powers: 1) to appoint the Board of Trustees and remove any appointed member thereof; 2) to approve any merger, acquisition, or dissolution of the Corporation or sale or encumbrances of the assets of the corporation; 3) to amend the Articles of Incorporation and make or amend the Bylaws.[39] In carrying out these functions, the Corporation Membership acts only after receiving the recommendations of the Board of Trustees. The Board of Trustees is the policy-making body of the college and selects the president of the college. The Board members assume their responsibility to "hold the College in trust," to preserve its mission and purpose. They do so by a careful selection of the president and through the establishment of sound policies which guide the college.

The relationship between administrators of the monastic community and the college also required a shift from informal decision-making by sister administrators in these two institutions. More formal structures were necessary when the majority of college administrators were lay members. Both institutions sought to develop collaborative structures and processes for the good of both institutions. While by their very nature collaborative relations are difficult, they are essential in this case. Documents in the archives provide insights into the types of challenges the administrators of both institutions faced. For example, Sister Emmanuel Renner stated in her 1984 President's Report:

> We are presently working to place our cooperative relations with the Monastery on a formal basis. This will improve the communication process and ensure that decisions which may have repercussions are not made by one institution without serious discussion. On a campus where two institutions share an administrative building, a power house, and roads, for example, we need a more formalized, joint long-range planning system on issues which affect both of us. We are, of course, two separate corporations and we need to be sensitive to preserving the autonomy of each as well as promoting better cooperation.[40]

To strengthen the commitment to collaborative relationship, the college and monastery designed a process for planning cooperatively. In addition, the two institutions created a master plan for buildings and grounds, planning and maintenance. Part of that process for cooperation was the establishment of a Joint Administrative Council (JAC), composed of officers of the monastic community and the college, who meet regularly to share information and make decisions that affect both institutions.

The shift from significant numbers of sister faculty members and staff to small numbers of sisters has led the monastery to form new means of involvement with the college community. Sisters who are not employees of the college as faculty or staff have established relationships with students. They have also developed ways in which lay faculty and staff can be introduced to Benedictine values so that they too are able to assume their responsibility to nurture those values in the college community. There are several ways in which this involvement is carried out, but two examples will suffice.

In 1977, the monastic community developed a program now known as the Benedictine Friends across the Campus. At the beginning of each school year, sisters in the monastic community invite the students to form a relationship with a Benedictine sister. Those students who do participate in the program have, in large part, found the experience to be both enjoyable and helpful in learning how to integrate their intellectual life with the emotional and spiritual aspects of their lives. Often the Benedictine friend is a retired sister, the age of the student's grandmother. Consequently, students find themselves talking comfortably about their families, their friends, their religious beliefs, and

Sister Carleen Schomer challenging chemistry students, Karla Ziegelmann and Bryan Johnson, in the college's new Ardolf Science Center.

Sisters extending a blessing for the students in the Benedictine Friends Program.

their doubts. The sisters, for their part, tend to be good listeners and enjoy their young friends who, in turn, are interested in the experience and wisdom of their Benedictine friend. The arrangement often provides occasions for students to pray with the sisters in the oratory and to share occasional meals together in the monastery dining room. In many cases, these friendships continue throughout the four years of college and extend beyond that time. The experience is enriching for both students and sisters. For those sisters who have not worked in the college, their young friends have increased the sisters' appreciation for the mission of the college as they observe the growing maturity of their student friend from her first year in college to her senior year.

Another example of attention to Benedictine values is that of a program offered every semester since 1990 for faculty and staff so that they are able to assume their responsibility to nurture the Benedictine values in the college community. The Benedictine facilitators invite faculty and staff as well as their spouses to participate in a semester-long dialogue on the "Benedictine Values" at these two college campuses. The program gives faculty and staff an experience of being with the monastic communities in their commitment to prayer, to reading and reflecting on the *Rule of Saint Benedict*, and to exploring the meaning of the *Rule* for their own spiritual lives. Since its origins, 217 persons have participated in the sessions and have given positive evaluations. One participant commented, "You did a great job of making the Benedictine *Rule* come alive by connecting it with your own monastic experiences." Another urged the continuation of the program and asked for a list of books, videos, or other relevant materials on the Benedictine experience, as well as a list of opportunities to join with the religious communities in prayer, reflection, and service activities.

Besides the legal relationship that emphasizes a juridic approach between the two institutions, the monastery and college administrators have been working together to articulate a cooperative relationship for daily shared responsibilities. For example, in 1992, under the leadership of Sister Mary Reuter, prioress, and Sister Colman O'Connell, president, the Monastic/College Joint Administrative Council drafted a document that describes their relationship arising out of their experience in the 1990s as equal partners in Benedictine education. Together they created "a joint mission of providing an environment that infuses Benedictine values into the lives of those who live, work and interact with our communities." They reaffirmed their commitment to the vitality and strength of each organization and reminded each other of the responsibilities and the resulting benefits of the two institutions acting as partners.[41]

The Partnership Working Document lists the responsibilities of each institution to the other. Moreover, it enumerates the benefits that both will share as a result of this partnership. These include vital intellectual and faith lives, formal and informal interaction, and participation in liturgies

Sister Ephrem Hollermann, prioress, and Mary Lyons, college president, giving a blessing to the senior students.

and cultural events. The document states that a solid mutual partnership must be intentional. It is built on a basic premise that both partners sincerely want the relationship and exhibit a give-and-take working association with each other.

As a further step in developing a more mutual relational approach, Sister Ephrem Hollermann, Prioress, and Dr. Mary Lyons, President, together with the administrators of both institutions, agreed on a Statement of Relationship on April 10, 2000, that acknowledges common values:

> They both share in a rich living tradition of Benedictine spirituality, love of learning, hospitality, respect, interdependence, authenticity, and loyalty. These and other values continue to be developed and nurtured in a Catholic Benedictine setting as interaction in areas of spirituality, fine arts, and scholarly learning takes place on a daily basis. Both the Monastery and the College hold the education and formation of women as a valued priority.

In addition, the statement also recognizes that their relationship is many faceted:

The partner relationship is expressed in the architectural blending of the college's latest addition to Mary Hall (bookstore, post office, and student and administrative offices) with the monastery chapel and Art and Heritage Place.

> The two function as neighbors, guests of each other, friends, partners, joint planners, teachers, and as two separate legal entities. They live side by side sharing a common history, separate but common missions, spaces, and resources, and they enhance each other's mission and purpose.

As the understanding of the relationship between these two institutions evolves, the leaders are searching for a satisfactory term to name the relationship. Neither juridic nor partnership adequately describes the cooperative relationship. The word "juridic" limits the relationship to the strictly legal aspects, and the word "partnership" is used to name the cooperative relationship between the College of Saint Benedict and Saint John's University as two liberal arts colleges. Furthermore, the term "partnership" has legal meanings that do not apply to the relationship between the college and the monastery. At present, words such as "mutuality" and "pastoral" are being considered to refer to the unique form of cooperation between the two institutions.

This concern to identify the appropriate word is important in forming attitudes that affect responses of the members of both institutions.

Summary

This chapter has described two significant topics that are relevant to understanding the history of the relationship between the monastery and the college. The first topic deals with the contribution of the sisters, especially during the period from the foundation of the college in 1913 to the 1960s. During that time Saint Benedict's Monastery founded the college; articulated its mission; provided the administrators, faculty, and staff and, as its initial Board of Trustees, established the policies for its governance. The monastery established a solid foundation for the college in its own right, providing the impetus for the college to develop in significant ways, including that of cooperation with Saint John's University.

The second topic dealt with the evolution of the relationship between the monastery and the college, especially since the incorporation of the college in 1961. Since the 1970s, the majority of positions of faculty, administration, and Board have been filled by lay women and men. This transformation occurred at a time of great change in the monastery, the college, and the society as a whole. The college and monastery have continued to play significant roles in preserving the college's original mission as a residential Benedictine liberal arts college for women in the Catholic university tradition. These two institutions are also continuing to clarify the function and meaning of their relationship as it evolves in the present and future.

There are numerous challenges and opportunities in the cooperation between these two institutions. There are also many benefits that have been opened to both institutions as they share their commitment to respect one another and to hold in trust their responsibility in carrying out the mission

12
INSTITUTIONS OF HEALTH CARE

Olivia Forster, O.S.B.

Introduction

Benedictine sisters traditionally embrace the needs they find in time and place and make it their "work." Surely health care is an unchallenged example of this. Before formal health care, the sick were cared for in homes with help of family and neighbors. The medical world of the late 1800s, however, became aware of possible dangers in home treatments. Other changes in society also, for example, the coming of railroads, brought about more mobility, and so public health care became necessary.

For the Sisters of St. Benedict, St. Joseph, Minnesota, Mother Scholastica Kerst (1880 to 1889), never one to miss an opportunity, took up the challenges presented by these changes in the health-care world in the last quarter of the nineteenth century. In 1885, Bismarck, North Dakota's, Lamborn Hospital (a former hotel), under the sisters' administration and management was to grow from a primitive frontier hospital to one of the best in the area, taking its place among recognized hospitals of the country. Its name was changed to St. Alexius Hospital in 1887. At about the same time, what would become the St. Cloud Hospital about

231

forty years later began as St. Benedict's Hospital on Ninth Avenue, St. Cloud, in February 1886.

Sister Grace McDonald, in *With Lamps Burning*, thoroughly chronicles these early stories of health care as carried on for seventy-one years by the Sisters of St. Benedict, St. Joseph, Minnesota.[42] Today, 2000, that record is revised to read 114 years. However, the brevity of a forty-year span since the McDonald history belies the momentous occurrences taking place in America's fast-moving society. This is eminently true in health care in which there were new and far-reaching trends, necessarily colored by significant events nationwide. Through it all, the sisters never lost sight of the goal they had set for themselves when circumstances first led them into health care in the late nineteenth century, in St. Benedict's words: "Care of the sick must rank above and before all else, so that they may truly be served as Christ . . . "[43] They reconfirmed this basic commitment in their Philosophy of the Health Service Apostolate: "Service to both spiritual and physical needs of people is a genuine Christian apostolate."[44]

Amid the many complexities in health care today—the mergers, creation of systems, closing of Catholic hospitals, the challenges of insurance companies and HMOs—the sisters found themselves in constantly changing milieux. At the time they started in health ministry, 1886, the Church was not able to build buildings, nor were the dioceses. So the sisters set about building buildings and, lest it be forgotten, they established the first nursing homes. They did this building carefully and well and were definitely in the public eye. However, in tune with the times and circumstances in which they found themselves, they moved from actually building health facilities to other programs of service in the Church.[45]

Vatican Council II's Impact on Health Care

The overwhelming changes in church, society, and traditional lifestyles of religious life brought about by the call of

Vatican Council II naturally also affected the sisters in health care. In 1965, 13,618 religious sisters staffed 803 hospitals in this country. The profound effects of Vatican II changes induced a gradual decrease in sisters' presence in health-care institutions everywhere. At Saint Benedict's Monastery, in the late 1950s and early 1960s, well over one hundred sisters were engaged in health care. The community sponsored, owned, and operated three hospitals and two nursing homes, as well as partially staffed three other homes owned by parishes. At St. Cloud Hospital alone there were ninety sisters. At the time of the 1973 *Priorities Study*, 110

Sister Mary Ellen Machtemes—surgery.

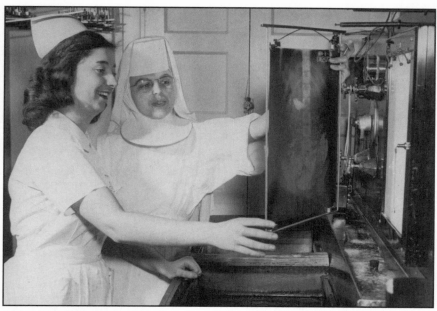

Sister Arles Silbernick—radiology

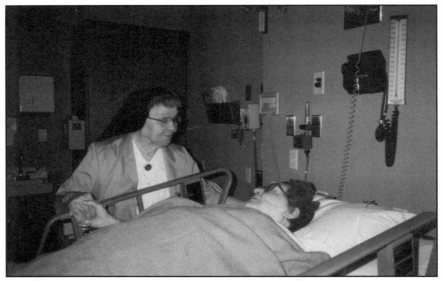

Sister Suzanne Helmin, member of the Spiritual Care Team at St. Cloud Hospital.

sisters were still in the health-care apostolates. Today, six sisters are corporate members on hospital boards: St. Cloud Hospital (two); Queen of Peace Hospital (four). Serving on Boards of Directors or Trustees are six: St. Cloud Hospital (three); Queen of Peace Hospital (three). As employees there are twenty-five sisters in health care plus eight serving as volunteers in health care facilities. Another seventeen are engaged in health-care service for the monastic community.

The phenomenon of many sisters leaving the religious life in the late 1960s and 1970s, thereby decimating the ranks of those serving in the health-care ministry, affected the identity of Catholic hospitals in that they could no longer be associated only with the strong presence of sisters. However, the Council's new emphasis on the role of the laity was a call for them to move into institutional health care and work along with religious communities.[46] In final analysis, this change did not spell the loss of the health-care ministry but a transformation.

As hospitals, due to pressures from third-party payers, more and more restricted care to the acutely ill, extended care for all age levels fell into the area of home health programs or hospice care. Health-care education gained great popularity, ranging from individual patient after-care education to programs running over many years. Spiritual care, as concomitant with physical care, received increasing attention. Wellness programs flourished in their emphasis on the healthy integration of mind, body, and spirit. At Saint Benedict's Monastery, too, while the breadth of health-care ministry may have narrowed, still it expanded considerably in other ways. Many sisters left the highly structured, corporate ministry of hospitals and chose to minister in less institutionalized, individual health enterprises. Some chose to serve in homes for the elderly, either as full-time nurses or in day care. A strong sister-patient visitor program in the sisters' former health institutions became available for semi-retired sisters.

Then in the 1960s there also arose a new awareness of the poor, of the need for social justice in the health care apostolate "because of the societal abandonment of the poor."[47] This inspired a few sisters to become involved in inner-city community programs that included a health-care element. Equally important, the community's need to care for its own growing number of elderly sisters called for the ministry of many care givers and sister-nurses and for a new program to administer community health care.

Clinical Pastoral Education (CPE) with its emphasis on counseling based on holistic and religious care, founded in 1920 and introduced by Catholics in the late 1960s and 1970s, attracted some sisters.[48] Also, the traditional model of a hospital chaplain gave way to a pastoral care model in which sisters teamed with other sisters, brothers, lay persons, Protestant ministers, and Catholic priests in the National Association of Catholic Chaplains (NACC), which opened its membership to women in December 1974. Some sisters became certified chaplains and served as staff members, directors of Pastoral Care Departments and Mission

Effectiveness, parish presiders, and prison chaplains. Sister Jonathan Herda became the community's first certified full CPE department supervisor in 1982, conducting the only NACC certified program in a five-state region in the mid-1980s. Pastoral Care Departments have offered sisters a unique opportunity to collaborate with others in giving Christian witness, in developing Christian values when ministering to patients, staff, and families.[49]

Conclusion

For the sisters, the term "health care" today may have connotations different from what it did fifty years ago. However, they are today, too, women in health care ministry and its "inherently public character,"[50] as they find themselves still relating to and involved in the largest private, not-for-profit system in the United States. Their interest is still in news, reporting the rapid advances made in medicine, surgery, rehabilitation, and preventative medicine, to mention but a few. They know about Health Maintenance Organizations (HMO), cutbacks in Medicare and Medicaid, union activities, mergers, consolidations, joint ventures, and acquisitions. The past forty years in health care may have been revolutionary, but the sisters have accepted the challenge, in society and within their own monastic community. Now, too, their courage does not fail as they keep their eyes steadily on the healing ministry of the Catholic Church and their "commitment to respond 'with creative adaptation to the changing and expanding requirements of society as time unfolds them.'"[51]

Hospitals

ST. CLOUD HOSPITAL

Many sisters' lives are woven into the history of the St. Cloud Hospital which had its beginnings as early as 1886. Dr. A.C. Lamothe Ramsay came to St. Cloud in 1882; after dickering and negotiating with the city, he opened his own hospital but wanted sisters' help so he could carry on his own medical practice. Instead, the sisters purchased a newly erected building for $2,000 and opened it as their own St. Benedict's Hospital on Ninth Avenue North in February 1886. No matter that the sisters were nurses without training; doctors trained them on the job from day to day. Almost from day one sisters were in administration.[52]

The well-known story of a cyclone on April 14, 1886, and the recognition the sisters earned in their care of victims, was the "sign from heaven" that launched them into building, managing, and administering hospitals. It led to a gift of five acres of land on the far east side of the Mississippi River and the building of St. Raphael's Hospital there in 1890. When promises of a bridge over the river and good roads leading to the hospital were not realized, the sisters had to close after ten years and return to Ninth Avenue North. There they built another St. Raphael's Hospital in 1900, next to the site of their original hospital, St. Benedict's. In twenty-six years, this hospital was totally inadequate for the St. Cloud area. The sisters then found land north of the city for a new site overlooking the Mississippi River. Here they formally dedicated St. Cloud Hos-

St. Cloud Hospital.

ST CLOUD
HOSPITAL
ST CLOUD MINNESOTA

ANNUAL
REPORT
FISCAL YEAR 1967-1968

Mother Henrita Osendorf
speaking for the Borad of Trustees

The Board of Trustees has completed its first year with lay members playing a significant role in its functions.

I am sincerely grateful to Mr. Edward Zapp, Mr. B. Howard Flanagan and Dr. E. LaFond for the generous and genuine manner in which they have represented the community and participated in the work of the Board.

I am grateful, too, to Mr. Gene Bakke, our first lay administrator, who has discharged his difficult duties with dedication. He has ably brought to the board the background needed to make judicious decisions, and he has implemented those decisions effectively.

Now, with expanded and improved facilities available to the residents of the St. Cloud area, we look forward to an ever-deeper commitment on the part of the hospital family to the enriching task of rendering high quality health care. To this end I am sure that we — Board, Medical Staff, Personnel, Sisters, Students — will continue to give the best of ourselves and our resources.

MOTHER HENRITA, O.S.B.
President, Board of Trustees

BOARD OF TRUSTEES: B. Howard Flanagan, Sister Mary Patrick Murray, Dr. E. LaFond, Mother Henrita Osendorf, Gene Bakke, Mother Richard Peters, and Sister Clyde Pavelski. (Missing from the photograph is Edward A. Zapp, Trustee)

pital on February 9, 1928. St. Raphael's Hospital, founded in 1900, became St. Raphael's Home for the elderly.[53]

At its present site, the sisters watched St. Cloud Hospital experience a strong, steady growth. By the late 1950s, it realized a critical need for expansion to serve the fast-growing city of St. Cloud and the outlying area. By 1961 the hospital was the third largest employer in St. Cloud and had truly become an area hospital.[54] Though growth was also steady in the 1960s, the sisters faced the constant challenge of keeping costs down but still providing good care. Since 1928 they had had no fund drive in the civic community. Now, when they had exhausted all sources for federal funds or grants and could not borrow further, they appealed to the civic community and received $900,000 toward the 1.6 million dollars cost of the new wing. This was part of the sizeable building program they undertook in 1968 through 1974 to add two new wings and to remodel, for the first time, the 1928 structure—at the cost of fourteen million dollars.[55]

Another momentous change for the sisters in the 1960s was a major shift in hospital management when the United States Congress passed its most significant piece of health-care legislation ever. The 1965 Kerr-Mills bill known as Medicare provided for private health insurance for all persons over sixty-five years of age, funded and administered by the Social Security administration. Private insurance companies acted as third parties or agents for the distribution. Medicaid was part of the bill to help the poor.[56] This bill, along with new technologies, profoundly affected not-for-profit hospitals, for now generating capital improvement funds, borrowing money, and issuing bonds became focal almost perforce. More and more, a hospital was viewed as a corporate model with CEO and "bottom line" rhetoric.[57]

For good or evil, Medicare had far-reaching effects. It also changed dramatically the sisters' relationship with the St. Cloud Hospital.[58] Though salaries were inadequate, the sisters had received many informal benefits. Now every element of daily living had to be separate and recorded financially: food, snacks, medications, laundry costs, supplies, household goods, use of car and gas, phone calls, and on and on. The federal government would reimburse the hospital costs only for activities related to the care of patients, not for upkeep of the sisters. However, for the sisters who were qualified to receive Medicare, a certain percentage of their medical bills were covered. Because of this, sisters could more readily take advantage of more procedures and medication.[59]

In the years preceding the Second Vatican Council (1962 to 1965), there was considerable stress and strain involved in the employment of professional women religious including those in health care. During the 1950s through the 1970s, the sisters engaged in health care at the St. Cloud Hospital, for example, lived together within hospital walls, then moved to the new convent next door in 1964. At this time, these sisters lived under a grueling schedule—it was work, work, and more work. They speak of it now, some with a tinge of bitterness, but at the time everyone thought it was the normal thing to do. In the 1960s, when sisters began to receive compensation comparable to that of lay employees, their salaries were important figures in the community's resources. This, perhaps, placed even greater emphasis on their work. Though their sense of community was very strong in their hospital group with their work as a common bond, they felt separated from the total community because of minimal opportunities to intermingle with other members. The custom was to come to the motherhouse for retreats, for Chapter meetings, and the like, but that was all. They would compare themselves to teachers who spent the whole summer at Saint Benedict's in summer school programs. When, due to changes wrought by Vatican II, they moved into other living arrangements, they felt the loss of their hospital sisters' community.[60]

With its ever wider outreach, St. Cloud Hospital ranked fifth largest in the state of Minnesota in 1973. Concomitant with this growth were difficult times with rising costs. The Minnesota Hospital Association encouraged the hospital not to increase beds but to have more out-patient services and to consolidate services whenever possible. However, as a referral center, which the hospital had by now become, it needed more space, and so the hospital launched a three-phase building plan to span 1971 to 1983. While it was a "faith-based and mission-driven" Catholic hospital,[61] the sisters still had to consider a certain element of competition with other health providers who were for-profit enterprises. Nor were the sisters in health-care service spared the dilemmas in medical ethics that face every Catholic administration as it implements Church teachings in a pluralistic, community-based Catholic hospital. As the sponsoring body of the St. Cloud Hospital, the sisters shouldered grave responsibilities in issues dealing with birth control, abortion, sterilization, family planning, euthanasia, and others. As recipients of federal funds, their hand could easily have been forced in deciding procedures. The Roe vs. Wade decision in 1973, for example, by which the Supreme Court legalized abortion was a significant point in the history of the sisters' relationship with the St. Cloud Hospital.

In dealing with this decision, Gene S. Bakke, chief executive officer at the time, guided the hospital in holding to its philosophy regarding the sanctity of all life. As a legal basis for refusing, he cited the Conscience Law, which gave hospitals or doctors the option of refusing to perform procedures in violation of their religious convictions. If, he maintained, a hospital were forced by law to permit what it considered an immoral medical practice, it would be the end of Catholic involvement in health care. He argued further: just as an institution can be curtailed by lack of funds, equipment, and personnel in offering every possible treatment in serving a community, so also a hospital can be "unable" to provide services that fall outside its religious and philosophical beliefs.[62]

With a marked increase in society's elderly, the sisters had to come to grips with their inability, in the 1970s, to continue their apostolate at St. Joseph's and St. Raphael's Nursing Homes in St. Cloud. Among other factors, a major one precipitating their closing was the burdensome regulations which state agencies prescribed. For the sisters, though, long-term and skilled care for the elderly in the area was an important mission, and they wanted it to continue, by all means. They were happy to have St. Cloud Hospital assume responsibility by opening St. Benedict's Center on April 25, 1978, as a corporate division of the St. Cloud Hospital. The site was twenty-five acres owned by the sisters and then sold to the St. Cloud Hospital, land adjacent to St. Joseph's Home which, seventy-five years before, had been St. Raphael's Hospital (1890). This twenty-five-acre campus

In twenty years, St. Benedict's Center grew into a village for the senior community.

afforded ample space for expansion to a whole continuum of care. In 1983, the Operating Committee for St. Benedict's Center began plans for an adjacent four million-dollar addition, that is, a congregate apartment housing complex for independent retirement living. Groundbreaking and blessing of this project, named Benedict Village, was on April 10, 1986, the formal dedication on January 9, 1987. St. Benedict's Center and the subsequent complexes around it became known as St. Benedict's Senior Community in January 1999.

Another concern for the sisters in their health-care apostolate was the threat of a second hospital in the area, proposed by Dr. Joseph C. Belshe during 1983. There were anxious moments, but the State Department of Health rejected the proposal because of the nationwide decrease in the number of patients, the surplus of beds in all area hospitals, and the high cost of medical equipment.[63] At the time of this writing, the Allina Health System of Minnetonka is proposing another hospital in St. Cloud. The issue has not yet been resolved. Currently a state law holds a moratorium on adding any beds in hospitals or nursing homes

Sisters associated with the St. Cloud Hospital School of Nursing felt the impact of the trends of the day. The school had started in 1908 at St. Raphael Hospital on Ninth Avenue North. It was a high-quality program to its very last graduating class in the spring of 1987. Graduates scored exceptionally high on licensure exams and met employers' expectations. Its closure marked the loss of "an educational program with a Christian/Benedictine philosophy at a time when complex and serious ethical issues confronted health care at all levels."[64] The hospital sisters' influence on nursing students was inestimable as they "modeled" attitudes of patient care in concern for spiritual and physical needs. The overriding reason for the school's closing was the threat of withdrawal of Medicare federal funds to hospital-based nursing education. A bill was introduced by Senator David Durenberger in October 1984 to end the current Medicare pass-through funds for hospital-based diploma program schools. It did not go into effect, but it did affect recruitment efforts. Then, too, the American Nurses Association proclaimed that, by a certain date, no nurses without a baccalaureate degree could be licensed. To this day this has not happened, but the publicity also had its impact on recruitment. In its seventy-nine-year history, the St. Cloud Hospital School of Nursing included 2,672 students; in this number were 112 men and seventy-eight LPNs accepted as second-year students.[65]

When John Frobenius came on the scene as the new chief executive officer in April 1985, he commended the sisters' long dedication to the health-care apostolate as found in the St. Cloud Hospital's "full line of services . . . as a unique and progressive approach to serving the region."[66] In an intent to continue in the sisters' footsteps, he resolved on a course to keep up with the times, to accommodate regional needs, to market the hospital's many services regionally, and to integrate these services with other health facilities and clinics. The crown of various alliances was the formation of an integrated health-care delivery system for central Minnesota along with the St. Cloud Clinic of Internal Medicine in 1995. It is known today as the CentraCare Health System. Currently St. Cloud Hospital is cited as one of the state's "8 Great Places to Work"[67] Like the sisters' and his lay predecessor's, Frobenius' has been a strong leadership in remaining true to the hospital's basic tenet, which the sisters had set up years ago: to improve the health and quality of life for people in Central Minnesota in a manner that reflects the healing mission of Jesus.[68]

To better document the gradual changes that brought the sisters from full ownership, management, and sponsorship of the St. Cloud Hospital to their present formal relationship with it, a word concerning governing structures is in order. From 1886 on, sisters were at the helm, very definitely involved in every aspect. These giants of women laid firm foundations at which lay administrators who followed could only marvel in awe. Acknowledged here are the sisters who were administrators and the years they spent in those roles. Sister Anselma Billig was the very first—in St. Benedict's

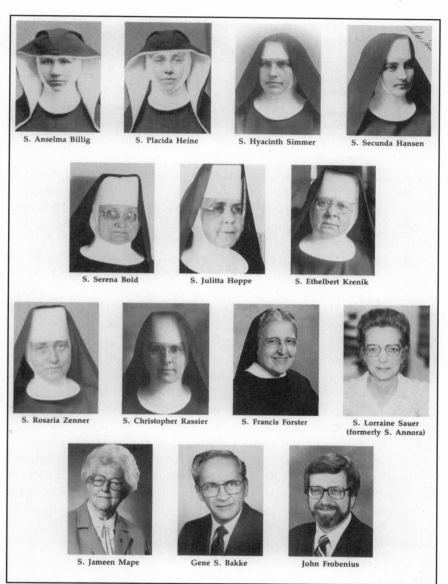

S. Anselma Billig   S. Placida Heine   S. Hyacinth Simmer   S. Secunda Hansen

S. Serena Bold   S. Julitta Hoppe   S. Ethelbert Krenik

S. Rosaria Zenner   S. Christopher Rassier   S. Francis Forster   S. Lorraine Sauer (formerly S. Annora)

S. Jameen Mape   Gene S. Bakke   John Frobenius

Administrators of the hospitals in St. Cloud from 1886 to 2000. (Photo from Dominic, John J., *That You May Find Healing*, St. Cloud Hospital, 1986, p. 49. Used with the permission of the St. Cloud Hospital.)

Hospital (January 1886 to summer 1886); Sister Placida Heine took over (1886 to 1890) until the move to St. Raphael's Hospital I (1890 to 1900) and in the next move to St. Raphael's Hospital II (1900 to 1902) as well. In this institution's twenty-eight-year existence, administrators following Sister Placida were Sisters Hyacinthe Simmer (1902 to 1908), Secunda Hansen (1908 to 1921), Serena Bold (1921 to 1923) and Julitta Hoppe (1923 to 1928). Sister Julitta headed the list of administrators at St. Cloud Hospital in its final location in 1928 (to 1929). Sisters Ethelbert Krenik (1929 to 1938), Rosaria Zenner (1938 to 1943), Christopher Rassier (1943 to 1948), Francis Xavier Forster (1948 to 1958), Lorraine (Annora) Sauer (1958 to 1959), and Jameen Mape (1959 to 1967) complete the roster.

By force of circumstances, governing structures took on gradual but significant changes in the 1960s, 1970s, and again in the 1990s. Since 1886, through changes in name and locations, the hospital was the total responsibility of the Sisters of the Order of Saint Benedict at St. Joseph, Minnesota. They owned two other hospitals and other nursing and retirement homes in addition to the motherhouse and college. All this was heavily operational, financially a burden, and a frightening risk; if one of the facilities failed, liability claims would touch everything the sisters owned. At the recommendation of the Catholic Health Association, they created the St. Cloud Hospital as a separate, not-for-profit corporation, officially incorporated when the Articles of Incorporation were filed with the Secretary of the State of Minnesota and a charter issued on September 6, 1962. The actual deeding of the land, together with all buildings and equipment, from the Sisters of the Order of Saint Benedict to the St. Cloud Hospital, was recorded with the Stearns County Register of Deeds on January 17, 1964. Though by virtue of its corporate status, this corporation is the owner of the hospital properties, yet its non-profit character sees the property as held in trust for the benefit of the people in the area served or who might be served by the hospital in the future. The sisters would keep full control of its operation as stated in the articles of incorporation and bylaws, but this new corporation, the Saint Cloud Hospital, would stand as a separate financial entity. Sister officials of the monastery comprised corporate membership; others would continue as members of the St. Cloud Hospital Board of Trustees, and some would become salaried employees. This allowed the hospital more flexibility and autonomy while at the same time giving sisters an opportunity to share responsibilities of operation by appointing lay persons to the governing board and to management positions.

As a first step in the sisters' decision to share responsibility for the hospital with lay persons, Gene S. Bakke was hired as assistant to the administrator, S. Jameen Mape, as early as August 1962, the first layman to hold such a managerial position in a Catholic hospital in Minnesota. Five years later, on April 3, 1967, Mother Henrita Osendorf, president of the Board of Trustees and prioress, appointed Gene Bakke to succeed Sister Jameen, thus he became the first lay administrator in a Catholic hospital in Minnesota. Early in 1969, the Board of Directors approved administrative reorganization making Bakke chief executive officer; he retired in 1984. He moved St. Cloud Hospital through four major building programs and a critical period of growth when Medicare and Medicaid were introduced.[69]

In the 1965 Bylaws of the St. Cloud Hospital, corporate members were the sisters resident at the St. Cloud Hospital, the president, vice-president, and secretary-treasurer of Saint Benedict's Corporation, and any other sister whom the president (prioress) designated. The Board of Directors, not fewer than five, was made up of the president, vice-president, and secretary-treasurer of the sisters, along with the local superior and the administrator of the St. Cloud Hospital. Note that members of the Corporate Board and the Board of Directors were all sisters. A lay advisory board was possible.

In amending the Bylaws and Articles of Incorporation 1967, each Chapter member of the Sisters of Saint Benedict became a member of the Corporate Board. Another very important change was that the Board of Directors would be at least seven: four sisters and three lay persons. Inviting lay persons to the Board was another implementation of Vatican II's recognition of the laity. They were Edward A. Zapp, B. Howard Flanagan, and Dr. Edward M. LaFond.

From the beginning of the corporation in 1962, the Articles of Incorporation, with each emendation, stated clearly that the sisters, though deeply committed to the St. Cloud Hospital, were not accountable or responsible, legally or morally, for any financial obligations related to the hospital. In 1969, Bylaws for the corporation changed Board of Directors membership to at least eight, equally four lay persons and four sisters, one of whom was the prioress or her designate. The term "sponsorship" appeared as the title of Article I, which explained that "the Sisters as a community of women religious, by their presence and influence in Board, administrative, and staff positions, would give Christian witness of love and compassion for the sick. Sponsorship," it stated further, "safeguards adherence to the principles of the Catholic Church, the tradition and ideals of the Sisters, and the policies and directives of the Catholic Hospital (1979: Health) Association."

Soon after, the 1973 Supreme Court decision of Roe vs. Wade elicited another significant change in the sisters' relationship with the hospital they had founded and funded since 1886. They felt the need of a broader support to maintain Catholic principles, including resisting the Supreme Court decision. So, in 1975, they asked the Diocese of St. Cloud to be a co-sponsor, making it the only Catholic hospital, at the time, to enjoy co-sponsorship with a diocese. Now Article I in the Bylaws became "sponsored by the Sisters of the Order of Saint Benedict and the Diocese of Saint Cloud . . ." And "the Bishop" will join the sisters in giving Christian witness. The Board of Directors would be "an equal number of lay persons and sisters or clergy." The Board of Directors in the St. Cloud Diocese joined the Executive Officers of the Sisters of Saint Benedict as the corporate membership of the hospital—five sister representatives; five diocesan officials. This made it a total Church community service.[70]

Then, for a span, there were no changes except that in 1987, a change in the Articles of Incorporation called for increased membership in the Board of Directors—no fewer than nine.[71]

In the early 1990s, this existing structure of co-sponsorship took on a quite revolutionary change when the idea of forming an integrated health-care delivery system for central Minnesota emerged. Representatives of the St. Cloud Hospital, the St. Cloud Clinic of Internal Medicine, and the St. Cloud Medical Group formed an ad hoc task committee in summer 1993. In 1995, the St. Cloud Hospital and the St. Cloud Clinic of Internal Medicine formed the proposed CentraCare Health System. This arrangement enabled the hospital and physicians to share resources and eliminate duplicate services, all the while maintaining the common goals of health-care quality and availability. Basic to the system was the commitment to maintain the St. Cloud Hospital as a Catholic hospital.

In May 1995, the Articles of Incorporation and Bylaws were changed to include as ex officio corporate members the bishop of the diocese and the vicar general (or delegates), the prioress and the subprioress (or delegates), and *two to four lay members* appointed by a majority vote of these ex officio members. Their primary function was the preservation of the hospital's Catholic mission.[72] Now, in the hospital's operation, the word "sponsorship" gave way to "under the auspices of the local church of St. Cloud," meaning the church as "a Catholic community comprised of laity, clergy, and members of religious institutions, under the leadership of the bishop."[73]

The sisters' calling of lay people to corporate membership for the first time was yet another step in the process that had begun with separate incorporation three decades earlier. It had been a tremendous change for the sisters, trying to understand what it all meant: ownership relinquished; sisters as the sponsoring body, as employees;

assets of land, buildings, and equipment transferred from the Sisters of St. Benedict to the new corporation in 1964[74] to be held in trust by the Board of the St. Cloud Hospital; lay people in administrative and managerial positions. The issue of including lay people as corporate members had been in the sisters' thoughts years before, but the time was not right. Instead, they had asked the Diocese of St. Cloud to co-sponsor the hospital in 1975. Now, in 1994, including lay persons as Corporate Board members spelled out the conviction that the local church is made up of clergy, religious, and lay people. "Just as St. Cloud Hospital has expanded to become a regional medical center in Central Minnesota, so corporate membership is expanding to include all groups of the local Catholic community"[75] Today St. Cloud Hospital's Corporate Board monitors and maintains the hospital's Catholic identity, according to the Ethical and Religious Directives for Catholic Facilities, September 1971, updated to Ethical and Religious Directives for Catholic Health Care Services in 1994, both versions by the National Conference of Catholic Bishops.

In its beginnings, the sisters working at the hospital and numbering more than ninety at one time, staffed and guided the St. Cloud Hospital. They shared its advances with the local community but shouldered the burdens themselves. This changed appreciably in the last three or four decades as the sisters gradually shared their responsibility for the hospital. On the one hand, they stayed involved, but they were actually moving away from being in control. The significance of this history of 113 years, though, is not lost. In that time, twelve sisters have served in the role of administrator (1886 to 1967); almost 300 (282 until 1986) passed through its halls in various capacities of ministry. "Always, in whatever era, their task has been more than a commitment or even a vocation; it has been an apostolate in the fullest sense of the word, carried out with dedication, always intent on providing healing service in Christ's name, for his sake, to his people."[76]

UTAH-COLUMBIA OGDEN REGIONAL MEDICAL CENTER

The story of how the sisters accepted an invitation on May 10, 1943, to become involved in health care in Utah is well told in Sister Grace McDonald's book.[77] The first Benedictine sisters arrived in Ogden on October 12, 1944. On September 18, 1946, Duane G. Hunt, Bishop of Salt Lake City, dedicated the first St. Benedict's Hospital at 3000 Polk.[78] This was a new venture in health care, not an expansion or rebuilding of a facility already in operation in a well known territory. At the time, there was only one Catholic hospital in the entire state of Utah. Considering the invitation a splendid missionary opportunity for the Church, Sister Mary Margaret Clifford, administrator (1946 to 1961), and nineteen Benedictine sisters quietly embraced the Ogden community in caring service.[79]

The hospital flourished. It made a medical first for Utah in an exsanguination (complete blood exchange of an infant because of the RH factor); "Dr. W. H. Anderson, pediatrician, performed it successfully on the first baby born in this condition to be saved in the Intermountain West."[80]

To add to their area of service, the sisters accepted an invitation from Bishop Joseph L. Federal of Salt Lake City, to take over St. Michael's Hospital in Richfield, Utah, in April 1960. Sister Arles Silbernick was the administrator. The effort was short-lived, for the Church of the Latter Day Saints officials opposed the sisters' presence and threatened

The first St. Benedict's Hospital in Ogden, Utah.

to build a new hospital in competition. The sisters, though reluctantly, offered to sell the hospital to the Latter Day Saints, and they assented. The sisters' efforts, however, did not go unnoticed or unappreciated. Among the tributes paid them are these words from an editorial published in the *Richfield Reaper*, January 3, 1963: "It is doubtful that anyone can deny the Sisters have done a marvelous job in providing the finest medical care and service possible in a hospital the size of St. Michael's. They have been cooperative in the community and lived up to their name and reputation as 'angels of mercy.' The community owes them a debt of gratitude."

A highlight of the 1970s was groundbreaking for a new hospital on October 30, 1974; in February 1977 Joseph L. Federal, Bishop of Salt Lake City, dedicated this new 204-bed St. Benedict's Hospital. However, more and more challenges were facing the sisters in their attempts to preserve Catholic health care in Utah. It was becoming increasingly difficult for a stand-alone hospital to survive at this period of time. Maybe a "system" of some sort would help, pooling

Board meeting at St. Benedict's Hospital: Left to right, standing: Sister Cassian Peters, Dr. L.D. Nelson, Dr. Donald Moore, Sister Francis Xavier Forster, Samuel Powell (legal counsel), Ralph Nye, Sister Stephanie Mongeon; seated: Sister Arles Silbernick, Sister Luke Hoschette, Mrs. Jean Morton, Sister Mary Patrick Murray, William Olwell, Sister Justin (Mary) Feeley, and Richard Hemmingway.

of resources and diversifying somewhat.[81] So, in 1982 they formed St. Benedict's Health System as a holding company to provide coordination of services to seven separately incorporated subsidiaries, each with its own Board of Trustees.

That, too, was not enough. A larger system was needed to alleviate the existing financial problems and, after serious consideration, the hospital forged an affiliation with Holy Cross Health System Corporation, South Bend, Indiana, in October 1986. By December 1, 1986, this affiliation was finalized; corporate members of Holy Cross replaced corporate members of St. Benedict's Health System. An equal representation by Sisters of St. Benedict and Sisters of the Holy Cross comprised the Board of Trustees. This turn of events prepared the sisters, in a way, for the ultimate loss they would experience in later developments.[82]

By affiliation of St. Benedict's Hospital with the Holy Cross Health System, many significant strides in quality health care became possible. However the new era that the Holy Cross Health System had opened took another turn in 1993 when this system concluded that it needed to leave health care in Utah. Then followed negotiations for the sale of St. Benedict's, Holy Cross, and Holy Cross Jordan Valley to HealthTrust, Inc., a for-profit corporation, as of August 15, 1994. This for-profit aspect definitely brought a new perspective to what was now called Ogden Regional Medical Center. Notwithstanding, it also strengthened the determination of the sisters to retain the Benedictine values they had nurtured so carefully.

Still another change followed on April 24, 1995, as HealthTrust, Inc., merged with Columbia/HCA. These changes in ownership were seen as necessary to ensure future viability, efficiency, and effectiveness. The "mission" of the Benedictine Sisters was to remain an important part of the culture of what became the Columbia Ogden Regional Medical Center. It is a non-Catholic, for-profit, proprietary hospital, owned by Columbia/HCA Health Care Corporation, Nashville, Tennessee. The changes that occurred since 1986 indicate that pressures from the outside prompted the sisters to accept the shifts, initially in governance and then in ownership, as a last resort.[83]

For more than fifty years, the sisters have rendered service to the Utah community. In almost thirty years within that span, five sisters served as administrators: Sister Mary Margaret Clifford (1946 to 1961) was the first in this role; Sister Estelle Nordick (1961 to 1967) followed; the convent was built in this era; Sister Luke Hoschette (1967 to 1971) initiated plans for the new hospital; Sister Mary Patrick Murray (1971 to 1974) purchased land for the new hospital. When the time was deemed opportune, the sisters handed over the management to lay people. In January 1975, Louis Prebil became the interim administrator until May 1, 1975, when Robert K. Eisleben became the first lay administrator.

Though some sisters of Mount Benedict Monastery have gone on to ministries outside formal health care, others still serve in various capacities at Columbia Ogden Regional Medical Center. The fiftieth anniversary of the Benedictine sisters' arrival in Utah in 1994 offered countless reasons to celebrate: deep roots in a state that had no Catholic religious foundation as late as 1979; acceptance by and cooperation with many Mormon neighbors; and a stalwart faith and willingness to risk autonomous status.

The question can be rightfully raised whether today's Medical Center really continues to uphold the Benedictine mission even though it is a for-profit facility. There is no easy answer, only a reassurance in saying that the Columbia mission and value statement parallels the one that made St. Benedict's Hospital what it was. The sisters do all they can to assure that this statement is carried out. Another reassurance is that many of the employees have been there for a long time and were witnesses to what happened. The name and ownership may be different, but the "caregivers" are the same and provide the same kind of care for which the Benedictine sisters have always been known.[84] Words in a recent brochure bolster this assurance:

> For fifty years, Columbia Ogden Regional Medical Center (CORMC) has delivered compassionate, person-

alized, quality healthcare to the people of Ogden and Northern Utah. Although our name has changed since the Sisters of Saint Benedict first established a community hospital in 1946, the tradition of quality and caring continues.[85]

As in their beginnings, the sisters are still breaking down misunderstanding of the Church and her work in the state of Utah. The memory of the lived experience of Benedictine caring and healing will not easily fade from sight in Ogden. Even after more than fifty years, Benedictine philosophy continues its healing touch. In a seemingly ever-changing milieu, it has been a bulwark of support for employees, physicians, volunteers, and members of the community throughout these years as St. Benedict's Hospital lived out its philosophy from the *Rule of St. Benedict*: "Before all things, care must be taken of the sick as if they were Christ in person."(*RB* 36:1)

QUEEN OF PEACE HOSPITAL, NEW PRAGUE, MINNESOTA

It all started with a gift. William L. and Eleanora Harvey gave their home to the civic community of New Prague when they moved to Minneapolis in 1923. In 1924 this home opened as the New Prague Community Hospital and operated as a private citizens' non-profit corporation until January 7, 1947, when the board transferred ownership and assets to the city. It was a time of optimism—right after World War II—and the city, in need of a new hospital, began construction in July 1950. When voters approved a $175,000 municipal bond issue, Hill-Burton funds became available from the federal government. St. Wenceslaus Parish donated the land. Citizens from the surrounding rural area raised additional funds. Health care in New Prague, from its very beginnings, was a cooperative enterprise, a significant factor in its development and progress.

Management, however, posed a problem. The townspeople and pastor prevailed on the Sisters of St. Benedict to take over this forty-two-bed hospital. They had asked Fran-

Queen of Peace Hospital, New Prague, Minnesota.

ciscan Sisters from Springfield, Illinois, twice, but to no avail. So in August 1951, the Sisters of St. Benedict accepted management responsibility and ownership—and assumption of the city's indebtedness on the bond issue ($143,000). Sisters Catherine Mc Innis (a medical records librarian, now a patients' advocate), Cor Marie Auer, Ella Schweitzer, Martha Schrantz, Mary Afra Guettler, Mary Jude Meyer, Ruth Ann Duclos, and Jameen Mape as administrator made up the original staff. Volunteers from the civic community came to help in great numbers.[86] On February 10, 1952, 3,500 visitors were welcomed at the open house for the new hospital. After six years of plans, dreams, prayers, and work, Community Memorial Hospital opened on February 14, 1952. Patient occupancy was above expectations. The medical staff came from surrounding hospitals, some from the Twin Cities area. It was now a Catholic hospital. Sister Mary Margaret Clifford accepted the role of administrator from 1961 to 1967.

Obstetrics was perhaps the busiest place and Sister Mary Afra Guettler, its central figure, a wonder to all. The

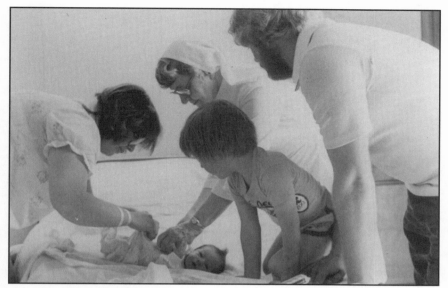

Sister Mary Afra Guettler, obstetrics.

Quinlan triplets brought Community Memorial Hospital international publicity, as far as Tokyo, Japan, in 1954. Arriving on December 31, just in time for a triple tax deduction for their parents, they were born to an Rh-negative mother; it took only a few days for them to show signs of Rh erythroblastosis. All required multiple transfusions and they survived. At the time only one other set of RH sensitized triplets was reported to have survived.[87]

As early as 1958, it was evident that Community Memorial Hospital would have to expand in order to meet the health-care needs in the immediate and surrounding areas. The result was a forty-bed, million-dollar addition completed in1963, funded through a loan, accumulated patient revenue, and Hill-Burton money. To emphasize its Christian values as basic, Community Memorial Hospital became Queen of Peace Hospital.

A well-known presence at Queen of Peace Hospital was Sister Ruth Ann Duclos with a thirty-six-year tradition in the clinical laboratory. Queen of Peace is one of the few

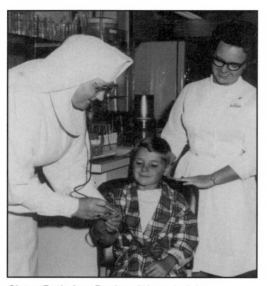

Sister Ruth Ann Duclos, lab technician.

Minnesota hospitals of its size to have its clinical laboratory accredited by the College of American Pathologists. Dr. Paul Stahler notes: "Ever since the sisters opened this hospital, the doctors have had great respect and admiration for the lab and x-ray."[88]

Despite difficulties encountered, hospital reviews were consistently favorable. Queen of Peace received its first accreditation in 1976 by the Joint Commission of the Accreditation of Hospitals (JCAH). Evaluators use the same national standards for Queen of Peace as for larger hospitals, subjecting each area of service to appraisal every three years. For the June 24-25, 1996, review, the hospital received the highest marks ever—ninety-three percent, a grade only about twelve pecent of hospitals achieve.[89] Accreditation "is a badge of excellent care," commented Dr. Paul Stahler.[90]

With an exceptionally supportive staff and civic community, Queen of Peace Hospital merited high commendation over the years. Sister Jean Juenemann, chief executive officer since 1977, has been a member in the American College of Health Care Executives, AHA, since 1987. On April 17, 1989, the Society for Healthcare Planning and Marketing, representing more than 3,300 health-care executives worldwide, gave her its CEO award for excellence in health care planning and marketing.[91] In the fall of 1991, Queen of Peace Hospital was one of the forty-nine hospitals in the

United States selected by the Hospital Community Benefit Standards Program because of its organized approach to community service beyond direct patient care.[92] Again, in 1994, the Wisconsin Healthcare Public Relations and Marketing Society recognized Sister Jean as outstanding in the categories of total marketing campaigns and special publications.[93] In 1996 the Minnesota Hospital and Health-care Partnership bestowed its Distinguished Service Award on Queen of Peace Hospital.[94]

New emphasis on caring for the whole person created many new service programs during the 1970s and 1980s. However, concomitant with improved care and expanded services, the administration experienced the usual difficulties in escalating costs and restrictive government polices. Advanced technology, skyrocketing insurance rates, rising personnel expenses, and an ever-growing need for staff edu-

Sisters with a long track record at Queen of Peace Hospital: Left to right, standing: Sisters Mary Alfra Guettler, Lydia Erkens, Jean Juenemann, Lawrence Kiff-meyer, Elizabeth Brannan; seated: Sisters Catherine Mc Innis, Jameen Mape, and Margaret (Leo) Schweiss. Sister Ruth Ann Duclos (not shown) was the photographer.

cation challenged hospitals financially nationwide, even leading to closures or mergers. Medicaid and Medicare cover only from fifty-five to eighty percent of hospital charges; the increase in paperwork involved was mountainous. Attitudes in patients changed, too, as they became more knowledgeable. Sister Jean Juenemann spoke of these very difficulties when she wrote: "A major challenge of the 1980s was keeping abreast of medical technology, finding space to accommodate the surge of outpatients, and continue providing health care in a manner consistent with patients' expectations."[95]

The 1990s ushered in a decade of continuing remarkable improvements. The number of programs possible in outreach services and education for community benefit seemed limitless. Nor was the Hospital hesitant to launch into new areas, even as a small-town health-care facility. In July 1997, Queen of Peace built a new outpatient center ($4.37 million), a facility that had already been declared a great need in the 1980s. In the August 5, 1990, issue of *Hospitals*, Sister Jean wrote an article about this phenomenon: "Outpatient Care: A Nationwide Revolution."

Another area seeking special attention in this decade was the provision of spiritual services for patients. With the decreasing number of sisters in key positions, it was necessary to intentionally provide a Pastoral Care Department with a chaplain. This department also began a Befriender Program, a parish/volunteer home-visiting program originating at St. Thomas University and adapted to a health care setting. Ecumenically orientated, this ministry is to the parish's homebound and to patients in the hospital's hospice program. The National Befriender Ministry cited the program for its visionary adaptation.

In order to offer the number and variety of programs needed for its own staff and to reaffirm an integral part of its mission to serve the community in health-care education, the hospital planned a conference center in 1988. The dedication of the Jameen Mape Conference Center, on March 28, 1990, honored Sister Jameen for her many contributions to health care, especially in the New Prague community for a span of thirty-eight years. Her years as administrator (1952 to 1958; 1967 to 1977), as chairman of the Board for sixteen years, and as a board member were ones of phenomenal growth and development at Queen of Peace Hospital.

Queen of Peace Hospital is true to its identity in adhering to the *Ethical and Religious Directives for Health Care Services* as outlined by the National Conference of Catholic Bishops in 1995. After careful study of these seventy directives, the hospital formed an ad hoc committee to address them as applicable to Queen of Peace. Sister Mary Ellen Machtemes, Director of Mission Effectiveness of the St. Cloud Hospital and Queen of Peace Hospital Board member, lent her expertise to a detailed study. The Board of Directors has approved the final draft; approval of the Corporate Board came in Spring 2000.

In 1964, the sisters changed the Queen of Peace Hospital ownership by having it form its own self-governing, locally owned, non-profit corporation, licensed in the state of Minnesota, governed and managed by a board of directors and a chief executive officer. Article 4 states specifically that the sisters sponsor the Corporation.[96] This sponsorship, not ownership, relationship has as "Its role . . . one of assuring that the institution be true to the purpose for which it was incorporated, and that the corporation not be dissolved without approval of the Sisters of Saint Benedict, Inc."[97] Article 6 lists Corporate members as the president, vice-president, director of finance, and the secretary of the Sisters of the Order of Saint Benedict, along with two additional sisters who are directors.[98] Members of the Board of Directors are selected from each town served by the hospital. They play a strong role in developing vision and charting a future direction as significant investments are made in building, renovation and expansion, and extension of services. At present, three Benedictine sisters and ten lay persons make up this board; they select, nominate, and elect new and additional directors, and also appoint the chief executive officer.[99]

Continuation of sponsorship by the Sisters of Saint Benedict is discussed regularly. Though Board members value this relationship highly and are grateful for the sisters' presence, they are realistic in viewing a future in which there would be no sisters staffing the hospital and so consider alternate models of Catholic sponsorship.[100]

Today, Queen of Peace Hospital is a licensed fifty-bed facility. It has flourished, despite neighboring hospitals in rural Minnesota having to curtail services, raise revenues through tax levies, or even close their doors. Observers single out community support as the main key to its success. It began as a community undertaking when myriads of community volunteers, staff members, and the Benedictine sisters saw the need in one rural community and went into action to meet its challenges. As a health-care facility, it has never lost that important ingredient of community backing; in fact, it has only widened in its reach, grown stronger in its dedication.

Homes for the Elderly[101]

The sisters at Saint Benedict's Monastery began their care of the elderly in 1900 when unfavorable circumstances led to the abandonment of the first St. Raphael's Hospital. It was, however, considered an ideal location for the elderly, and so it became St. Joseph's Home. From that time forward, the sisters tenaciously clung to care for the elderly as an important value in their mission. In the decades following, they were to extend their care far beyond St. Joseph's Home: to St. Raphael's Home in St. Cloud, to four other homes in the area, three of which were parish owned but staffed by the sisters, and to two in North Dakota.

ST. JOSEPH'S HOME FOR THE AGED

Since the first St. Raphael's Hospital had proved impractical, especially in its location of two and one-half miles southeast of downtown St. Cloud, the monastery Chapter voted, on February 27, 1899, that "the present building . . . be changed into an asylum [sic] for the reception of the old and infirm." In May 1900, patients transferred to the new St. Raphael's Hospital. Eight of the patients stayed behind and formed the nucleus of the newly established St. Joseph's Home for the Aged. It reached a capacity of eighty residents by 1904; after adding to the building, its number stabilized at about ninety. State Department of Health requirements for licensure and certification as a nursing home prompted the building of a new wing in 1964, increasing capacity to 115. In its origins, acreage property was 5.45. Over the years, purchase of surrounding land increased land holdings to 250 acres, 170 of which were used for farming.

From its beginnings, the sisters owned, managed, and partially staffed St. Joseph's Home. Although they separately incorporated it in 1966, it was still under their direction. In 1975, they merged it back into the Corporation of the Sisters of St. Benedict. Increased government regulations, the need for a larger Catholic facility for the care of the elderly in the area, and the decreasing number of sisters available for the work at St. Joseph's Home forced its closing. In April 1978 residents left it for the newly completed St. Benedict's Center. Again, the hand of Providence was evident, for St. Joseph's Home proved to be an ideal home for the increasing number of elderly and in-need-of-care sisters. In the summer of 1978, the sisters needing skilled care moved from the infirmary at Saint Benedict's Monastery to St. Joseph's Home, now renamed Saint Scholastica Convent. At present, it flourishes as one of the important centers of the community.

ST. RAPHAEL'S REST HOME

When a new St. Cloud Hospital welcomed patients and staff from the second St. Raphael's Hospital on Ninth Avenue North in May 1928, St. Raphael's Hospital, which had been in operation since 1900, became St. Raphael's Rest Home, a home for the aged. For the next thirty-three years or so, resident census was about seventy. In 1961, the sisters built an addition to certify it for nursing care as well as board and care. Further demands by the State Health Department resulted in another small addition, bringing capacity to ninety-three. Although the sisters always owned and managed the home, it was separately incorporated in 1966, and then returned to the Corporation of the Sisters of St. Benedict in 1975. Try as they might, they were unable to meet increasing demands of government regulation or the pressure of ethical concerns in a Catholic home for the elderly, and so they closed it to lay persons in October 1975. The sisters themselves were looking about for a retirement center for their members, and St. Raphael's became home to many retired sisters until January 1999 when decreasing membership did not warrant having this center.

ST. ANN'S HOME; ST. BENEDICT'S HOME—DICKINSON, NORTH DAKOTA

On September 29, 1944, Saint Benedict's Monastery Chapter in St. Joseph, Minnesota, voted to open St. Ann's Home for the aged in Dickinson, North Dakota. The building had been purchased by Bishop Vincent Ryan of the Bismarck Diocese. A year later, September 18, 1945, the same Chapter voted to purchase the Wilson school building to be remodeled into St. Benedict's Home for the aged, also in Dickinson. The sisters of Annunciation Monastery were to supply the funds for said purchase. When Annunciation Monastery's status changed to an independent diocesan community in 1947, the sisters there took complete charge of both of these homes.

MARY RONDORF HOME

Upon request of Pastor Ferdinand Falque for a sister to act as superintendent of the parish operated facility, a home for retired people of Sacred Heart Parish and of the town, Sister Sophonia Lang took this position at Mary Rondorf Home in Staples, Minnesota, in 1953. That summer, four sisters joined the staff, and in 1954, the monastery Chapter accepted the home as a community mission. The sisters started with twenty-nine residents; later this expanded to eighty-four. Unable to meet state standards in 1977, the home transferred the patients to a new non-parish nursing home, and the sisters withdrew.

St. Mary's Home—Long Prairie

In 1957, the monastic Chapter accepted a request of delegates from Long Prairie to convert a former hospital into a home for the aged. Sisters Eulalia Siebels, Noel LeClaire, and Gudilia Duclos opened it as St. Mary's Home. It was leased to the monastery and later separately incorporated. The census began at twenty-seven guests and remained at this level for ten years, making necessary renovations to meet state standards financially unfeasible. The lease arrangement was ended and the residents moved to a new facility in the area.

Mother of Mercy Nursing—Albany

The monastic Chapter voted on July 19, 1959, to lend support to the new parish-owned nursing home in Albany, Minnesota. Sisters Ivan Schaefer, Hildelia Auer, and Aelred Stang opened and helped staff it. The first residents came in August of that same year. Its peak census was sixty-one. From its opening until now, sisters have and continue to serve in various capacities—Sister Mary Zierden for twenty-six years.

Assumption Nursing Home—Cold Spring

This parish-owned nursing home opened in September 1963. Sisters Rosemary Yost and Carolinda Medernach were sent to help operate it; the facility is licensed for sixty-eight residents. On July 25, 1964, the monastic Chapter approved helping staff this home on a permanent basis; this service continues to the present time.

Conclusion

These ventures show that the sisters answered the call to care for the elderly whenever possible. An appreciable number of sisters spent many years in these nursing homes in dedicated, loving care, with long hours and arduous tasks. It is true, changing circumstances in time narrowed their possible courses of action, but even in limited numbers, they remained true to their mission in providing quality care for those who came to them. In their focus on the ethical and spiritual dimensions of care for the elderly, a constant was the promotion of human dignity, independence, wellness, and life. Giving reason to hope, to experience God's love for each person was the core of their theology, their whole attitude toward life and death. That spelled out precisely the distinction of a Christian home for the elderly. It is still a characteristic maintained by the few sisters who are serving directly in the care for the elderly today.

Mary, mother of God and model of contemplative service, was a favorite subject of the art of Sister Thomas Carey. ("Indian Madonna and Child," 1954)

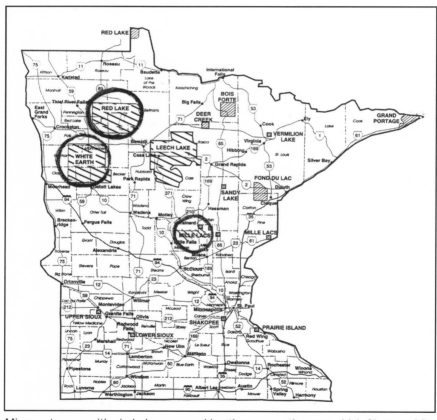

Minnesota map with circled areas marking the reservations on which Sisters of St. Benedict lived and ministered: White Earth, Red Lake, and Mille Lacs.

13
NATIVE AMERICAN MINISTRY

Carol Berg, O.S.B.

Introduction

History is replete with examples of powerful nations and institutions that lack respect for those who differ from them. This is true from the dawn of recorded history into modern times. The nineteenth century, for example, was a time of world colonization by several western nations, such as Great Britain, France, Germany, and the United States, nations that conquered other peoples, usually attacking their culture as well. Nationalism ran amuck, as in previous ages, bringing an era of colonization that forced change upon smaller, less powerful nations. Unfortunately, the churches—Catholic and Protestant—often were accomplices of that nationalistic zeal. Yet, as Timothy McCarthy states in his book, *The Catholic Tradition*, long before the post World War II period, when colonialism was in decline, various popes were advocating a more flexible, open-minded approach to peoples of diverse cultures.

Pope Gregory the Great, who served from 590 to 604, gave directives to missionaries to show respect for native cultures, blending their beliefs and rituals with Catholic ones when possible. But after the Council of Trent (sixteenth century), a church on the defensive was less open minded, and "pagan" culture was scorned as ignorant, or worse, satanic. This attitude prevailed until the early twentieth century. Benedict XV (1914 to 1922) gave three principles for missiology in his apostolic letter, *Maximum Illud* (1919): (a) formation of a native clergy, (b) reunification of nationalism, and (c) appreciation for the native culture. His successor, Pius XI (1922 to 1933), in his encyclical *Rerum Ecclesiae* (1926), reaffirmed these principles. He stated clearly that "the church of Christ, the faithful depository of the teaching of Divine Wisdom, cannot and does not think of deprecating or disdaining the particular characteristics which each people, with jealous and intelligible pride, cherish and retain as a precious heritage."[102]

Piux XI was also aware of a major problem faced by most missionaries through the ages: the language barrier. In a passage from his writing on native clergy, the pope noted that ". . . the foreign missionary, because of his imperfect knowledge of the language, often finds himself embarrassed when he attempts to express his thoughts with the result that the force and efficacy of his preaching are thereby greatly weakened."[103] Generations of missionaries can attest to this.

One of the most scholarly popes was Pius XII (1938 to 1958), unusual in his ability to read and speak twelve languages. His encyclicals, *Summi Pontificatus* (1939) and *Evangelii Praecones* (1951), have long passages encouraging respect for other people's cultures and traditions. His successor, John XXIII (1958 to 1963), writing on the missions, native clergy, and lay participation, stated that the training of seminarians for the missions should "open up and sharpen the minds of seminarians in such a way as to enable each individual to evaluate correctly his own and his country's particular kind of culture."[104] Convenor of the Vatican Council II, John XXIII, opening his mind and heart to the peoples of the world, became much beloved.

In the late twentieth century, the concept of inculturation was becoming accepted: the mixing, mingling of older native cultures with new or foreign ones. Pope John Paul II (1978-) has traveled extensively around the globe, interacting with many diverse cultures, showing much openness to them while never failing to proclaim the Gospel of Jesus Christ. He and missionaries of all denominations have had to come to terms with people's attachment to their own customs and traditions. The post-Vatican II teaching has come true: "If, in the past, missionaries thought they had much to give and teach, they now acknowledge that they have much to receive and learn about diverse ways of being human, religious and holy."[105] As the following cases evidence, Benedictine mission experiences with American Indians and among peoples in Asia and the Caribbean, show at times an ethnocentrism but also a steady growth in understanding and appreciation of native cultures.

The Missions

(Note: The term Indian will be used instead of Native American since the former term has become so embedded and generally accepted in historical writing.)

For both St. Benedict's Monastery and Saint John's Abbey, the Indian missions had become a major apostolate by the late nineteenth century. In 1875, thirteen years after the Sioux Uprising and eighteen years after the monks came to Minnesota, Abbot Rupert Seidenbusch was named Vicar-Apostolic of the newly created Vicariate of Northern Minnesota. Archbishop Seidenbusch was very conscious of the large Indian population, barely reached by the efforts, albeit heroic, of such priests as Fathers Francis Pierz, Joseph Buh, and Ignatius Tomazin. The total population of this area included 14,000 whites and 25,000 Indians, primarily Ojibwa.[106] Archbishop Seidenbusch called upon his successor at Saint John's Abbey, Alexius Edelbrock, to furnish priests for work among the Ojibwa in northern Minnesota.

Open to this appeal, Abbot Edelbrock asked his Chapter for approval. Although approval was granted, there was concern with what some monks termed "excessive activism."

There was a fear that too much missionary work would weaken the Benedictine spirit and that the contemplative dimension of Benedictine life would be submerged under the active life. Abbot Edelbrock reminded his monks that the long history of the order attests to a missionary impulse in response to the needs and call of the Church.[107]

Abbot Edelbrock in turn asked Mother Aloysia Bath (appointed prioress from 1877 to 1880) to supply sisters for the mission. This she did, and in November 1878 a trio—Father Aloysius Hermanutz, Sisters Lioba Braun and Philomena Ketten—began what would be fifty years of work at White Earth, the first of three Minnesota Indian missions undertaken by the Benedictines.

Father Aloysius and Sisters Lioba and Philomena knew little of Indian life in general and of Ojibwa culture in particular. In this, they were among the majority of missionaries, before and after them, who served the tribes, ignorant of the Ojibwas' rich traditions and values. Across the United States, little of Indian culture was understood or even tolerated by non-Indians. It took many years of living among the Indians before some missionaries grew to know and respect them in the context of their cultures. Part of the problem was a lack of preparation for this work. Moreover, many missionaries, because of common stereotypical images of Indians, feared or scorned them. It is a safe generalization to say that few missionaries—Catholic or non-Catholic—possessed the willingness or ability to adapt to Indian culture, even well into the twentieth century. Good will and zeal were present from the start, but these did not compensate for ignorance and a failure to appreciate Indian culture over many decades of missionary activity.

Some sisters volunteered for the Indian missions, but most were assigned by the prioress (called Mother Superior before the 1960s). Mother Aloysia Bath (elected prioress from 1889 to 1901) sent the first sisters to White Earth, and her successor, Mother Scholastica Kerst (1880 to 1889) sent some to Red Lake, Minnesota. Unfortunately, these missionaries kept no diaries or journals of their experiences.

White Earth and Red Lake

THE EARLY DECADES

White Earth, the first Indian mission for the Benedictine Sisters and monks (1878 to 1969) was followed by missions at Red Lake, sometimes "Redlake" (1888 to present), and Mille Lacs (1941 to present). These missions were opened at the pleas of local bishops and priests who wanted the sisters to conduct a school on each reservation. The twin goals of "civilizing" and Christianizing were cited nationwide for all missionaries to the Indian tribes, helping to "save their souls" and at the same time preparing them to take on the rights and duties of United States citizenship. (An industrial school for Indian girls, partner to one for boys at Saint John's, was operated with aid of government funds at Saint Benedict's Convent from 1884 to 1896.)

While many sisters grew to love the people at White Earth, they also found it difficult to adjust to Ojibwa culture. They attribute this problem mainly to a lack of preparation for their

Benedictine sisters in White Earth in 1918 (third and fourth from the left —Sister Lioba Braun and Philomena Ketten, the pioneers).

assignments. A questionnaire and interviews with former missionaries, conducted between 1980 and 1994, make it clear that most of these sisters have bittersweet memories of their time on the reservations. When asked what knowledge they had about the Ojibwa prior to going to the reservation, the majority replied, "None." What information they did have was often negative, the usual stereotypes of "wild, savage, heathen Indians." Thus, obedience to religious superiors sent sisters to a task for which they were ill-prepared.

By the time of the questionnaire (1980), Vatican II (1962 to 1965) had exerted a major influence on how Catholics viewed different cultures and faiths. The *Decree on the Church's Missionary Activity* addresses the vocation of missionaries. A significant section reads:

> Christ himself searched the hearts of men, and led them to divine light through truly human conversation. So, also, his disciples, profoundly penetrated by the Spirit of Christ, should know the peoples among whom they live and should establish contact with them.[108]

Key phrases here are "know the people" and "establish contact with them." The decree called for a familiarity with the people, and participation in the local cultural social life was not only encouraged but prescribed.

The majority of the sisters serving on reservations lived most of their religious life in a pre-Vatican II milieu. But not all "narrowness" of thought and action can be laid solely at the feet of either the Church or the religious order. Sisters were and are participants in and observers of an American milieu that can strongly influence their thinking and behavior.

Sadly, few sisters learned the Ojibwa language, or, at best, they learned only a smattering of words and phrases. Lack of opportunity and time played a role here, of course. Nor did it help that before 1940, many of the early missionaries were of German stock. For them, English was already a second language; struggling with Ojibwa would seem an impossible task. Furthermore, by federal decree, native languages were banned in the schools. This must have been a relief to most missionaries. The Indian children often forgot their tribal language after some time in the schools, an effect favored by both teachers and government officials.

Conditions generally were severe at the reservation missions, with poor housing and lack of good and easy transportation the major problems for both missionaries and Ojibwa. However, the potential at both White Earth and Red Lake was such that early difficulties there were endured in the hope of long-range success.

Along with harsh living and working conditions at White Earth and Red Lake, the sisters were far from the monastery, making it difficult to attend Chapter meetings, retreats, or cultural events open to those living at or near the monastery. Unable by custom, at least during the first years, to attend Indian celebrations, the sisters hungered for more cultural activities—to see a play, to view an art show, or to hear a concert. Lacking these opportunities, the sisters were dependent on one another for daily support and companionship. Religious training and faith, above all, provided the necessary cohesion. Records show that most sisters were able and willing to relax by participating in school bands, church and school choirs, student and faculty plays, and outdoor diversions such as hikes, skating, and sledding. While there are letters attesting to some occasional friction among the sisters—enclosed for long periods of time in cramped quarters—and between the sisters and the pastor(s), harmony reigned most of the time. The wonder is how seldom such conflicts became unmanageable. But in that era, harsh situations were "offered up," and it was not often that a sister requested or even demanded a change of assignment.

The White Earth and Red Lake missions flourished between 1900 and 1940, each averaging ninety to 100 students annually. Financial aid came regularly from St. Benedict's, Saint John's Abbey, and the Bureau of Catholic Indian Missions, with additional aid from tribal funds after 1908. A number of court battles were fought between 1904 and 1908 over the constitutionality of using trust funds for

The combination boarding school and convent in White Earth.

The combination of boarding school and convent and the mission church at Red Lake.

contract schools (those schools having a contract with the federal government, which paid them per capita for teaching Indian children), but the Supreme Court settled the issue in May 1908 in a decision to allow use of tribal funds for sectarian schools that emphasized the free exercise of religion.

At White Earth and Red Lake—and later at Mille Lacs—the missionaries were heavily reliant on aid from St. Benedict's and Saint John's. Both centers gave generously of personnel and funds over the years. The sisters and pastors received little or no salary in the first decades of the missions, and, when they did, $150 yearly was the norm. Under such circumstances, a great deal of self-sufficiency was required of the missionaries. The maintenance of gardens and a farm took much time and effort on the part of staff and students well into the 1950s. The large, productive gardens were a major source of food; since most vegetables were homegrown, food bills were reduced somewhat. Picking potatoes; canning carrots, beans, cucumbers, beets; and shucking corn were major jobs each summer and fall for both sisters and students. There was always a steady supply of milk, too, from the mission dairy herd, and most of the eggs came from the mission's own chickens.

Few sisters requested to be changed from the Indian missions, in spite of starkly simple conditions. Most rose to the challenge, physically and mentally, aided in no small measure by a deep faith that they were doing a valued work. Nor did this go without notice. An article in the *Indian Sentinel*, a publication by the Bureau of Catholic Indian Missions, credits the work of the sisters for many general improvements in the White Earth mission physical plant. The anonymous writer states:

> After [thirty-two] years of hard labor and economy we are blessed with a most wonderful heating plant, and water system. How did the sisters ever save the amount? By hard labor. Instead of hiring help during the summer, the sisters do all the work in their own garden which provides the vegetables. It was nothing unusual to see seven sisters in the grain fields pulling out wild mustard and other noxious weeds, hoeing, and cleaning [twelve] acres of potatoes and even helping to shuck the grain.[109]

Summer and fall months were the busiest at the missions, for outdoor work at least. Clearly, the sisters had little time for vacations.

At both White Earth and Red Lake, the sisters supplemented government, tribal, and other donations by selling needlework, giving music lessons, and operating a second-hand store. Normally, the money was put into a general fund for the schools. Over the years, selfless, hardworking, low-paid personnel were the major means by which the monastic centers subsidized the Indian missions. The Ojibwa apostolate was given high priority, evident in the efforts made to keep the missions going.

SISTERS' MEMORIES—PRE-1960

Musing on relations between missionaries and the Indian people, adults and children, one might ask what were helps and hindrances to their interactions. Mainly through interviews with both sisters and Ojibwa, it is possible to gain insight into how two such different cultures were able to interrelate. Sister Thea Grieman, who retired at St. Scholastica Convent, St. Cloud, Minnesota, as of 1974, speaks freely and glowingly of her experiences at White Earth. It was her first mission, and she stayed twenty-three years: 1921 to 1944.

Young and energetic, Sister Thea went to White Earth immediately after professing first vows, to teach music and play the organ. As the 1920s advanced, Sister Thea's tasks broadened, and she soon became a classroom teacher, giving music lessons on Saturdays and after school. At one time or another, Sister Thea taught all the grades. By 1944, though, she was ready to leave. But her "memories contain many [more] good and happy times than sad ones."[110]

Sister Thea Grieman in her last years at Red Lake at her favorite ministry, playing the organ.

A companion of Sister Thea for most of her years at White Earth was Sister Mary (Hilaire) Degel. Officially retired in 1978, Sister Mary was always ready to relate stories about her years on the reservation. Like Sister Thea, Sister Mary went to White Earth immediately after professing temporary vows, remaining there from 1922 to 1938. During her first ten years at the mission, Sister Mary taught first and second grades. Later, she had all the grades in turn, finding the students to be "diligent" for the most part, though, like all students anywhere, needing to be motivated.

Sister Mary's fondest memories were of the home-economics cottage she managed for the seventh and eighth graders. She helped them plan meals, budget, can fruit and vegetables, and learn childcare. During the 1930s, she began a 4-H Club at the mission, enrolling an average of fifty to sixty girls at one time. Members put on plays, gave readings, sewed, raised vegetables and flowers, and baked bread and pastries. Many of the girls won ribbons at fairs and other exhibits.

Sister Mary Degel and two assistants collecting maple syrup.

Asked her impressions of the Indians' character traits, Sister Mary found them affectionate, good-natured, and a happy people. She cited as basic requirements for success in working with them both honesty and an understanding of Ojibwa background. Sister Mary made many friends among the White Earth Ojibwa and kept up a correspondence with a large number of them long after leaving the reservation.[111]

Much younger than either Sister Thea or Sister Mary, Sister Debora Herda served at White Earth from 1940 to 1943. Twenty-four at the start of this new assignment, she recalls being lonesome and "craving to talk to someone my own age"; all but one of the sisters were over forty. She recalls that the only steady visitors to White Earth were government inspectors, sisters' parents, and the pastor's relatives.

Sister Debora was a prefect for the pre-schoolers and the girls from first through fifth grades. Besides this, she taught cooking for the girls, fifth grade and up. For a prefect, the hours were always full. Sister Debora was in charge of the girls outside classroom hours, getting them up in the morning, tucking them in at night, supervising the playroom and their manual labor. She and another prefect slept in the dormitory all night, in case a child needed help as well as to ensure order and quiet. Sister Debora regrets that she could rarely recreate or pray with the other sisters. For Benedictines, praying the Divine Office, later called Liturgy of the Hours, is a central feature of religious life, and this deprivation was felt keenly.

Like Sister Mary Degel, Sister Debora points to having learned much from the Ojibwa about their culture. She lists doing beadwork, dyeing, ricing, and tapping maple trees. Overall, she says her years at White Earth were mostly happy ones.[112]

Sisters' experiences at Red Lake mirror those of the sisters at White Earth. An interview with Sister Adelma Roers covers the years 1934 to 1952, with a second term running from 1956 to 1974. When first told by the prioress that she was to go to Red Lake, Sister Adelma was "sick about it." She had heard tales of how difficult conditions were at the mission.

Teaching the students the art of child care (left) and rug weaving (right)—Sister Benno (Marlene) Schoenberg.

Preparing food for one hundred hungry boarders—Sisters Elaine Schindler, Karen Nordick, and Erna Miller (1950s).

At Red Lake, Sister Adelma spent most of her time sewing and teaching sewing to the girls. After school, Sister Adelma also taught needlework. There were some seventy to one hundred girls and ninety to one hundred boys at the mission during her years there. In 1936, Sister Adelma began to run the mission store, which featured second-hand items, mostly clothing. The store was non-profit in its first year, but it was enlarged during the 1940s and became quite profitable. Besides teaching sewing and running the

Sister Alice Alcuin Deutsch with her students at Red Lake.

store, Sister Adelma became a prefect, with more direct contact with the girls. Over the years she grew to love them dearly.

There were sixteen sisters at Red Lake during Sister Adelma's first term there, and, with an affectionate tone, she recalled most of their names and the positions held. She also referred to the mission priests. Father Simon Lampe, pastor, was "a great big husky man with a voice that could knock you over." Father Florian Locnikar, his assistant, was "big on sports," and spent much of his time with the boys. She added, "Father Florian was strict, but he didn't interfere with the teachers; he let them go their own way."[113]

The daily schedule was set by the goals and needs of the boarding school. The sisters rose at 5:00, recited the rosary, and then attended Mass. The prefects would get the children up at 6:00, after which followed the students' Mass, breakfast, and then chores. Classes began at 8:30 with lunch at noon. The afternoon was divided among classes from 1:00 to 3:00, playtime 3:00 to 4:00, sewing and chores from 4:00 to 5:30, supper and playtime between 5:45 and 7:30, with bedtime for the younger students at 7:30 and 8:00 for the older ones. Clearly, both sisters and students were kept busy during the day. With slight variations, this schedule was followed at White Earth, too.

The boarding school became a day school in 1940, and the schedule and workload lightened somewhat as a result. At both White Earth and Red Lake missions, the number of sisters rarely fell below fifteen or seventeen in the pre-1960s. This allowed a sharing of joys and sorrows, success and failure, a generally supportive environment. But at Mille Lacs Reservation, in south-central Minnesota, the situation was considerably different from the start.

Mille Lacs

BEGINNINGS TO 1957

Youngest of the three Minnesota Benedictine Indian missions, Mille Lacs (the section called Vineland), was a one-woman operation for many years. At the request of Bishop Joseph Busch, head of the Diocese of St. Cloud, Sister Laura Hesch (1882 to 1972) went to Mille Lacs in 1941. At that time, there were few Christian Ojibwa, since no resident missionaries had ever settled closer than Onamia.

Approximately 400 Ojibwa lived at Mille Lacs when Sister Laura arrived. During her first eleven years there, she worked alone, living with other sisters in Onamia, commuting ten miles daily. A nephew, Louis Gottwalt, built a small cabin for her in 1944, and by 1951 Sister Laura began living there regularly, often having one or more Ojibwa girls stay with her overnight.

Times were hard on the reservation for both missionary and Ojibwa. The number of Ojibwa living below poverty level was very high, most living in tarpaper shacks and subsisting on fish, rice, oatmeal, and macaroni. Necessarily, Sister Laura became adept at chopping wood, cutting brush, and doing minor repairs. She felt keenly the lack of a companion, but this did not deter her from going deep into the bush, visiting Ojibwa families, introducing herself, and inviting them to send their children to her for religious instructions. After several months, she became a familiar presence. Success, if measured in the number of converts, came slowly, and it was the 1950s before significant numbers could be counted. Parents did send their children frequently for catechism, noting that Sister Laura fed them milk, cookies, and fruit.[114]

Most of Sister Laura's days were spent in catechesis and distributing used clothing. During the first few years, other sisters came on a trial basis. All left, defeated by the harsh conditions (especially by the abundance of woodticks) as well as by the loneliness and frustration. In 1952 Sister Mary George Ortmann arrived, soon becoming a boon com-

Sister Mary George Ortman canning in Little Flower Mission.

panion to Sister Laura. The monastery subsidized both of the sisters, while the Diocese of St. Cloud paid for a car and its upkeep.

In 1954, a church was built next to the convent and was named for St. Theresa, the Little Flower, patron of missionaries. Priests from the nearby Crosier monastery came to celebrate Mass once a week. Diocesan funds and donations helped pay for

The convent, Little Flower Inn, and mission church in Mille Lacs.

Sister Laura Hesch with a friend on Mille Lacs reservation.

the church, which had Indian decor, a source of pride to the missionaries and their Indian converts.

Much of what is known about life at Little Flower Mission is found in a series of newsletters that Sister Laura wrote and mailed to hundreds of supporters nationwide in an organization called the Spiritual Mothers' Union. She began this group in 1938 while stationed at Red Lake, continuing it when she moved to Mille Lacs. The newsletter, entitled *The Stray Lamb,* was chatty in style, giving updates on events at the mission, usually closing with a plea to the "mothers" to write letters and, if so inclined, to send gifts to individual Ojibwa children.

Some excerpts from the newsletters give a sense of what Sister Laura considered important and/or interesting:

SPRING 1946 Most of our Indians belong to the Grand Medicine Lodge and they are very hard to convert yet the work is both interesting and fascinating.

OCTOBER 1949 Now for the greatest highlight in all my years here. On September 22 we had twenty of our converts confirmed with the Bishop presiding and seventeen priests in attendance.

FALL 1956 94 Catholic and pagan [sic] Indian children receive Catholic instruction weekly.[115]

A gymnasium, built in 1954, proved immensely popular and brought many youngsters to the mission; as Sister Laura wrote, "Our gym is the center of attraction for our young people. How they love to play basketball, volleyball, and even roller-skating. Our agreement was that before the practice afternoons they have to come to the house for religious instructions. Use of the gym declined significantly after April 1968, when a community center, funded mainly by Housing and Urban Development (HUD) and the Bureau of Indian Affairs (BIA), was completed by the Indian community.

Like many pre-Vatican II missionaries, Sister Laura and her companions evangelized, sometimes ignorant, sometimes intolerant of native religious beliefs. The Gospel message they brought was both welcomed and resisted, while the messengers were often admired and even loved by many.

Sisters' Memories—Post-1960

Comparing experiences of the reservation sisters in post-1960 with those of earlier decades, one finds changes occurring, though slowly. But there was also some continuity. Sisters still faced a culture strange to them, mainly a culture of poverty. And, sadly, not much was yet being done to prepare them for their work. A real breakthrough in this area came during the 1970s, a period when Native American Studies—stemming partly out of the American Indian Movement (AIM) with its call for Red Power—was becoming popular in United States colleges and universities. Meanwhile, sisters continued to serve the three missions, now more often by volunteering than by assignment.

Long after the White Earth Indian school changed to a day school (1945), Sister Delice Bialke was there (1962 to 1969), with a second stint from 1975 to 1980, the latter years as a volunteer. With no training behind her, she recalls "having been scared." From 1975 to 1980, Sister Delice was a catechist at both White Earth and at nearby Ogema. She also worked occasionally in the mission store at Ogema. By the 1970s, home visits to Ojibwa families were becoming more common, and Sister Delice saw these as very important, since they showed the sisters' care on a more personal basis. Overall, Sister Delice liked being at White Earth, especially during her second stay there.[116]

At neighboring Red Lake, Sister Elizabeth Theis was experiencing the pain of transition—moving from the weight of past expectations into new models—both in and out of the classroom. She spent the years from 1974 to 1979 at Red Lake, supposedly as a "free" principal. But her duties soon included supervising breakfast and the noon lunch programs as well as doing the nurse's work, since the one appointed by the Indian Health Services frequently failed to appear.

One of Sister Elizabeth's major tasks at Red Lake was to change the way the school was run. In addition to teaching and gardening, the sisters were doing much of the custodial work, severely straining their time and energy. At a meeting with the pastor, the local bishop, the superintendent of Catholic schools in the Crookston Diocese, Abbot John Eidenschink of Saint John's Abbey, and Sister Evin Rademacher, prioress of Saint Benedict's Monastery, it was decided that the Benedictine Brothers would do the custodial work in school and also that the seventh and eighth grades would be dropped. This eased the workload considerably, at least in the school.

Conflict arose not only over job expectations but also over finances. Sister Elizabeth served five pastors in five years. They controlled the budget for the entire mission complex until Father Peter St. Hilaire, O.S.B., became pastor. He requested that the sisters take over this responsibility. They were ready to do so by this time, having had more educational opportunities than the previous sisters in charge of the school. With the aid of a McKnight grant, Sister Elizabeth was able to get a separate account for the school. Her top priority was the purchase of new texts, updating the school curriculum.

Asked whether she saw her years at Red Lake as "successful," Sister Elizabeth replied that she was successful in some ways, such as in getting rid of the custodial work in school, upgrading the curriculum, and establishing a Board of Education that helped with budgeting, with establishing policies for operating the school, and with funding. Also, she noted that the spirit among the sisters at Red Lake was generally high. There were thirteen to fourteen living together during her years there. A "good community spirit" was aided by lots of parties—even "some foolishness"—in celebration of special feasts. The Divine Office, daily Eucharist, and private prayer were central. All the sisters sang in the church choir, "whether we could sing or not."

Challenging the status quo was not pleasant, Sister Elizabeth states. Yet her memories of the years at Red Lake are mainly good ones; in fact, her years there were "the best community years I had—we had a wonderful group and we worked together."[117] It is a tribute to their strong character and faith, that despite many hardships, so many sisters agree: the spirit was good and enabled them not only to survive but to become stronger.

The Missions in Crisis: 1950s to 1970s

In the post-World War II era, the federal government implemented the policies of termination and relocation, attempting to move most Indians off the reservations and into towns or cities. It was a blatant move to end the special relationship between tribes and the federal government, as the movement to assimilate Indians into mainstream society was pushed even against the will of many Indians. At both White Earth and Red Lake, many families, younger ones in particular, relocated to the Twin Cities. This adversely affected school enrollments. By the late 1950s, the White Earth mission school—more so than Red Lake—faced declining enrollments annually and a slight decrease in staff as well, though some of the latter was due to expansion of parish schools elsewhere and increasing requests by pastors for sisters to teach in them.

After 1955, letters between the prioress at Saint Benedict's Monastery and the pastors at White Earth and Red Lake refer to the desire and the need of the former to remove one or two of the sisters from the reservations for service elsewhere. Desperate to meet these needs from a continually shrinking pool of personnel, Mother Richarda Peters wrote to Father Valerian Thelen at White Earth in June 1950, suggesting that he "purchase an electric mixer and a potato peeler" so that she could remove one of the house sisters. Father Valerian was displeased at the thought of losing sisters, but by the late 1950s the number at White Earth was gradually reduced, and by the mid-1960s it was becoming clear that the school itself might have to close.

In the mid-1960s, the shortage of sister-teachers was so acute that Bishop Bartholome, bishop of the St. Cloud Diocese, became alarmed. He wrote a three-page letter to

Mother Henrita Osendorf, detailing his concerns, urging that she and her council give priority to the elementary schools in the Diocese of St. Cloud so as not to "allow the Faith to deteriorate because of other interests that are not nearly as basic or important." However, as the decade progressed, the shortage of sisters worsened, and White Earth was one of the hardest hit missions.

In the summer of 1968, Mother Henrita asked Father Alban Fruth, pastor at White Earth, to hire a full-time lay teacher for grades five and six. Alongside the sister shortage, she was very conscious of the rising ability and desire of the laity to participate more fully in the church's worship and work. Vatican II produced the *Decree on the Apostolate of the Laity* that stressed the laity's role in the Church's missions. The decree stated that "the laity ought to collaborate energetically in every apostolic and missionary undertaking sponsored by their local parish."[118] Albeit reluctantly, pastors began hiring the occasional lay teacher. But it was too late for the White Earth school; it closed in May 1969, as enrollment dropped from over 120 students to seventy-eight in a period of just six years.

Father Alban wrote to Mother Henrita, acknowledging the necessity of the closing but also indicating further service possibilities for the sisters:

> I have written to the Abbot saying that if this school is closed, then one priest could easily take care of both Ogema and White Earth. . . . Perhaps the Sisters could do visitations, conduct adult education classes or summer schools, and make their headquarters here in the center. Perhaps much more good could be accomplished in that they would work with the people who actually stay here in the community.[119]

From 1970 to 1980 several sisters volunteered to continue ministry at White Earth. They taught catechism at Ponsford, Ogema, Waubun, and Naytahwaush. In 1972 a team approach was begun with the sisters and priests conducting Bible study, liturgies, teacher training, and home visiting. However, in 1980 the sisters were recalled from

White Earth. Advancing age for some and pressing needs for the younger sisters to serve elsewhere dictated the move.

In 1975, the community's personnel director, Sister Linda Kulzer, with the advice and aid of the prioress and her council, put out a community questionnaire asking which ministries should have priority, given the dwindling resources of personnel and finances. Among the fourteen listed apostolates, the Indian missions ranked ninth. Sisters between the ages of thirty-four and sixty-four indicated the most openness to continuing this apostolate. Those willing to serve at Red Lake, White Earth, or Mille Lacs were asked to sign a form. Though the number of volunteers was small, it was sufficient to keep the missions going.

In comparison with events at White Earth, the picture was brighter at Red Lake from the 1960s into the mid-1980s. In June 1965, a foundation was dug for an addition to the school, and the personnel numbered twelve sisters. Ten years later, that number remained the same, but by the early 1980s, the enrollment declined drastically and debts mounted. Support for the school weakened, and, by the mid-1980s, discussion began as to the viability of the school. In 1985-1986 sister-personnel numbered eleven, with most being support staff in school and in the convent. The first lay principal, Gene DeYoung, was hired.

Unlike at Red Lake, the situation at the Mille Lacs mission approached its crisis much earlier—in the 1970s. Sister Laura Hesch turned eighty-eight in 1970 and gave over more duties to Sister Mary George, who took charge of Little Flower Mission in 1972 upon Sister Laura's retirement. Sister Laura returned to Saint Benedict's Monastery, dying in June of that same year. Many of her Ojibwa converts and friends from both Red Lake and Mille Lacs assisted at the funeral Mass, drumming before, during, and after it. At their request, Sister Laura was buried in the Little Flower cemetary on Mille Lacs Reservation. Sister Mary George chose to continue at the mission, with an occasional assist from one or two other sisters.

Reassessment: 1980s and 1990s.

At the monastery, a Chapter meeting held September 26, 1985, devoted much time to a discussion of continuation of the Red Lake ministry. Sisters who had served there shared their experiences and their hopes for the mission. Small-group discussion followed, and sisters were asked to give reasons to keep or to close the mission. Positive responses included a preferential option for the poor and the needs sisters could fill by adult education, religious education, home visiting, and continuation of the store—the latter a major way to meet the people and to bring in much needed revenue. At the end of the Chapter meeting, volunteers were sought, and several sisters indicated an interest and willingness to serve at Red Lake.

Sisters (and monks from Saint John's Abbey) at Red Lake in the late 1980s: Left to right, first row: Brother Julius Beckermann, Sisters Ruth Anne Schneider, Mary Minnette Beutz, and Delphine Heier; second row: Brother Douglas Mullin, Sisters Jane Weber, Constette LeFevere, Laurita Wydra, S.S.S., and Gilmary Kempf; third row: Father Aelred Tegels, Sisters Dorothy Ann Marx, Barbara Zinzer, Delice Bialke, Ansgar Willenbring, and Philip Zimmer.

The monastic community set up an Indian Ministry Task Team, and their Minutes of March and April 1978 show an increasing sensitivity towards the needs and aspirations of the Ojibwa people. Needs were addressed, among them development of leadership skills and building community with and among the Ojibwa people. Questions were raised as to why there were no Ojibwa teachers in the Indian school and why the Indian mission had not become self-sustaining. The task team compiled a list of assumptions about the Indian ministry and, along with the national reassessment of the place of Indians in society, concluded that the Ojibwa people were becoming more capable of taking control of programs instituted on their behalf.

Among the assumptions of the task team were that "Sisters who choose to work with the Indian people must be able to respect their values and way of life and not set out to change it. Sisters planning to work in the Indian apostolate must have prior training and instruction in the Indian culture and way of life. Leadership is emerging among the Indian people themselves." These statements reveal a complete turnabout in attitude toward Indians and their potential. Additional comments and assumptions refer to the sisters being able to "gain much from the Indians if they are open to the culture and giftedness of the Indian people." From these Minutes, it is clear that the sisters were becoming aware of the richness within Native American culture and values.

The Indian Ministry Task Team Report of December 15, 1978, articulated the rationale for continued involvement in the Indian ministry and gave some recommendations or action plans. The rationale stressed an "incarnational witness of Christ's love, care, and sense of dignity which the sisters' presence brings to the Indian people alongside an education and training in leadership which will promote the Indians' learning to help themselves." Recommendations included "that the sisters working among the Indians be orientated and educated in values clarification and leadership training in order to facilitate the goals and objectives for this" and, further that "community members explore new ministries on each of the Indian missions: dietary consultants, retreat work, home nursing, etc." New thinking is evident in this report: no longer could missionaries see themselves in the usual narrow roles or as sole arbiters of what is best for the Indian people. A case in point is Red Lake.

Missionaries of the late 1980s were becoming more sensitive to the needs and expectations of the native people, as is made clear in comments given in a cover story in the *St. Cloud Visitor* of October 1986. Brother Douglas Mullin, O.S.B., principal at Red Lake from 1986 to 1989, is quoted, "I think the Church as a whole has a lot to learn from traditional Indian spirituality. We as Church have to get accustomed to the idea that the experiences of the true faith can take place in many ways."[120]

Unfortunately, the financial needs of the mission proved too much, and by 1989 the Red Lake school board voted to close the school, though needing the Crookston Diocesan Board's approval. The Board voted to keep the school open another year, and, in the fall of 1989, the second lay principal, Jean Thompson, arrived. She asked to live with the sisters, as did a Sister of Social Service, Laurita Wydra, hired to direct the religious education program. This brought to eleven the number living in a convent originally built for twenty to thirty sisters. In the school, grades one through six were all that could be managed, and enrollment remained very small, an average of fifteen in each grade.

At almost the same time, a feasibility study of the Mille Lacs apostolate began in 1990-1991, led by the monastery administration and Bishop Jerome Hanus, head of the Diocese of St. Cloud. A report prepared for the prioress as part of the reassessment process reaffirmed an earlier report that stated "we have to look to some way of being effective other than that which was visualized by Sister Laura when she set up the mission. The needs of the Indians are quite different because the social conditions are greatly altered." Focus was now finally put on training the native people to take more leadership.[121]

At Red Lake, the personnel dropped drastically by 1990, down to five for the 1991-1992 school year. Funds from Saint Benedict's Monastery and Saint John's Abbey, along with a tribal contribution, helped keep the school operating. But the problem of staffing continued. As of September 1998, four Benedictine sisters were at Red Lake, only two as teachers.

A new state-of-the-art public elementary school across the field from the mission offers stiff competition. But Sister Philip Zimmer, in her eleventh year of teaching at Red Lake as of 1999, believes that the sisters' presence is very important. She says, "We are a beacon light in people's lives. People come when in need and just to talk."[122] She feels that the sisters are highly respected and that the school itself is regarded as a safe environment as well as a center of good academics and values. Not least is the value of the mission as a prayer center in the midst of the Ojibwa people—great prayers in their own right.

Epilogue

In these years since the monastery task team's reports and recommendations, the Benedictines are much reduced numerically on the Ojibwa reservations. This is not entirely negative; the Ojibwa people have been gaining a new sense of their worth and identity. They are developing local leadership and demanding more rights. The mission personnel now see themselves as partners in these endeavors.

Those who served on reservations may find that too much of this mission history has focused on hard work and other difficulties. A positive side did exist. Sister Gudelia Duclos, who served at Red Lake from 1943 to 1955, surely speaks for many when she says, "I think outside of bodily hard work, I had it the nicest there on that mission. The closeness to my sisters, the trust we had in each other. There was kindness there."[123] That kindness went beyond convent walls.

Author Michael Dorris, himself a member of the Modoc tribe, asked a penetrating question: "How do we plumb a plundered past without condescending, romanticizing, or fabricating?"[124] Without ignoring the often painful exchanges between missionaries and the Ojibwa people over many decades of interaction, the history of this interaction at White Earth, Red Lake, and Mille Lacs reveals a steady pattern of mutual help and friendship. Both groups found benefits in the crossing of cultural boundaries.

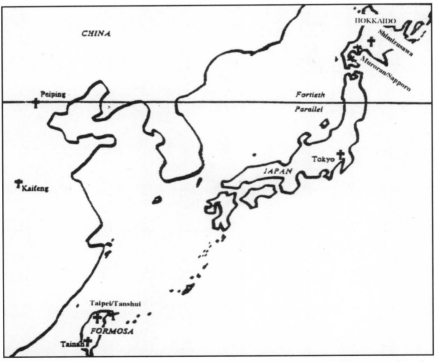

Asian map with crosses marking the sites of Saint Benedict's Monastery's mission work.

14

DISTANT MISSIONS MOVING TOWARD AUTONOMY

Carol Berg, O.S.B.

Introduction

Prior to 1930, the Benedictines of Saint Benedict's Monastery worked exclusively within the United States and primarily within Minnesota. Benedictine monasticism has never tied itself to a particular work or location; rather, Benedictines over the centuries responded to requests from bishops and clergy to help when and where needed. Such requests brought our sisters to the foreign missions. Before Vatican Council II, these foreign missions were viewed in a less than open manner, too much emphasis being on changing them to fit the mold of the missionary homelands. Vatican II's *Decree on the Apostolate of the Laity* pointed to a more respectful attitude and thinking towards peoples of other cultures. Chapter 3 of the Decree ends with the admonition to missionaries—lay and religious—that "All who work in or give help to foreign nations must remember that relations among people should be a genuine fraternal exchange in which each party is at the same time a giver and a receiver."[125]

Just as pointed is the *Decree on the Missionary Activity of the Church*. In this document, the specific purpose of missionary activity is stated as "evangelization and the planting of the Church among those people and groups where she has not yet taken root. Thus Churches can be adequately established and flourish the world over, endowed with their own vitality and maturity." Further on, the document lists specific ways in which missionaries can assist in bringing the Gospel to these missions: "Let the faithful labor and collaborate with all others in the proper regulation of the affairs of economic and social life. With special care, they devote themselves to the education of children and young people by means of different kinds of schools."[126] Educational endeavors dominated efforts in the foreign missions, although healthcare and retreat work were also significant. The history of Benedictines in Asia and the Caribbean attest to much zeal and good works, albeit without always an accompanying appreciation of the native culture.

China Mission—Beginnings to 1950

In August 1929, Father Francis Clougherty, a Benedictine from Latrobe, Pennsylvania, and missionary to China, came to St. Joseph, Minnesota, seeking sisters to work in China. He requested sisters to establish a women's college in connection with Fu Jen University (then all male) in Peking, China. On September 1, the Chapter voted to accept his call. Volunteers were invited to apply, and, in 1930, Mother Rosamond Pratschner chose six sisters out of approximately 100 volunteers: Sisters Francetta Vetter, Regia Zens, Ronayne Gergen, Rachel Loulan (who died and was buried in China), Donalda Terhaar, and Wibora Muehlenbein. They arrived in China on September 24, 1930.

The sisters' first two years were spent studying the language, and by 1932 they felt ready to begin the women's college classes. Due to financial problems, caused mainly by the deepening of a worldwide Depression, they withdrew from Fu Jen in 1935, the Benedictine fathers having withdrawn in 1932. The Divine Word Fathers took over Fu Jen in 1933, informing the sisters that they would not be able to help them financially.

In 1935, Monsignor Joseph Tacconi, Vicar Apostolic in Honoan Province, invited the sisters to Kaifeng (about 375 miles south of Peking) to work in education and to open a medical dispensary. The monastic Chapter granted approval in late March 1935. The sisters opened a middle school and a medical dispensary, the latter very much needed within two years as war broke out between China and Japan.

Two more sisters arrived in China in October 1936: Sisters Annelda Wahl and Ursuline Venne, a nurse and a musician respectively. By 1937 the small community was facing fears of Japanese bombing and of local bandits. When the United States State Department urged all missionaries to leave China or to withdraw from the danger zones, the sisters stayed to open relief shelters. Train loads of wounded—mostly soldiers—came into Kaifeng by 1937-1938, and ten camps were staffed by the varied missionary orders to handle the wounded and refugees. (This is chronicled in Sister Wibora Muehlenbein's brief, yet detailed, history, *Benedictine Mission to China*, published in 1980.)

After Pearl Harbor, December 7, 1941, the sisters and other missionaries were treated as hostiles and were interned as prisoners of war from December 8, 1941, to August 17, 1945. All missionaries were interned in religious houses in Peking, the Benedictine sisters staying with the Spanish sisters at Christ the King Convent.

In October 1946 they returned to Kaifeng. But that same year the Chinese civil war broke out—Mao Zedong's Red Army versus Chiang K'ai-shek's Nationalist forces. The sisters fled to Shanghai in April 1948, a few days before the communist army captured Kaifeng. They took refuge with the Madames of the Sacred Heart, helping teach in their schools. Much discussion ensued about the future. Many missionaries returned to their home countries, but when in December 1948 a ship set out for Taiwan (formerly Formosa) carrying refugee missionaries, among them were the Benedictines.

As in China proper, establishing a mission in Taiwan was a response to circumstances. Saint Benedict's Monastery soon found itself sponsoring a second Asian mission, although letters to Mother Rosamond make it clear that, while a Taiwan mission certainly looked promising, the sisters' hearts were still in China. Opportunities for teaching at both undergraduate and graduate levels opened, and in 1949 the sisters were engaged in a variety of works: teaching middle school, teaching English at National Taiwan University in Taipei, operating a hostel, staffing St. Benedict's Home for Children, and giving catechetical instruction.

Again, peace was short-lived. In the fall of 1949, Mao Zedong proclaimed the People's Republic of China. There was much bellicose talk of retaking Taiwan, considered by Peking as a province of China. The United States State Department encouraged missionaries to consider leaving Taiwan, anticipating an invasion by China. Many missionaries did return home, but many also moved to neighboring Japan, then still under military occupation by the United States.

Sisters Francetta and Regia left for Tokyo on June 25, 1950, and Sister Ursuline joined them in August. Sister Wibora resisted leaving Taiwan, and in a letter to Mother Richarda remarked: "If it is at all possible to stay, morally we don't feel we have the right to withdraw. Is it too much, Mother, for a community of 900 sisters, after having had a mission for twenty years, to suddenly have two missions in the Orient?"[127]

Taiwan Mission

THE 1950s TO THE 1970s

The sisters' most successful work in Taiwan during the years immediately after World War II came through their teaching in public universities. As the years passed, letters home tell of increasing numbers of student converts. Giving religious instruction and teaching English were the major sources of revenue and of reaching the Taiwanese. In a letter to Mother Richarda early in 1952, Sister Wibora observed that "two years ago the number of Catholic students at the national university was [seventeen]; now it is [sixty-seven]."[128]

Sister Bendu Han, a convert herself shortly before joining the Benedictine Order, stressed the sisters' role as visible signs of Christianity. In a letter to Mother Richarda in 1958, she wrote: "In Formosa, one can sense the observing eyes and the thinking minds very keenly as you walk on the crowded streets. People see you and they connect a religious with the truth of God. People like to talk with a religious and they ask surprising questions. . . . One can sense their sincerity and deep interest."[129] A recurring problem, however, was the inability of the non-native sisters to speak the language and to allow for cultural differences. In earlier letters from mainland China, the sisters had already expressed their regret about an inability to comprehend the language and/or customs of the people. Sister Bendu's letter to Mother Richarda in the summer of 1958 gets at this problem: "I hope that Sister [refers here to one particular sister

Convent in Taipei.

with whom she was in conflict] will slowly find out that Christianization of China depends on a deep appreciation and understanding of the 'Chinese soul' and Chinese cultural refinement."[130] Ignorance or failure to appreciate native language and customs would appear in all the overseas missions.

In 1959, there were seven professed sisters of Saint Benedict's Monastery in Taiwan: Sisters Wibora Muehlenbein, Ronayne Gergen, Annelda Wahl, Mariette Pitz, Bendu Han, Bernard Marie Liang, and Barbara Loe, plus four aspirants. Roots had sunk deeply enough so that the sisters could consider building a motherhouse and opening a novitiate. They were making payments on land at Tanshui, some twenty miles northwest of Taipei, in preparation for building a convent, a novitiate, and a school. The monastic Chapter voted in 1960 to give $50,000 for the new convent, but finances were always strained, and many letters arrived, asking for more aid. The groundbreaking at Tanshui was on July 11, 1961.

Convent, orphanage, and retreat center in Tanshui, built in the early 1960s.

On December 11, 1961, Sister Glenore Riedner, chief dietician at the St. Cloud Hospital from 1949 to 1961, arrived as the first regional superior (appointed), a role she held until her return to the States in August 1970. On February 19, 1962, the Formation House was moved to Tanshui, and

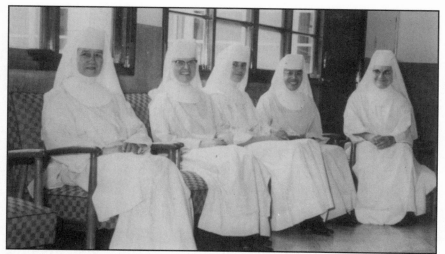

Sisters Ronayne Gergen, Jacinta Roemer, Loraine Bischof, Telan Hu, and Annelda Wahl (c.1963).

eight days later there was a reception of three novices. By September 1963 the orphanage had also been moved to Tanshui (from Taipei), and a student center opened there in 1965.

In several letters to Mother Henrita Osendorf, Sister Glenore confessed that she was experiencing much trial and error due to her lack of language skills. She also proved to have the wisdom not to initiate major changes without knowing why things were being done as they were. In a letter of

Sisters Ronayne Gergen and Wibora Muehlenbein, with orphans.

late December 1961, she writes: "I pray that I can be of constructive help—now I merely 'go along' for the most part. . . . There's a reason for things being as they are and until I know I won't suggest change."[131] Some of the frustration breaks through, occasionally. She observes in a January 1961 letter: "This sound barrier really is time and patience consuming. The sisters are willing enough to interpret, but much gets lost in the shuffle. They translate ideas rather than phrases, which I'm sure is the right thing to do."[132] Language difficulties aside, Sister Glenore was happy in Taiwan, returning there in March 1973 to celebrate her Golden Jubilee with the sisters in Tanshui.

During Sister Glenore's administration, Sister Josue Behnen arrived in Taiwan in October 1966 for a ten-year stay, primarily in nursing. She helped in the orphanage and studied Chinese with a tutor. Letters home reveal her concern for both monastic renewal and more spoken Chinese. Language was a challenge for both the American sisters and those indigenous to the culture and language in each of the

The St. Benedict Monastery community in Tanshui, Taiwan, today. From left to right: Beppo Wang, Emmanuel Hsiang, Cordis Chen, Rosalyn Tsai, Luca Chin, Gertrudis Lu, Jose Tung, Austin Chang, and Maria Hsu.

foreign missions. Sister Josue thought that too much English was being used for the benefit of the American Sisters. In a letter to Mother Henrita, May 1967, she wrote: "missionary effort requires delving into the culture and society as it is, and then slowly, by the spirit and attitude that we carry, change their thinking to a Christian thinking."[133] Studying the language full time, she argued, would help her to do that necessary delving. The following September, Sister Josue took language courses at the university four days a week. In her zeal to learn the native language, she was in tune with the directives of Vatican II where, in Chapter Three of the *Decree on Missionary Activity of the Church*, it is stated: "Let missionaries learn languages to the extent of being able to use them in a fluent and polished manner. Thus they will find more easy access to the minds and the hearts of men."[134]

Mother Henrita was most supportive in this endeavor. Her letter to Sister Josue, in November 1968, noted her knowledge of and agreement with Vatican II thinking: "In the past we have not been able to give our sisters the preparation they needed and there was even a time when it did not appear that anything more than a normal amount of virtue, the desire to convert pagans, and the willingness to be martyred was requisite to the good missionary. Times have changed."[135] She then proceeded to appoint native sisters as regional superior.

On March 27, 1970, Sister Telan Hu, a native of Taipei, appointed the first native regional superior in Taiwan, arrived August 3 to take up her duties and served into 1972. Sister Bernard Marie Liang followed her, becoming 'the first elected regional superior' in April 1975 and re-elected in 1979.

The 1970s saw some major developments for the Benedictine Taiwan mission—one of them a proposal to found a Spirituality Center in cooperation with the Jesuits. This plan was dropped, and instead the sisters opened a retreat house in December 1975 in Tanshui. The Taiwan Chapter had voted on January 2, 1975, to focus on retreat work and to phase out the orphanage. As of 1976, apostolates includ-

Sister Katherine Howard with Sisters Luca Chin and Bernard Marie Liang.

ed hosting prayer meetings, small-group retreats, and marriage encounters.

A sign of their growing stability and confidence, the Taiwanese sisters applied for dependent priory status on January 5, 1975. The monastic Chapter vote on February 8, 1976, gave them overwhelming approval. A new convent opened in Tanshui in fall 1983, and the last sisters from St. Benedict's Monastery assigned to Taiwan left that same year. The Taiwan Benedictines had come of age.

THE 1980S AND 1990S

Ten years after becoming a dependent priory, a move towards autonomy was well underway. A discernment workshop was held in June 1986, and Sister Luca Chin, regional superior from 1983 to 1988, reported to Sister Katherine Howard, prioress, that the Taiwan sisters were calm and ready for the big change. Application for autonomy followed in 1987, with a Visitation held in January 1988. At that time, there were eleven professed members, two junior sisters, one postulant, one aspirant, and one affiliate. The monastic Chapter voted to grant autonomy on March 19, 1988, and the Federation Chapter gave Taiwan membership in July 1988.

The 1990s saw the deaths of two pioneer missionaries from the original China mission: Sister Ronayne Gergen, who celebrated her Diamond Jubilee in Taiwan in March 1977, died on January 18, 1991, and Sister Mariette Pitz passed away on November 13, 1996. Both had arrived in

Taiwan in 1949 and stayed on as members of the priory after 1988. They are buried at Tanshui. The Taiwan Benedictines are wholly native now, and, as they tell in their community history, *Beyond the Horizon*, published in 1980, they continue to face the future with pride in their accomplishments and with deep faith in their continued role as religious, dedicated to God and to the service of their people. As of 2000, the Taiwan community numbered nine members.

Pioneers, Sisters Mariette Pitz and Ronayne Gergen, with Sister Luca Chin (center).

Japan—Mission and Priory

BEGINNINGS TO 1960

In flight from a predicted invasion of Taiwan by the Chinese Red Army, Sisters Francetta Vetter and Regia Zens arrived in Tokyo on June 29, 1950. Sister Ursuline Venne joined them on August 12. Wryly, while still in Taipei, she wrote to Mother Richarda Peters: ". . . It makes no difference where we work just so we spread the Faith among those who do not know God. I've moved around so much since I've come to the Orient that I have developed a sort of 'wanderlust.'"[136]

A handicap carried over from the China mission was that of language. Sister Ursuline alludes to this in a letter, a little over two weeks after arrival in Japan: "I am sure I will

like it here but it was not easy to leave Formosa (Taiwan)—
for it meant I was leaving China and I found this harder
than leaving the U.S.A. Being here means the study of a new
language. One consolation is that so many of the characters
are the same as the Chinese but the pronunciation is entirely different."[137]

The sisters were welcomed warmly by the Benedictine
fathers at St. Anselm's Parish and Rectory in Tokyo and
lived in temporary housing next to them. The house, crowded though it was, allowed the sisters to have a home-economics kitchen, a classroom, and a small music room. By
1951 both American women (military wives) and Japanese
were asking for cooking lessons. On February 2, 1952, the
Saint Benedict's Monastery formally accepted the mission in
Japan.

Shortly before the Benedictine sisters arrived in Tokyo,
two Japanese women came to St. Benedict's in May 1950 as
aspirants, becoming postulants in December. Catherine
Haruko (Renata) Mori and Agnes Masako (Imelda) Deguchi
were sent by Father Hildebrand Yaiser, pastor at St. Anselm's Church. On June 16, 1952, they were received as
novices, completing that canonical year and most of their
juniorate before returning to Japan in 1955. It would be
1958 before the Japan mission opened its own novitiate in
Shimisuzawa, Hokkaido.

In a new home by fall of 1952, the sisters in Tokyo were
busy teaching religion classes—during vacation and the regular school terms—as well as increasing their cooking class
sizes. The religion classes were taught at the American air
force base in Tachikawa, outside of Tokyo. These two apostolates brought in steady revenue for the first few years of
the mission.

Sister Benedice Schulte from Saint Benedict's Monastery
joined the three pioneers in late September 1954 and began
helping to teach religion classes as well as studying the language in preparation for beginning a novitiate. The small
community gave most of their time and energy to the cooking school. In a letter to Mother Richarda in April 1954,

In Tokyo, Sisters Francetta Vetter and Regia Zens conducted cooking classes for both the Japanese women and the women at the American Air Force base.

Sister Ursuline noted that spring cooking classes had begun a week earlier and that fifty-six women had appeared for class, causing an emergency. Three morning and three evening classes were offered.

Sister Benedice praised the cooking school highly. In a general letter to Saint Benedict's Monastery, she wrote: "I can never stop marveling at the good will created among these many non-Catholics through these classes. One after another will tell us that they never knew sisters before, or were afraid to speak to them."[138] Later, however, she regretted what she considered excessive cost of the lessons, prohibitive for most Japanese women. The classes continued until 1966, when a decline in students and lack of teaching personnel, in particular the death of Sister Francetta, made the school unprofitable as well as too difficult. By all measures, the school had been a great success. Royalties came in for many years from the publication of Sister Francetta's book, *The Art of Chinese Cooking*, first published in 1956, going into a total of twenty-six printings.

By 1955-1956, the sisters were planning for a novitiate. They disagreed on where to place it: Sister Benedice favored Hokkaido as the site, but the older sisters dissented. Due to bad health, Sister Ursuline left Japan in January 1957 and died on March 18, 1957. She had been one of the unifiers within the community and was sorely missed as dissension continued over placement of the novitiate.

A novitiate was clearly needed by 1957 since there were three aspirants at the time. With their superiors differing over this issue, the two youngest professed, Sisters Renata and Imelda (final profession in 1956), were caught in a confusing, tension-filled situation. Their immediate superior, Sister Benedice, left for Hokkaido on February 21, 1957, to settle on a site for both a novitiate and a proposed high school. Soon after, Mother Richarda Peters visited Japan, stopping off in both Tokyo and Hokkaido. Her decision was to have the novitiate in Hokkaido.

Hokkaido seemed far from Tokyo in the minds of the older sisters and the younger community members. The distance between Tokyo and Shimizusawa was twenty-five hours by train and ferry and three hours by plane. Sister Benedice was sure that part of the problem was that Hokkaido, in the eyes of many Japanese, was viewed as a "wilderness." However, her desire for a novitiate in a rural area was consistent over several years. Already in November 1955, she had written to Mother Richarda: "We seem to be just an island of American life living comfortably here. . . . I am convinced that our convent in Japan must be Japanese. We must speak Japanese, provide strictly Japanese meals at least for the Japanese sisters."[139] Sister Benedice believed strongly that the native culture should be respected and followed as much as possible. In this, she anticipated advice to missionaries from Vatican II documents.

On February 27, 1957, a mission opened in Shimizusawa, Hokkaido, with the Bishop of Sapporo Diocese formally granting approval on March 19. In April a kindergarten opened, followed in 1958 by a nursery. Sisters Benedice, Renata, and Imelda formed the community and were joined in 1958 by Sister Euphrasia Ruhland.

The pioneers at the Shimizusawa mission on the northern island of Hokkaido, Japan, Sisters Imelda Masako, Benedice Schulte, and Renata Mori.

Is Sister Euphrasia Ruhland teaching English or learning Japanese?

The Shimizusawa property had been purchased from the Maryknoll Society and needed much repair and clean up before being truly livable. Situated in Sapporo Diocese, Shimizusawa was a coal mining and farming city, and the people were quite poor. The parish numbered approximately 150 people, but Sister Benedice believed that the potential for converts was high.

On March 21, 1958, the first postulants were received in Shimizusawa, and one month later the Sacred Congregation for Religious granted permission to erect a novitiate there. Sister Benedice suggested keeping the Tokyo house as a base for educational and business purposes. Teaching kindergarten and catechism and doing parish work occupied most of the community's time and energy. Sisters Olivia Forster and Alisa Ogata arrived in Japan in September 1959, with Sister Alisa joining the Shimizusawa community while Sister Olivia stayed in Tokyo to do language study.

On March 24, 1959, Saint Benedict's Monastery Chapter voted to begin a high school in Muroran, Hokkaido. Groundbreaking began on May 11, 1960. Finances were a constant burden from the beginning. Another major problem was the amount of "red tape" embedded in Japanese law. Sister Benedice persevered in pushing ahead with the high school, consulting with the monastery and with Japanese contractors on an almost rotating basis. She asked Mother

Combination high school and convent in Muroran, Hokkaido, built in 1960.

Richarda for permission to build a convent next to the school. Permission was granted, though funding was a constant problem.

The question of how the Benedictine presence was to be solidifed in Japan was much debated during the late 1950s and early 1960s. In a letter to Mother Richarda dated May 15, 1959, Sister Benedice observed:

> I have felt this school worth every sacrifice because I believe it can give our community in Japan the beginning of a real stability. We need some such institution, spiritually and economically. Without it I do not see how we can ever progress from the situation we find ourselves in here in Shimizusawa where we are a heavy financial burden, unable to help ourselves. We can find plenty of work here for the church to keep us very busy, but until we have a school or hospital or the like we will never approach becoming self-supporting.[140]

The school became the heart of the Japan mission, well into the 1990s.

By Lent of 1959, the community at Shimizusawa had more than doubled in size. There were eleven members: four perpetually professed, three novices, and four aspirants. In March 1960, the first profession was held in Shimizusawa, and, in February 1961, the Bishop of Sapporo agreed to the erection of a religious house in Muroran, next to the proposed high school.

Post-1960

In February 1961, Sister Olivia Forster moved to Muroran, joining Sister Benedice. The new convent was completed in September 1963, and the community then numbered eight professed sisters, two novices, three postulants, and three aspirants. The novitiate moved to Muroran in 1963, and the first reception of novices took place there on January 13, 1964. The novitiate had a considerable odyssey: Shimizusawa-Muroran-Tokyo-Muroran-Sapporo, with Sapporo becoming the permanent site in 1982.

In 1962, Sister Mary Gertrude Maus arrived as superior of the entire mission, while Sister Alisa Ogata took charge of the aspirants and novices. Top priority went to the high school, which by April 1962 had an enrollment of 346, most of these non-boarders. Needs were listed as a larger chapel, a playground, a carpenter shop, and a dormitory to accommodate boarders.

Sisters Jane Weber and Shaun O'Meara arrived in Japan in 1962 and 1965 respectively, Sister Jane becoming superior at Shimizusawa and Sister Shaun superior at Muroran in 1966. The mission years were difficult for Sister Shaun, not least due to the language barrier. She wrote to Mother Henrita Osendorf: "Please pray for the gift of tongues—if the Holy Spirit doesn't know Japanese, I'm sunk."[141] She took language lessons in Tokyo for over a year but never mastered the language. This failure took a toll on her physically and emotionally.

In the spring of 1968, plans were laid to open a kindergarten in Muroran. A loan from the Maryknoll Society made it possible to start building that August. The kindergarten was blessed on September 8, 1969, and ninety children had registered as of April 1970, the formal opening. Ironically, as the kindergarten flourished, the middle and high school began to slightly decline in numbers. Meanwhile, a school for the mentally retarded opened in Shimizusawa in 1967, and a new convent and nursery followed in 1970. The two missions were deeply rooted and open to the many needs of the people around them.

By the late 1960s, Vatican II's directives for missionary activity were being widely disseminated. Sister Shaun, for one, was giving voice to new thinking. In a letter to Mother Henrita in June 1970 she wrote: "I think foreign missions should have greater autonomy. So much is said about trusting others—well, then I think the U.S. has to learn to trust those on the mission even if they don't understand sometimes."[142] Control of the missions was to be given, when possible, to the native religious, and the monastic Chapter was amenable to this new thinking.

In part, the switch to native control of the Japan mission could occur relatively smoothly because the oldest missionary sisters were no longer there. In 1957, Sister Ursuline returned to the United States. Sister Francetta died in Tokyo in 1966 and was buried there. Sister Regia, the last of the original missionary trio, returned to the United States in 1969. Sisters Ursuline, Regia, and Francetta, had given their best years to the mission fields, first in China and Taiwan, then in Japan. But all had developed in a pre-Vatican II milieu that colored strongly their views on how a mission should be run. The three refused to move to Shimizusawa and later Muroran, keeping Tokyo as their "motherhouse." In the late 1960s, "a changing of the guard" was occurring, however, allowing the Japanese Benedictines more control on how to live out Benedictine monasticism in a Japanese setting.

As in Taiwan, so in Japan: the 1970s were a time of increasing leadership by native sisters. In 1973 there were twenty-three Benedictine sisters in Japan, only five of them American. (In 1965 Sister Benedice had returned to the United States. From 1969 to 1978, she was back in Shimizusawa, working as a parish minister.) The intent was clear: the mission would be turned over to the native sisters when feasible. Sister Renata became superior in Tokyo in 1969 and in 1972 was appointed regional superior, succeeding Sister Shaun. Sister Renata continued living in Tokyo and also remained director of Formation to April 1975. Elected regional superior from 1975 to 1983, Sister Renata was succeeded by Sister Bernardin Sakurai, elected for 1983 through 1985 and re-elected for another term.

By 1973-1974 the move for dependent priory status was underway, and, on February 8, 1975, Saint Benedict's Chapter granted this status. Members were sufficient in number to open a convent in Konopporo in 1979, but the Shimizusawa house closed in 1980, mainly because coal mining was dying out and the population had decreased.

A veteran of twenty years in the Japan mission, Sister Olivia Forster has mostly fond memories of those years, though she admits that the first five-six years were difficult. From 1966 to 1975 she served as principal of the Muroran high school, gaining a deep love and respect for the Japanese people and their culture. One of the few American missionaries who learned to read, write, and speak Japanese, Sister Olivia was the last of the Saint Benedict's Monastery sisters stationed in Japan. Only partially in jest, she remarks that in 1980 she was "dragged home kicking and screaming."

On October 7, 1984, the Japanese Benedictines requested autonomy. The monastic Chapter granted this on October 27, 1984. Federation membership came on July 4, 1985. Formal erection of the independent priory and election of its first prioress, Sister Bernardin Sakurai, occurred on October 10, 1985.

While the sisters dug deep roots in Hokkaido, the Tokyo house, little used, was falling into disrepair by the 1970s. In 1986, the sisters sold a third of the land they owned in Tokyo and built a three-story building, blessed by the bishop of Tokyo in 1987. The new convent provided a place for sisters from other orders to stay when they came to Tokyo as well as a place for the Japanese Benedictines to stay when taking courses or visiting in Tokyo, but by 1998, the Tokyo property was placed for sale. Economics and dwindling, aging personnel were the major reasons. The last sisters left the house in March 2000, moving to Hokkaido, and closing out a half-century of Benedictine history in Tokyo.

Reminiscing about the years since gaining autonomy, Sister Alisa Ogata stresses the desire of all the Japanese Benedictines to "give our witness in a Japanese way." She sees that way as based on living in peace, love, and mutual trust: "We are convinced that our witness as Benedictines is given by living our monastic life itself. . . . We are worthwhile not by what we do but by what we are."[143] The sisters therefore began phasing out some of their administrative duties in the teaching apostolate.

Apostolic activity has its costs—in time as well as in money and energy. The sisters were the responsible body for the School Board Corporation to which the girls' high school and the kindergarten belong. As of 1985, they agreed to ask that a lay person rather than one of the sisters be director general of the School Board. The sisters would still be able to teach or work in the school. In August 1995, Sister Alisa resigned as principal of the girls' high school in Muroran, a position she had held for twenty years. A Christian layman succeeded her.

Wanting a larger focus on contemplative life, the sisters considered alternative work. They decided to start a retreat house in Sapporo, and in 1991 most of the construction was

St. Benedict's Monastery in Sapporo (top) and Muroran (bottom), Hokkaido.

finished. Twenty people can be accommodated for spiritual exercises and rest. "In this way we can stay in the convent to serve them instead of going out. . . . At the present time many Christians and non-Christians use the house for spiritual renewal. We think that this is a successful project."[144]

The major building project was in Muroran. In 1994 the monastic Chapter voted to buy land near the school on which to build a new convent. They purchased the land in 1995, starting construction in April 1996. The building was completed in fall 1996, allowing the sisters to move out of the school building into a separate home.

The Japanese sisters are determined to lead a full monastic life, giving much time and energy to the Liturgy of the Hours and to cultivating an environment of silence for deeper prayer life. As of 1999, Saint Benedict's Monastery in Japan numbered seventeen members, all perpetually professed.

The Benedictines in Hokkaido on an outing.

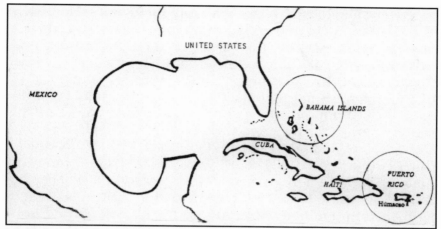

Circles indicate the areas of mission activity of St. Benedict's Monastery in the Caribbean: Puerto Rico and The Bahama Islands.

Puerto Rico Mission and Priory

BEGINNINGS

Minnesota monks from Saint John's Abbey established a monastery in Puerto Rico in 1947, and the Sisters of Saint Benedict came a year later. Bishop James P. Davis, bishop of San Juan, wrote to Mother Rosamond Pratschner, asking for three to four sisters: "Recently additional property for a school and convent were bequeathed to the parish and I am most eager to see a real parochial school begin in Humacao. No less desirous of this are the Fathers, for it is most apparent to them that without a school much of their labor will remain fruitless."[145]

Replying to Bishop Davis, Mother Rosamond told him that there were no sisters to send. Another letter of request arrived from Father Basil Stegmann, O.S.B., describing the need for the sisters. He noted that "The parochial district has about thirty thousand Catholics but many of them are only nominal." He added: "The main reason for the indifference is lack of instruction for centuries and hence to save what is to be saved requires more priests and sisters." A reply letter informed him that Saint Benedict's Monastery was dividing its members into two new priories and the percentage of sisters left at Saint Benedict's Monastery was uncertain. But Father Basil, undaunted, wrote to Mother Rosamond again: "We must have sisters for the organization of regular religious instruction for the thousands of children. At present, our lay teachers make generous sacrifices to help along but they are themselves not deeply rooted in the truths of the Catechism and are too irregular because of other preoccupations. The children and their parents want Sisters."[146] Mother Rosamond, possibly worn down by this time, said that she would send two to three sisters to Humacao to "look over the situation."

In May 1948, Mother Rosamond went to Humacao, Puerto Rico, investigating things firsthand. Interviewed years later, she reminisced: "Now this was even less than a year after the Fathers had established themselves, and these good people and the entire environment were difficult to resist. So it was easy for me to go back to Minnesota and assure the sisters of the fine opportunity we had in the growth of the church."[147] The monastic Chapter voted on July 15, 1948, to accept the Puerto Rico mission. Three sisters arrived in Humacao on August 1: Sister Adeline Terhaar, teacher and superior; Sister Jeanette Roesch, teacher; and Sister Agnes Herwers, housekeeper and sometimes teacher. The people gave generously of money, linens, utensils, and furniture to help the sisters get settled.

First sisters from Saint Benedict's Monastery to explore the mission field in Puerto Rico, Sisters Jeanette Roesch, Agnes Herwers, and Adeline Terhaar.

THE 1950S . . .

Due to illness, Sister Jeanette returned to Saint Benedict's in 1951. The pastor of Humacao, Father Julian Simon, wrote to Mother Richarda Peters on July 18, 1951, inquiring about her replacement and telling of the need to hire even more teachers. He added: "The sisters you send should be fairly young so as to be able to learn to speak Spanish fluently and to be able to stand up under the stress of the heat and work. It is so important that they learn to speak Spanish."[148]The sisters did stand up under the heat and work, but the language skills did not come easily.

Sister Jeanette Roesch's letters give details of the first years in Puerto Rico. She and Sister Agnes began teaching English classes, with Sister Adeline helping out occasionally. Sister Jeanette informed Mother Rosamond: "I am making enough progress in Spanish to scold my unruly class in Spanish. Teaching arithmetic and reading in Spanish also helps, as the children do not understand enough English to understand English explanation." She also describes relations with the Benedictine fathers. "They often help us and we had a turkey from their *finca* [farm] for our Christmas dinner. They receive help from us in the mending and washing of some of their clothes, like habits and church linens." She stressed that if more sisters come, they should know the language, "for the school day begins at eight and when prayers are added to the school day there is little time left for study and class."[149]

In fall 1950, the sisters were asked to teach religion to the children of United States servicemen at the navy base (Ceiba) sixteen miles from Humacao and agreed to do so. There were four Benedictine sisters in 1950, five in 1954. A new school/convent complex opened in 1951—two stories, with eight classrooms, a chapel, and living quarters for the sisters.

Sister Agnes Herwers' correspondence gives much information on the first decade in Puerto Rico. She informed Mother Richarda that "Father Rupert brought us a radio so that listening to the Spanish will aid us in learning to speak it. Mrs. Mediavella comes here quite regular to help us with the Spanish."[150] There were 297 pupils in school, and Sister Agnes helped out by teaching English to grades one to four. Some laywomen were now helping to cook and do laundry.

On November 2, 1954, the sisters moved into a new house across the street from the school. Sister Brendan Maiers arrived in 1955—remaining until 1971—and she highlights an on-going problem: "Not knowing a word in Spanish other than counting to ten, it was especially frustrating to try in a very limited way to show the people that I was sent to serve them when I couldn't even speak a word in their language. However, as the years went on, I began to get more confidence."[151] But few of the United States sisters ever became truly fluent in Spanish. One who did was Sister Anne (Antone) Malerich, who arrive in Puerto Rico in 1954.

Poverty was high, Sister Anne observed: "In the 1950s it was still very much like a Third World country where you have a few rich, sugar cane people and so on, people who owned all of that land and then the rest were poor. There was veritably no middle class."[152] By the late 1960s and early 1970s, Sister Anne was involved in parish work, as she wanted to be among the neediest people, mainly those in rural areas.

In 1955 the first Puerto Rican novice, Sister Josefina Bobonis, made her novitiate at Saint Benedict's Monastery. She returned to Puerto Rico in 1957, remaining there as a community member until leaving the order in 1975. Although Sister Josefina could read, speak, and write English, she preferred her native tongue, and it disturbed her that so many United States sisters could not speak or read Spanish. In a letter to Mother Richarda in early 1960, Sister Josefina alludes to a culture clash when she wrote: "The problem that creates most of the trouble is the difficulty to explain why we follow certain customs or rules existing in our school due to our own Puerto Rican culture. . . . Some things are done differently in the schools of Puerto Rico than in Minnesota."[153]

Sisters with their students from Academia San José in the plaza of Humacao (1965).

THE 1960s

By 1964, the sisters were engaged in two schools: Academia San José, an elementary school, and Colegio San Benito, a boarding high school for girls that later became a co-ed day school. During the 1960s, the Benedictine community in Puerto Rico doubled: there were eighteen sisters in 1968, seven from the United States. In 1963, the first native-speaking sister, Sister Gaudalupe Bonfil, was appointed superior from 1964 to 1968, followed by Sister Lois Wedl from 1968 to 1974.

Sister Lois arrived in Puerto Rico in 1964, where she was assigned to San José as superior, acting principal, and eighth-grade English and religion teacher; she also taught high school English classes at Colegio San Benito. The sisters were living in three places at this time: five at San Benito, five at the monastery (cooking, cleaning), and ten at San José.

Sisters Lois Wedl and Josefina (Maria del Carmen) Bobonis with Carmen Solis.

The sisters from Saint Benedict's Monastery were consistently welcomed by the Puerto Rico sisters and lay people. This warmth and support were strongly felt by Sister Lydia Erkens when she came to the island in 1963, unprepared but open-minded. Reflecting on her twelve years in Puerto Rico (1963 to 1975), Sister Lydia refers fondly to those years. In an interview, she shared that, although she had no knowledge of the Spanish language nor any history of the island when she first came, her years there were "rich ones, among the most pleasant in my life."[154]

Since the new boarding high school was under construction when she arrived, Sister Lydia stayed at the monastery until the school was completed. She was the only non-native sister at San Benito during the first year, but the native sisters who knew some English were very helpful. However, she was forced to learn Spanish because she worked in the kitchen with persons who knew little or no English and had to go to the town market to purchase food from the Spanish-speaking merchants. Sister Lydia and Lois commuted to Rio Piedras (city) during one summer to study Spanish.

For all the sisters, the 1960s and 1970s proved to be expansive decades, with education clearly the dominant apostolate. Academia San José had over 400 pupils in 1966, and Colegio San Benito's enrollment increased rapidly in 1969 when it became a co-ed day school rather than a girls' boarding high school. Another major change resulted from the presence of many English-speaking families who moved into the Humacao area because of the massive industrial development on the island. These companies generously contributed money, supplies, and builders to make it possible for their children to attend the Catholic schools.

In 1968, Sister Lois wrote to Mother Henrita Osendorf: "We have to double rooms of every class from kindergarten to sixth—plus fifty students in both the seventh and eighth grades—plus two sections of freshmen, [forty-four] sophomores, [twenty-seven] juniors, and [seventeen] seniors— with more and more matriculations coming in."[155] By1970, the schools were filled to capacity with little room for expansion. After much consultation with Mother Henrita Osendorf, and the administration of San Antonio Abad, a male boarding school, the decision was made to merge Colegio San Benito with San Antonio Abad. Although the decision was most difficult, San Antonio Abad did have all the needed facilities such as extra classrooms, labs, a gym, a swimming pool, and a football field. To ease the painful transition, most of the faculty members from Colegio San Benito moved with the students to San Antonio Abad in 1971.

THE 1970s

In August 1971, all the sisters (sixteen) moved together to live at San Benito; seven commuted daily to San Antonio Abad to teach at the newly merged high school where Sister Lois was the first woman administrator. The other sisters taught at San Benito or worked in pastoral care. Sisters

Justina Diaz and Carmen del Valle visited and cared for the poor in the *campos*, while Sister Rebecca Schmidt worked in health care.

The 1970s were an exciting, somewhat disruptive decade—not least politically. A rising nationalism, even more widespread than that of the 1950s, was evident. In a letter to Mother Henrita in October 1970, Sister Lois informs her that "The political picture is not the brightest. The latest tactics of the Independence Party have been the bombing of power plants, generators . . . causing power failures all over the island. Four schools were evacuated Friday because of bomb threats."[156] In September 1971, she referred again to trouble in San Juan due to the Independence Party whose campaign is very anti-United States. They "have plastered every wall, telephone post, and sign with posters of 'Yankee-Go-Home." The people of Puerto Rico were divided into three major parties: for independence, the status quo (commonwealth), or statehood. Interestingly, Sister Josefina had an interpretation of the times that saw the positive side of this virulent nationalism. Her letter to Mother Henrita in 1968 referred to "a new and let us say psychological or sociological awakening in the character of the Puerto Ricans. For many years—better, for all history— we have been living under colonialism which creates in a sense an inferiority complex that others are better or many times conformist, just accept and that's it." She suggested that better educated and higher-economic Puerto Ricans are claiming their right and that "Some have developed anti-Americanism, others a desire to improve or better themselves to show that we have the potentiality to do what others do."[157] She saw the stirrings of this in the Benedictine community, too.

Politics aside, there was a growing sense of maturation and stability with the religious community. Much of the tale can be found in Sister Myriam (Rosarito) Pacheco's correspondence. She was assigned to teach high school in San Benito in 1966, finding it a postive task. Her letter to Mother Henrita in 1967 stated, "We are seven Sisters in the house, but work as one. . . . Sister Guadalupe continues to do her great work as principal with love and generosity. She is very well loved by the students and by the parents." Several years later, in 1975, Sister Myriam wrote to Mother Evin Rademacher, prioress, referring to the establishment of study groups to plan for dependent priory status. She noted:

> We looked at the pros and cons of being a Dependent Priory. . . . Each had the opportunity to speak out, ask questions, share fears, and point out responsibilities. We decided on December 8, feast of the Immaculate Conception, to sign the petition. On December 12, we presented our request to the Bishop of the Diocese of Caguas, Rafael Grovas, and he was very happy with the idea.[159]

The time was ripe for this step.

In 1974, Sister Lois, finishing her tenth year in Puerto Rico, returned to the United States. As in Asia and in the Bahamas, American sisters gradually left Puerto Rico, turning affairs over to Puerto Rican control. That same year, 1974, Sister Myriam Pacheco was elected the first Puerto Rican regional superior, succeeding Sister Lois.

Years later, Sisters Lois Wedl and Myriam Pacheco celebrating memories with former students at a reunion.

At the June 8, 1974, Chapter meeting there was discussion and acceptance of a policy for establishing a dependent priory in Puerto Rico. Requirements for such status included a sufficient number of native sisters, financial stability, and a definite community identity and rootedness. On all counts, Puerto Rico met the requirements and, along with the Bahamas, Japan, and Taiwan, requested dependent priory status, which was granted by the Chapter on February 8, 1975.

The 1980s and 1990s

Continuing issues from 1975 into the 1990s have revolved around buying or building a new convent, the relationship with Colegio San Benito, personnel, types and scope of service to the people, and preparation for independent priory status. Much help—funds and financial legal aid—was provided by Saint Benedict's Monastery administration, which sent Sister Kathleen Kalinowski, liaison between the prioress and the dependent priories, to advise the sisters in their financial affairs.

Application for autonomous status was in the minds of many of the Puerto Rico sisters long before the 1990s. But the desire and drive for this status peaked around 1994-1995. In a letter to Sister Mary Reuter, prioress, Sister Carmen Davila, regional superior, wrote: "In our Quasi-Chapter, we decided to begin our process for INDEPENDENCE [sic]. We were in peace, happy, and had a beautiful discernment."[160]

The date was set for 2000, very appropriate with the new millenium. This was agreed to by vote at a meeting of the Puerto Rico sisters on January 21, 1995, with Sisters Mary Reuter and Kathleen Kalinowski present.

In 1998, the sisters in Puerto Rico (twelve perpetually professed and one novice) celebrated the fiftieth anniversary of the arrival of sisters from Saint Benedict's Monastery in Minnesota in 1948. Currently they live in two houses: Monasterio Santa Escolastica, the main monastery, and Convento San Benito. On March 25, 2000, the Saint Bene-

San Benito Convent and Colegio.

Monasterio Santa Escolastica.

dict's Monastery Chapter voted to grant autonomy to the community in Puerto Rico. By a vote on July 22, 2000, the Chapter of the Federation of Saint Benedict granted them canonical membership in that organization. On September

16, 2000, the community of Monasterio Santa Escolastica elected their first prioress, Sister Mary Ruth Santana.

The fourteen members in the Puerto Rico monastery engage in a variety of services. Some are teachers, others are in social work, parish ministry, youth ministry, ministry to shut-ins, and in nursing. This expansion in apostolic works has been possible thanks to the sisters' increasing professional training and education—several of them earning Bachelor of Arts and Master of Arts degrees in educational administration, nursing, social work, and theology.

The Santa Escolastica Community at the time of becoming autonomous in 2000.

Utah Mission and Priory

BEGINNINGS—THE 1940s AND 1950s

Ogden, Utah, is the site of an unusual apostolate for Saint Benedict's mission outside Minnesota. World War II was the catalyst for this, as noted by Sister Estelle Nordick in her history of St. Benedict's Hospital. She cites the great population increase of some 30,000 civilians in Ogden, working directly or indirectly for the military.

In 1943, Monsignor Wilfred J. Giroux, pastor of St. Joseph's Catholic Church in Ogden, wrote to Mother Rosamond Pratschner asking for a few sisters to open and run a hospital. She replied that she was "mildly interested." A week later, the monsignor was in St. Joseph, Minnesota, pleading his cause in person. He was very persuasive; on May 10, 1943, the Monastery Chapter accepted sponsorship of a new 150-bed hospital that, together with the well-established Thomas Dee (Mormon) Hospital, would meet the people's needs.

Ground was broken on October 3, 1944, and the new St. Benedict's Hospital was dedicated on September 18, 1946. Nineteen sisters were stationed in Ogden, living at first in the School of Nursing, which was completed before the hospital. In Sister Estelle Nordick's judgment, "Living in Utah as a minority group did much for our Benedictine family. Our desire and willingness to do all we could to make the hospital a success resulted in our being a closely-knit group, striving to make our Benedictine community life a more perfect observance."[161]

Upon its opening, the hospital's isolation ward was filled with polio patients, over 100 during the years 1946 through 1947. The sisters constantly stressed the hospital's philosophy: "Each patient's worth and dignity is derived from the relationship of love in Christ that God has for each individual. Here all persons are cared for regardless of creed, race, color, ethnic origin, sex, or financial status."[162]

The School of Nursing was founded in 1949, lasting until 1968, after which time Weber State College and the University of Utah took over this training. Directors of the School of Nursing were Sisters Mary Gerald Maiers, Berno Flint, and Cassian Peters. The Utah State Board of Examiners approved the School of Nursing on April 12, 1947. In July 1957 the National League for Nursing accredited the three-year diploma program.

The 1950s saw the sisters and their hospital become fully accepted and respected in Ogden. Relations with the physicians were good from the start. It took a little longer with the populace as a whole. Sister Arles Silbernick, who arrived in Ogden in 1950 as an x-ray technician and would serve there for thirty-six years, recalls that the general public was "somewhat cool" to the sisters, but that this changed in a few years "as the people saw the dedicated service given by the Sisters and their hospital."

THE 1960s

The 1960s was a decade of great activity and expansion: among the additions in service were a four-bed coronary care unit, a twelve-channel autoanalyzer (installed for blood tests), a ten-bed intensive care unit, and a comprehensive poison control center. The departments of Pastoral Care and Social Services were organized to more fully care for the whole person. The sisters also moved into their new convent; the old one, the east wing of the hospital, was then renovated as a pediatric ward.

In the early 1960s, a new mission was begun in Utah-one that would be cut short, due to circumstances beyond the sisters' control. In March 1960, Bishop Joseph L. Federal, co-adjutor of the Catholic Diocese of Salt Lake City, asked the Ogden Sisters to take over a privately owned hospital in Richfield, two hundred miles south of Ogden. It was a thirty-bed hospital with an attached home for the aged.

Mother Richarda Peters called a Council meeting to discuss the proposition and visited Utah to get first-hand information. She convened a special Chapter, which, on April 2, 1960, voted approval for the purchase. Official takeover of the hospital was on April 16, 1960, and the first Mass was celebrated there on Easter Sunday, April 17, 1960.

To run the hospital, sisters from Ogden filled in as needed, traveling between Ogden and Richfield. As of July 23, 1960, St. Michael's Hospital had its own staff of sisters, meant to be permanent: Sisters Arles Silbernick (administrator and superior), Benora Gaida, Mary John Sweeney, Job (Norma) Zimmerman, and Noel LeClaire.

Almost from day one, there was talk of a new Mormon hospital being built in Richfield—though the Mormons had turned down the first chance at the old one. According to Sister Benora, a "war of nerves" began. The little hospital did well at first. But a surprise was in store within nine months of its opening. On December 10, 1962, the Utah sisters were informed by Mother Henrita Osendorf that the Latter Day Saints (LDS) would build a new hospital in Richfield. St. Michael's Hospital would not be able to compete financially. On December 12, 1962, a letter was sent to the presiding bishop of the LDS church, offering to sell St. Michael's Hospital. An agreement was reached on December 18, 1962. LDS officials arrived at St. Michael's on December 27, 1962, to tour the facility and to complete plans for the takeover. The hospital's name was changed to Sevier Valley Hospital of the Church of Jesus Christ of Latter Day Saints.

On January 1, 1963, St. Michael's Hospital and convent were officially closed. Sister Benora writes in her memoirs, "All these happenings seemed like a bad dream . . . we felt stunned . . . many tears were shed."[164] Some anger was felt, since the negotiations had begun and were carried out seemingly without the active participation or knowledge of the Utah sisters. The sisters moved to Ogden on January 5, 1963, awaiting new assignments. Ironically, in 1976, a new LDS hospital and nursing home were built in Richfield, the old one having become too small to meet the needs of a growing area.

By the mid-1960s there was a need for a new hospital in Ogden, too. Much discussion ensued, and in March 1971 the first lay governing board was established, consisting of half sisters and half physicians and business leaders. Their first order of business was to plan a new, larger St. Benedict's Hospital. The State of Utah approved plans for a 133-bed facility, and on October 30, 1974, ground was broken.

The 1970s

Although most were employed in the hospital, some sisters moved into educational fields. In 1968 two sisters joined the staff of St. Joseph's High School in Ogden; in 1970, a sister began service as diocesan coordinator of secondary education. In 1971 another became director of the resource center in the Office of Education, and one became a teacher at Judge Memorial High School, with two more joining her the following year. Above and beyond this, the sisters were active in parish work and vocation promotion.

By the late 1970s, the Utah Sisters began plans for a dependent priory. At a meeting on March 18, 1979, a five-member committee was established to prepare a statement of the Utah situation and the desire for dependent status. Among advantages cited were broadening of the scope of apostolates, encouraging of vocations, strengthening of the local church and building/gaining more credibility. Task teams were set up: Philosophy, Recruitment and Formation, Finances, and Election Process.

On March 23, 1979, three members of the Priory Planning Committee met with Bishop Joseph L. Federal in Salt Lake City, informing him of their goal to become a dependent priory and also of plans for a sesquimillenial celebration in 1980. Bishop Federal was very supportive of both. The Monastery Chapter, on June 9, 1979, approved the beginning of study towards dependent priory status. Initial membership would be restricted to the sisters assigned to Utah as of February 1980. Mother Evin Rademacher visited the Utah community in late January 1980, and she asked that a report be readied for the February 1980 Monastery Chapter.

The 1980s

On February 16, 1980, the Monastery Chapter gave an overwhelming vote for dependent priory status. As of February 17, the priory took the name Mount Benedict Priory. An election committee prepared for election of the first regional superior and two Council members. Election was held on April 13, 1980, and Sister Francis Forster became the first Regional Superior with Sisters Maxine Kaiser and Jacquelyn Dubay as council members. In 1981, Sister Francis added the duties of president of the board of St.Benedict's hospital.

On October 5, 1980, the Sesquimillenial Celebration of the birth of St. Benedict was celebrated in the Cathedral of the Madeleine in Salt Lake City, with Bishop Federal as principal celebrant. The occasion was a grand stage on which the sisters could express their identity, goals, and commitment as an indigenous community, identified with the church in Utah.

Service to the people of Utah is broader than through the hospital or schools. The sisters are able to offer much help, thanks to two charitable organizations that give sufficient funds to support varied programs. One of these is the Hemingway Trust, established on December 14, 1962. A donor gave the initial funds—stock worth over $20,000—to support the ministries of the Sisters of St. Benedict. That trust was now worth over two million dollars in 1997 and earns an annual income of approximately $85,000. The St. Benedict's Foundation was set up in October 1976 with the goal of raising money for St. Benedict's Hospital. After 1993, a legal change allowed the Foundation to change that goal. Now it supports programs to help the needy at large, especially women and children. The Sisters of Mount Benedict Priory are the corporate members and exercise buying and selling powers. The sale of St. Benedict's Hospital to Health Trust, Inc., brought approximately two and one-half million dollars to the Foundation. This has enabled the sisters to give generous aid to many needy people in Ogden and the nearby region. For example, funds have gone to therapy for abused children and for women at risk for prenatal care.[165]

A change in hospital ownership occurred in 1986: St. Benedict's Hospital affiliated with the Holy Cross Health System based in South Bend, Indiana. This was somewhat worrisome to the sisters, as a financial strain was felt due to

Front entrance to Mount Benedict Monastery.

The community of sisters in 1998: Left to right, first row: Sisters Luke Hoschette, Virgene Marx, Francis (Xavier) Forster, Stephanie Mongeon; second row: Sisters Judine Suter, Danile Knight, Marilyn Mark; third row: Sisters Jean Gibson, Jeremia Januschka, Iris Beckwith, and Mary Zenzen.

high indebtedness. In the fall of 1993, Holy Cross Health System sold its Utah hospitals to Health Trust, Inc. While the sisters received a one million-dollar gift from Holy Cross, this severance from ownership/sponsorship was traumatic. However, several sisters remained on the hospital staff. As of 1995, Health Trust, Inc., merged with Columbia, a corporation with headquarters in Nashville, Tennessee. The hospital is now officially titled Columbia Ogden Regional Medical Center.

Sister Jean Gibson, x-ray technician at the hospital since her arrival in Ogden in 1975, thinks that this transaction was "a blessing in disguise. We could now concentrate and focus on being a Benedictine community serving the people in a more spiritual way. We could now ask ourselves what is truly important."[166]

On July 11, 1982, Sister Marilyn Mark professed final vows in Utah, the first final profession in the priory. The second election of regional superior was held April 23, 1984, with Sister Francis Forster being re-elected. She was succeeded by Sister Jeremia Januschka in May 1987, who was re-elected in 1991.

THE 1990s

During 1991 and 1992, a total of six Utah sisters, after discerning whether or not to stay with the Utah priory once it became independent, returned to the monastery, leaving eleven members in Mount Benedict Priory. Plans were firming up to request independent priory status. On May 9, 1992, eleven sisters signed a covenant, expressing their desire to form an independent priory. This covenant was submitted to the St. Benedict's Monastery Council in January 1993. On June 12, 1993, the Monastery Chapter granted independence, and in July 1994 the priory joined the Federation of St. Benedict. Sister Mary Zenzen was elected prioress in 1994 and re-elected in 1998. Also in 1998, Sister Francis Forster, who arrived in Utah in 1958, celebrated her Diamond Jubilee of profession, the first sister there to reach such a milestone.

Ten sisters comprise Mount Benedict Priory as of 2000. They completed building a monastery in August 1999. Prior to this, the sisters lived scattered among three houses. The new monastery can house fifteen sisters comfortably. Sister Jean Gibson, priory treasurer, sees this monastery as a drawing card, a visible manifestation of the Benedictine charisma and an opportunity for the sisters to "get back to our roots." While the sisters came to Utah primarily for the healthcare apostolate, their situation has changed and new opportunities continue to open. There is much excitement and joy as the sisters face a new century in Utah.

The Bahamas

BACKGROUND

Saint John's Abbey, in Minnesota, sent Father Chrysostom Schreiner to Nassau in February 1891; two years later, he opened a priory and a small school. Father Chrysostom predicted that the school would be the main source of converts, noting the work of the Sisters of Charity from New York who were the majority teachers in the islands. Two newly ordained priests, Fathers Gabriel Roerig and Melchior Bahner, went to the Bahamas in June 1894, but the mission remained small and rather poor for the next forty years.[168]

A key figure in the development of Catholicism in the Bahamas was Father Paul Leonard Hagarty, at work in the Bahamas since 1937. Appointed bishop vicar-apostolic in 1950, he made Catholic education his priority and exerted strong leadership in this area. In March 1951, Bishop Hagarty petitioned Mother Richarda Peters to send sisters to help the native Blessed Martin de Porres Sisters (Blessed Martin de Porres was canonized in 1962) to affiliate with a religious order of pontifical status. He wrote:

> What would be ideal for us would be a sister or sisters who could live with these colored sisters, not so much

as superiors but rather as guides and counselors with one of the Native Sisters being the Mother, the native Sisters having their own council, etc. Whereas the Benedictine Sisters would not only help them to form themselves spiritually but intellectually as well by giving them special classes in the convent to bring them up to high school graduate level, so that we could send them north to college perhaps two at a time.[169]

Mother Richarda's response was neither a firm yes nor no. She suggested that they discuss the matter after Easter.

The Sisters of Blessed Martin de Porres, Nassau, Bahamas.

In existence since 1937, the Nassau Sisters of Blessed Martin de Porres numbered eight professed, three novices, and three postulants in spring of 1951. The Sisters of Charity of Mount St. Vincent-on-the-Hudson were helping the small order by having one of their sisters live with the native community, counseling, directing, and instructing them in the religious life. Because the Sisters of Charity were planning to withdraw some personnel in the early

1950s, they could no longer supply mentors for the native sisters.

The 1950s

In September 1950, Sisters Teresa Symonette and Maria Rahming left the Bahamas to attend college with the Franciscan Sisters in Clinton, Iowa. During the summer of 1951, they visited Saint Benedict's Monastery, prior to their returning to the Bahamas. They were the first Bahamian sisters to do so. That summer, June 1951, Mother Richarda consented to send two sisters to the Bahamas: Sisters Alfreda Zierden and Margaret Rose Kamp, a teacher and registered nurse respectively. They left St. Cloud for Nassau on August 6, 1951, arriving there on August 9th. Inevitably, some tensions occurred, seemingly due to different temperaments and different notions of the appropriate way to live religious life. Still, much effort was made by both sides to live harmoniously.

Sister Alfreda, in particular, was sensitive to the situation. She wanted to be open to the needs and desires of the native sisters. Her letter in August 1951 to Mother Richarda stated: "I can see much that could be done, but for the time being I think we will quietly live their schedule and wait for an opening or whatever opportunity they will give us to help them. They have a multiplicity of prayers as one would expect and their frugality is severe."[170]

Some obstacles faced by Sisters Alfreda and Margaret Rose were the intense heat, unaccustomed foods, and little sleep—the latter due to the noise of dogs and what seemed an invasion by insects. However, the two pitched in and tried to meet the needs of the small community and the neighbors. Sister Margaret Rose visited the sick in their homes and gave short periods of instructions to the sisters on how they could help the sick. Sister Alfreda studied the British educational system to learn how she could expand on it to help the younger members of the community. She also taught some liturgy classes. Many of the Martin de Porres sisters had no more than ten years of formal schooling—at the most a high school diploma.

Neither Benedictine sister stayed more than one year. Sister Margaret Rose returned to Saint Benedict's Monastery in late November 1951, and Sister Alfreda returned in August 1952. Contact had been made and some ties forged, however slight. When the Sisters of Charity no longer supplied a mentor for the Martin de Porres sisters, the governance of the small community was shared among three of their own members: Sisters Elizabeth Claridge, Maria Rahming, and Marie Agnes Rolle. They continued in office until amalgamation with Saint Benedict's Monastery began in 1962. Between December 17, 1956, and January 8, 1957, two Martin de Porres sisters, Sisters Marie Agnes Rolle and Rosella Harvey, visited St. Benedict's Monastery. From 1960 to 1962, Sisters Mary Bernard (Telzena) Coakley and Bernadette Powell attended the College of St. Benedict, for their junior and seniors years, earning their B.A.s in 1962.

AMALGAMATION: THE 1960s

By 1960 Bishop Hagarty, first bishop of the newly created Diocese of Nassau, was pressing for amalgamation, merging the Martin de Porres sisters with the Sisters of St. Benedict. In a letter to Mother Henrita Osendorf, April 26, 1962, he described how he convened the Martin de Porres sisters on April 25, 1962, to vote on amalgamation. The majority vote was affirmative—with choices being to receive dispensation from their vows, to transfer vows to another community, or to amalgamate with Saint Benedict's Monastery. By an overwhelming number, the Saint Benedict's Monastery Chapter voted for amalgamation on July 21, 1962.

Bishop Hagarty was very pleased with events. He wrote to the Cardinal Prefect of the Sacred Congregation for the Propagation of the Faith, May 15, 1962:

> One great benefit to the Missions of the Bahamas will be the fact that this will enable us to integrate completely our native community of sisters with white Sisters and colored Sisters. At the present time, our native Sisters are entirely of the colored race, white applicants having

rarely been interested. By joining the Benedictine Community . . . I feel that the new community in the Bahamas will be almost from the start an integrated community of both colored and white Sisters.[171]

Mother Henrita planned an abbreviated novitiate of three-month duration for the professed members of the community, as suggested by Father John Eidenschink, monk and canon lawyer from Saint John's Abbey. There would also be an exchange of professed sisters to and from Saint Benedict's Monastery, expenses to be borne by the Diocese of Nassau, if possible.[172] Four sisters from St. Benedict's arrived in Nassau on August 21, 1962: Sisters Harvette Hockert (superior), Eunice Antony, Loren (Lauren) Keppers, and Louis (Dorothy) Manuel.

As of 1963, four Bahamian sisters were teaching in Minnesota parish schools, three were in the Juniorate and four in the Novitiate at Saint Benedict's. What these sisters thought of the process and results of amalgamation appar-

Mother Henrita (center) with Sisters Eunice Antony, Louis (Dorothy) Manuel, Harvetta Hockert, and Loren (Lauren) Keppers, and Bahamian Sisters Marie Agnes Rolle, Maria Rahming, Joan Dean, and Cecilia Albury.

ently was not asked. It seemed taken for granted that amalgamation was a logical, positive step. May 1, 1963, was the deadline for the Bahamian sisters to indicate their individual choices on joining Saint Benedict's Monastery. Most decided in favor of amalgamation.

In a letter to Bishop Hagarty, in January 1963, Mother Henrita and Father John told him of their decision that the Bahaman sisters in perpetual vows need not profess temporary vows after the condensed novitiate but could "go right into perpetual vows. There is enough insecurity connected with this amalgamation for them without our adding more to it unnecessarily."[173] The Sacred Congregation of Religious empowered Bishop Hagarty to issue a decree incorporating the Sisters of St. Martin de Porres into the Benedictine Order. The bishop was pleasantly surprised at how "quickly and smoothly" the amalgamation had gone.

In the Bahamas, Sister Harvette and her colleagues were settling in—though not without some difficulty. In a letter to Mother Henrita, Sister Harvette tells of being exhausted with teaching due to heat and the lack of materials. She was also concerned with some "old bills" coming due. Nor was

Sister Eunice Antony at St. Bede's School, Nassau, early 1960s.

she convinced that all the native sisters were pleased with the new order of things. Mother Henrita advised gradualness, going slowly in introducing Benedictine customs.

Serving in the Bahamas for eight years and in charge of the aspirants for several of them, Sister Eunice Antony wrote to Mother Henrita August 25, 1962, giving her view of the process of amalgamation: "The sisters all work together so well that work is finished quickly. They are making speedy progress with the Divine Office also. Everyone seems happy and eager to comply with any suggestions of changes. . . . Operation Amalgamation seems very promising right now, but it has a very humble beginning. The Sisters here would be a great asset to our community."[175] She was very right in her observation. Both sides, the Bahamas and St. Joseph, Minnesota, benefited greatly from their close relationship over the years. A remark made by Sister Maedene Russell at the time of Bahamian independence from Britain in 1973, attests to one positive major effect of amalgamation: "I have seen a tremendous growth in the sisters in Minnesota in the exposure that they are all receiving in understanding the world and different cultures."[176]

However, less than a year later, in late March 1963, Sister Eunice reports that there is some resistance on the part of several Bahamian Sisters to Benedictine practices, though she is hopeful and optimistic about the situation. In a letter in spring of 1963, she tells of some reaction to Bishop Hagerty's letter (Decree) requiring amalgamation, noting "reactions of depression, heaviness, and unhappiness . . . like a 'bomb' the order to amalgamate had been given, and the Sisters just weren't ready for it."[177]

In an interview conducted on November 19, 1988, at St. Martin's Priory, Sister Mary Benedict Pratt summarized how she understood amalgamation: "we were told it was the wish of the Holy See that a community like ours, being so small, should amalgamate with a larger community which is more stable . . . if we weren't happy with the possibilities, then we could do three things: we could either go with the community that would take us all, we can join another community that we know and feel more comfortable with as individuals, or we can leave. That was what was thrown out; there was no discussion."[178] Additional interviews with other priory members affirmed Sister Mary Benedict's recollection of events. The process, more than the results, saddened and even angered some of the sisters.

Coincidentally, the amalgamation project and Vatican II were occurring at about the same time—at least for the first years, 1962 to 1963. However, they were clearly independent events, and Vatican II had no direct impact on the amalgamation process as it evolved. Amalgamation had church approval as of March 19, 1963, and Vatican Council II opened on October 11, 1962, closing on December 8, 1965.

POST-AMALGAMATION, THE 1960S

In the early years, the candidates for the community went to Saint Benedict's Monastery for their education and formation. The community rejoiced in the influx of new members. By the fall of 1964, there were seven novices. Sister Eunice was responsible for their formation as aspirants in the Bahamas. She was optimistic in a letter to Mother Henrita: "Things look much differently [sic] here now than they did a few months previous. I am so happy that you didn't allow us to give up when things looked gloomy . . . the [candidates] appear quite happy and peaceful."[179] Adding to her pleasure was the fact that three new aspirants came that fall.

Along with responsibility for aspirants, Sister Eunice was headmistress of St. Joseph's elementary school, having 850 pupils, fifteen lay teachers, one aspirant, and three sisters on staff. As of 1966, she no longer had the aspirants, and she became a member of the Diocesan Liturgical Commission in the spring of 1967. She also made home visits on Fridays, supervised CCD (Confraternity of Christian Doctrine [religious instruction]) classes on Saturdays, and helped conduct adult education classes two nights a week. By 1968, Sister Eunice was working almost completely in religious education, a move happening for some Benedictine sisters back in Minnesota, too.

Much information on the years 1963 to 1973 can be gleaned from the correspondence of Sister Aloysius Weber, who served in the Bahamas from 1963 to 1974. Her work was mainly giving the sisters classes on the Rule of Benedict and on the Declarations and related readings. On trips outside the convent, Sister Aloysius describes a visit to Cat Island and being haunted by the poverty. She also praises the monks of St. Augustine's Monastery for being very kind, giving solid advice, and occasionally inviting the sisters to pick fruit—grapefruit, oranges, and tangerines—from the monastery orchard.[180]

In a revealing letter to Mother Henrita, January 1965, Sister Aloysius writes: "The school and the convent would probably fall apart if it would not be for Sister Rosella. She backs us both [Sister Eunice and Sister Aloysius] one hundred percent. . . . Often she helps us see the situations from the Bahamian angle and helps the Bahamians see situations from our angle."[181] Although the amalgamation was in its third year, obviously there were still rough spots to iron out.

Sister Mary Patricia Russell.

Sister Mary Patricia Russell, superior at St. Martin's Priory from 1967 to 1974, wrote a three-page report, dated July 6, 1968, and called "Our Apostolate in the Bahamas." In the report she gives a background to the current situation and, among other things, explains that most Bahamians are good Christians, although not Catholics: "At least [seventy-five percent] of us came into religious life from Anglican, Baptist and Methodist families . . . any missionaries coming to the Bahamas are not coming to convert pagans, but will find people who are Christians having a great respect and love for the Bible."[182]

She describes the work being done on four islands: New Providence, Cat Island, Grand Bahama, and Bimini. This includes five grade schools, one high school, CCD centers, and visitation to hospitals, youth corrective homes, and a prison. The high school was the newest apostolate at that time, and the "only one we began since becoming Benedictines, and it is staffed chiefly by lay teachers and by three of our American sisters."[183]

Toward the end of her report, Sister Mary Patricia reveals her hope for the future. She declares: "We look forward to the time when those who are away will return to serve the people of God in the Bahamas better. We are deeply appreciative for those from other lands and they can help to a certain extent, but we Bahamians must be the catalysts for effective and needed change in our Catholic school system and in other areas of our apostolate."[184] She also expresses a desire for more flexibility on how to live the Benedictine life in a Bahamian setting.

THE 1970s, 1980s, AND 1990s

As with other foreign missions, the native members of the Bahamian mission assumed more control during the 1970s. In August 1970, Mother Henrita appointed Sister Mary Patricia Russell as regional superior—the first native Benedictine superior after amalgamation. Sister Mary Benedict Pratt became the first elected native regional superior in 1974, just one year after the Bahama Islands gained their independence from the mother country, Great Britain. As of 1975, the sisters from Saint Benedict's had returned home, with the exception of Sister Christian Morris, whose stay covered 1974 to 1976 and 1979 to 1980.

By 1974 much discussion about and planning for becoming a dependent priory had begun. The sisters petitioned the Saint Benedict's Monastery Council in early February 1975 and were given Chapter approval that same month. Sister Mary Benedict asked for a clarification that

American sisters were still sought to work alongside the
Bahamian sisters. She feared a misconception that the
Bahamians did not want any American sisters after attain-
ing dependent priory status. During an interview she gave
at Saint Benedict's Monastery in March 1991, Sister Cecilia
Albury paid tribute to the efforts of the many Minnesota
Benedictines who served in the Bahamas. "I think those
people who succeeded really were very open to the culture,
open to what we had to offer, and worked from there. I don't
think there's anybody who came to the Bahamas and were
a part of us that I could really say did not succeed."[185]

The fortieth anniversary of the founding of St. Martin de
Porres Convent was celebrated in 1977. Bishop Hagarty was
chief celebrant at a High Mass, and the governor-general of
the Bahamas was also present. The Bahamian Benedictines
were taking leadership, becoming ever more vocal about
their hopes and desires. Election for the regional superior
was held on March 27, 1978, and Sister Mary Benedict Pratt
was re-elected.

Some major events occurred during Sister Mary Ben-
edict's administration. In 1979, the College of St. Benedict
began its Freshman Extension Program in Nassau, with
Sister Annie Thompson as director. On July 25, 1980, the
Silver Jubilee of Sisters Agatha Hunt, Cecilia Albury, and
Ena Albury was celebrated.

The Benedictine sisters in the Bahamas in the 1970s.

In 1986, Sister Mary Patricia Russell was elected regional superior, succeeding Sister Agatha Hunt, who served from 1982 to 1986. By this time, there was talk of requesting independence as a priory. Various committees were set up: building, election, handbook, liturgy, formation team, hospitality, coordinator, and an independence process committee. On the topic of independence, Sister Cecilia Albury stated: ". . . many sisters want independence, and this includes myself; we have this relationship with St. Ben's and we never want to lose that. So how can we be part of St. Ben's as an independent priory? I think the federation answers that; that's no problem."[186]

Mother Henrita visited them during the anniversary celebration of the Golden Jubilee of the founding of the sisters of St. Martin de Porres in 1987. Sister Mary Benedict recalls that visit, stating: "She realized that the life was not easy for us at the time of transition from St. Martin de Porres sisters to Benedictines in 1962-1963, but she wanted us to know that she loved us all and that we were dear to her heart . . . she would like before she dies to see us become an independent priory. It was touching, and she didn't waver. She spoke clearly."[187] Mother Henrita did not live to see the joyous occasion, dying on February 12, 1992.

St. Martin Monastery, Nassau, The Bahamas.

The Bahamian community became autonomous in 1994, and elected Sister Clare Rolle as their first prioress. They are clearly fulfilling Sister Mary Patricia's hopes, stated twenty-six years earlier, of being "the catalyst for effective and needed change" among the Bahamian peoples, serving in a variety of apostolates while maintaining and enriching their Benedictine monasticism. As of 2000, there are fourteen professed sisters in the community.

Sister Maria Rahming, one of the first three women who became Blessed Martin de Porres sisters in 1937, pondering the changes of the past sixty-three years.

AFTERWORD

Part I and **II** showed how Saint Benedict's Monastery had shifted its orientation to claiming its monastic charism as it raison d'être. In no way does that imply a lessening of the sisters' desire to be of service to the Church and the world. To claim the monastic charism is a responsibility the sisters cannot take lightly in view of the crying need in the world for the values that monastic life espouses. It demands of them to be of service in new ways, ways they themselves need to discover for the contemporary milieu. The new millennium challenged the sisters to a deepening of the monastic call personally and communally, to holding the God-quest more consciously, and to living more simply, freely, and compassionately in the self-emptying way of Jesus.[188]

Part III revealed that the various ministries in which the sisters have been engaged have prepared them for this moment of the new millennium. Their service has been a mutual ministry in which they have received as well as given. Saint Benedict's Monastery has become rooted in central Minnesota. The sisters are the daughters of the unbelievably courageous pioneers and early settlers of the Midwest. They have inherited the staunch faith of the people of Stearns and the surrounding counties. They have been affected by the

351

deeply spiritual culture of the Native Americans. The sisters have been challenged by the ideals of the young, the wisdom of the elderly, the witness of ordinary people with extraordinary faithfulness, and the needs of the poor and suffering people with and to whom they have ministered. It was the resources from this area that built this monastery and its ministries. It was the women from this area who gave their lives in joining the community that enabled Saint Benedict's Monastery to make its resources available for the educational, health care, and social ministries through which the sisters gave of their lives in return. Though the sisters venerate their founders Benedict and Scholastica and their foremothers from Bavaria, they know that their lives are now inexorably intertwined with the people in central Minnesota among whom they have lived and worked. Perusal of the names on the Membership List and the Necrology attest to the fact that St. Benedict's is truly indigenous to the upper Midwest. The sisters' future is therefore intertwined with the future of the people of this area as their lives and services continue to be shaped and supported by the sacred mutuality that has characterized the past 150 years.

Of the first group of sisters traveling up the Mississippi River, Sister Grace McDonald wrote:

> No one saw in this group the tiny flame of sanctity and culture that was being carried to the Midwest, nor the nucleus of an organization of over a thousand members, who in course of time were to educate and mold the minds and hearts of thousands in the upper Mississippi River valley.[189]

In the same way, the future of the sisters of Saint Benedict's Monastery in the new millennium lies hidden. Just so was the tiny flame of Christendom hidden in the band of the first disciples. However, Jesus had great expectation of his followers: "I have come to set the earth on fire, and how I wish it were already blazing (Luke 12: 49)!" Though God waits for the tiny flames of human endeavors, history reveals that in God's time, the Spirit blows them into an amazing blaze of divine love.

*It takes just
a tiny flame
passed on
from age to age
to start a blaze!*

The flaming urn placed on Mother Benedicta Riepp's grave during the sesquimillennial celebrations.

Notes to Part III

CHAPTER 11: COLLEGE OF SAINT BENEDICT

1. Catholic University educated only men until 1911 when they established a sisters' college, located near the university, to meet the educational needs of sisters. Most religious communities, however, could not easily send their sisters that far away to attend college.

2. Mary Oates, ed., *Higher Education for Catholic Women: An Historical Anthology* (New York: Garland Publisher, 1987). The historical background for the origins of Catholic women's colleges is included in the Introduction which is unnumbered.

3. Grace McDonald, O.S.B., *With Lamps Burning* (St. Paul: North Central Publishing, 1957), pp. 100-101.

4. Some students took a scientific core in which they substituted more sciences courses, four years of Latin. A few students took a commercial program, which centered more on accounting and secretarial skills, but they received a certificate rather than a diploma. In addition, the academy emphasized music and the arts (Bulletin 1913).

5. Saint Benedict's Academy continued until 1973.

6. Between 1913 and 1932 the frontispiece of the Catalog announced that the college was under the patronage of the bishop of the St. Cloud Diocese, a statement that they had borrowed from the catalog of the academy. After 1932 that statement was omitted.

7. The college borrowed from the tradition of conservatories of art, music, and theater, a tradition that blended theory with creation and performance. By the 1950s the college offered majors in music, theater, and the visual arts.

8. The inclusion of such vocational subjects was likely influenced by the 1860s Morrill Acts that provided for land-grant colleges. These colleges added courses in agriculture and the mechanical arts to the regular college curricula; for women, domestic science was introduced in order to promote the liberal and practical education of the industrial classes. Saint Benedict's later added majors in education, social work, and nursing, undergirded with strong general education requirements in the liberal arts.

9. As the student life program developed, Sister Grace Donovan (Vice President of Student Development, 1961 to 1980) played a very important role in articulating and initiating a developmental

philosophy to shape the student development program. As a result of her leadership in this area, the educational experiences in student life have been one of the main strengths of the College in integrating the emotional, spiritual, and ethical aspects of students' lives with their intellectual development provided in the academic courses.

10. SBMA: RG 22-4A-2, f.1.

11. SBMA: RG 22-4A-2, f. 3.

12. SBMA: RG 2-4-2, f.1.3.

13. Sisters Mariella Gable wrote the script, Firmin Escher composed the music, Alfreda Zierden and Clarus Himsl designed the costumes, and Marcine Schirber directed the early productions. Constance Zierden, one of the very few lay teachers at the time, choreographed the dances. All faculty and students were involved in the production. In the mid-1960s the Pageant had to be discontinued due to the growing cooperation with St. John's University that no longer allowed the shortening of classes for rehearsal in late spring and early fall.

14. Annual Report, 1933-1934.

15. SBMA: RG 22-4A-1c. In response to Philip Gleason's essay, "The Erosion of Racism in Catholic Colleges in the '40s," *America* 173:12-15 (November 18, 1995), Kathleen Yanes Waynes, CSB 1942 graduate, relates her positive experience at the College of Saint Benedict. *America* (February 17, 1996), p. 38.

16. *Benet,* March 1943.

17. Notes from an interview by Sister Emmanuel Renner of the alumnae from the class of 1948, in June 1998.

18. John Harriott, "The Nun's Tales," *The Tablet,* 12 August 1989, p. 1.

19. John Cogley, *Commonweal,* 22 December 1950.

20. Introduction by Sister Nancy Hynes, O.S.B., editor of Sister Mariella Gable, *The Literature of Spiritual Values and Catholic Fiction,* 1996. In her introduction, Hynes also relates the painful censures by Bishop Bartholome of the Saint Cloud Diocese which resulted in removal of Sister Mariella from the faculty at the college between 1958 and 1962. She was able to return to teach at the college in 1962 when Bishop George Speltz became a new coadjutor bishop in the diocese.

21. Mother Richarda Peters worked two years seeking incorporation of the several health-care institutions founded and managed by the sisters, primarily to protect the monastic community from liability for these hospitals and nursing homes. Actually, the idea

of incorporating the college related more to the issues of management and the possibility of getting government grants for building dormitories than to issues of liability. See Mother Richarda's letter to William Consedine on May 12, 1961. John Eidenschink, O.S.B. was the canon lawyer in preparing for incorporation of the monastery's health-care institutions and the college.

22. Kathleen Kalinowski, O.S.B., "Sponsorship of Benedictine Institutions by the Sisters of the Order of St. Benedict," 29 April 1993, (Personal copy).

23. Over the years the monastery transferred to the college some land, buildings, and equipment to be held in trust by the Board of Trustees.

24. Sisters employed by the college did not receive full salaries and fringe benefits until the Board approved a change of policy in 1974-1975. Between 1961 and 1981, monastery audits reveal direct contributions or endowments to the college of over $10,000,000; this gift includes payment of one-half the cost of the Benedicta Art Center. (Kathleen Kalinowski, O.S.B., "Sharing and Shaping: College and Convent Interaction," April, 1981).

25. College of Saint Benedict Archives: Letter to Sister Mary Grell, President, 24 February 1966.

26. College of Saint Benedict Archives: College Board Minutes, 16 September 1967.

27. Robert Witte, Board member from 1971 to 1982, was the first lay person to become the chair of the Board from 1977 to 1982. Since that time all chairpersons have been lay men and women.

28. The history of cooperation between the College of Saint Benedict and St. John's University is yet to be written, but fortunately that history is well documented in the archives of both institutions. While this part of the college's history is not directly part of the history of the college's relationship to the monastic community, it nevertheless has played a role in that history. The continuously evolving relationship among four interdependent institutions, in this case the two Benedictine communities and the two colleges, presents growth-filled challenges and opportunities for everyone involved.

29. College of Saint Benedict Archives: Letter of Sister Nora Luetmer to the college community 1 March 1974.

30. Since Dr. Idzerda's term, two other lay persons have been presidents: Dr. Beverly Miller (1974 to 1979) and Dr. Mary Lyons (1996-).

31. *Directions for the Future,* September 1972, II: pp. 65-66.

32. The information about the changing demographics in the monastery is given in an unpublished report by Sister Kathleen Kalinowski O.S.B., "Community Resource Study of the Sisters of the Order of Saint Benedict," April 29, 1989.

33. Nora Luetmer, O.S.B., *Priorities Study*, 1974, p. 3.

34. Mother Henrita also expressed her continuing commitment to the sponsorship of the college despite the fact that the nature of the relationship between the monastery and the college had changed by the separate incorporation in 1961. She stated, "It has always been understood that the College continues to be one of the chief apostolic works of this Benedictine Community" (CSB Board Minutes, January 5, 1973 in College Archives, 2-1-1 f.8).

35. *Directions for the Future*, pp. 65-66.

36. Alice Gallin, O.S.U., "Sponsorship as Partnership," *Current Issues in Catholic Higher Education*, 4: 2 (Winter 1984), p. 7.

37. Alice Gallin, O.S.U., "Introduction," *Current Issues in Catholic Higher Education*, 11: 2 (Winter 1991), p. 3.

38. Ibid., p. 4.

39. Articles of Amendment to the Articles of Incorporation of the College of Saint Benedict, 1 October 1976. In 1979 the By-Laws were restated to restrict approval to the College Board of Trustees.

40. Emmanuel Renner, O.S.B., "Report of the President," *Annual Report*, 1984, p. 4.

41. Partnership Working Document, 29 January 1992.

CHAPTER 12: HEALTHCARE

42. McDonald, p. 132.

43. *RB 1980*, 36.1. (Collegeville, Minnesota: The Liturgical Press, 1982).

44. Luetmer, p. 211.

45. Interview: Colleen Haggerty, O.S.B., 30 July 1998.

46. Christopher J. Kauffman, *Ministry and Meaning* (New York: The Crossroad Publishing Company, 1995), pp. 299-300.

47. David Hilfiker, M.D., *Not All of Us Are Saints: A Doctor's Journey with the Poor* (New York: HarperCollins, 1994), p. 194.

48. Kauffman, p. 284.

49. Interview: Jonathan Herda, O.S.B., 10 March 2000.

50. Kauffman, p. 2.

51. Luetmer, p. 211.

52. McDonald, p. 132.

53. John J. Dominik, *That You May Find Healing* (St. Cloud, Minnesota: St. Cloud Hospital, Inc., 1986), pp. 6-16.

54. Ibid., p. 24.

55. Ibid., pp. 27-28.

56. Christopher J. Kauffman, *A Commitment to Health Care* (St. Louis: The Catholic Health Association of the United States, 1990), p. 43.

57. Kauffman, *Ministry*, p. 280.

58. Interview: Paula Revier, O.S.B., November 1999.

59. Interview: Mary Jude Meyer, O.S.B., July 1999.

60. SBMA: 3-3-9h. f. 4.1: Notes from Brainstorming Session of Community Health Care Personnel, 29 January 1994.

61. John F. Kavanaugh, "Ethical Commitments in Health Care Systems, " *America* 179: 14 (7 November 1998), p. 20.

62. Dominik, p. 34.

63. Ibid., p. 42.

64. Mary Jude Meyer, O.S.B., July 1989, (personal copy).

65. Interview: Mary Jude Meyer, O.S.B., July 17, 2000.

66. Dominik, p. 43.

67. CentraCare Health System Timeline.

68. *St. Cloud Hospital* (St. Cloud Hospital; CentraCare Health System, 1999), pamphlet.

69. Dominik, p. 43.

70. *Bylaws of the Saint Cloud Hospital,* 1975.

71. *Amended Articles of Incorporation of the Saint Cloud Hospital,* 1987.

72. *Complete Amendment to the Bylaws of the Saint Cloud Hospital,* May 25, 1995.

73. *Today* (St. Cloud Hospital weekly publication), August 1994.

74. Luke Hoschette, O.S.B., "Sponsorship in This Hospital," 2 May 1973, (personal copy) ". . . on September 23, 1962, a charter for the St. Cloud Hospital Corporation was signed by the Secretary of the State of Minnesota. . . . [However], the deeding of the land, together with the building and equipment from the Sisters of the Order of St. Benedict to the St. Cloud Hospital Corporation was recorded with the Stearns County Register of Deeds on January 17, 1964. It was not thought necessary at first to make this transfer, but in the intervening two years from 1962 to 1964 it was becoming clearer that a complete separation was wise."

75. *Today,* August 1994.

76. Dominik, pp. 45-46.

77. McDonald, pp. 172-175.

78. *The History of St. Benedict's Hospital, Ogden, Utah* (personal copy).

79. *The Courage to Lead, the Courage to Grow—Benedictine Sisters' Call to Utah*, 21 December 1995, (personal copy).

80. *Deseret News Magazine*, 27 March 1949.

81. Luke Hoschette, O.S.B. (personal notes, 13 November 1999).

82. Ibid.

83. Ibid.

84. Ibid.

85. *Building a Future on the Foundation of the Past: Columbia Ogden Regional Medical Center* (Brochure: circa 1996).

86. Paulette Cervenka, *A Community Story: Queen of Peace Hospital* (New Prague, Minnesota, 1989), pp. 3-7.

87. Ibid., pp. 14-15.

88. Ibid., p. 19.

89. *Peace Profile*, 18: 3 (Fall 1996).

90. Cervenka, p. 19.

91. *Peace Profile*, 10: 2 (Summer 1989).

92. Ibid., 13: 3 (Fall 1991).

93. Ibid., 16: 1 (Winter 1994).

94. Ibid., 19: 1 (Fall 1997).

95. Ibid., 11: 5 (Winter 1990).

96. *Amended and Restated Articles of Incorporation*, 12/9/97, p. 2, Queen of Peace Hospital, New Prague, Minnesota.

97. Cervenka, p. 24.

98. SBMA: *Corporate Relationships; Revised Hospital Bylaws and Articles*, 12/9/97, pp. 4-5.

99. Cervenka, p. 24.

100. Jean Juenemann, O.S.B., (personal notes: 15 November 1999).

101. SBMA.

CHAPTER 13: NATIVE AMERICANS

102. Claudia C. Carlen, I.H.M., ed., *The Papal Encyclicals, 1939-1958* (McGrath Publishing, 1981), p. 11.

103. Ibid., p. 286.

104. Ibid., p. 47.

105. Timothy McCarthy, *The Catholic Tradition* (Chicago: Loyola Press, 1998), p. 156.

106. Colman J. Barry, *Worship and Work* (Collegeville: The Liturgical Press, 1958), p. 128.

107. Ibid., pp. 165-166.

108. Virginia M. Hefferman, *Outline of the Sixteen Documents,*

Vatican II (New York: The America Press, 1965), p. 94.

109. *Indian Sentinel*, 10 August 1923, p. 11.

110. Interview: Thea Grieman, O.S.B.,12 August 1980.

111. Interview: Mary Degel, O.S.B., 22 July 1980.

112. Interview: Debora Herda, O.S.B., 21 January 1981.

113. Interview: Adelma Roers, O.S.B., 15 July, 1984.

114. SBMA: *Circular Letters*, RG24-SGS, f. 24.

115. Ibid.

116. Interview: Delice Bialke, O.S.B., 14 July 1980.

117. Interview: Elizabeth Theis. O.S.B., 14 February 1995.

118. Walter Abbott, *Documents of Vatican II* (New York: Herder and Herder, 1966), p. 501.

119. SBMA:RG: RG 5-10-11, f. 71, 6 March 1969.

120. Nancy Bauer, O.S.B. "Benedictine Mission to Red Lake: Nearly a Century Old," *St. Cloud Visitor*, 30 October 1986, p. 12.

121. SBMA: RG: 3-1-3, f. 8, *Council Meeting Minutes*, Executive Committee Meeting, 18 September 1989.

122. Interview: Philip Zimmer, O.S.B., 29, March 1995.

123. SBMA: GIS-4-1 f 2.

124. Dorris, Michael, *Paper Trail* (New York: HarperCollins Publishing Inc., 1994), p. 49.

CHAPER 14: FOREIGN MISSIONS AND UTAH

125. Walter Abbot, *Documents of Vatican II* (New York: Herder and Herder, 1966), p. 506.

126. Ibid., p. 598.

127. SBMA: RG 27-2D-4, f. 21.

128. Ibid.

129. SBMA: RG 27-2D-4, f.10.

130. Ibid.

131. SBMA: RG 27-2D-3, f.2.

132. Ibid.

133. SBMA: RG 27-2D-4 ,f.1.

134. Abbott, 617.

135. SBMA: RG 27-2D-4, f.1.

136. Ibid., f. p. 48.

137. Ibid.

138. SBMA: RG 27-4-3, f. 37.

139. Ibid.

140. Ibid., f.28.

141. Ibid.

142. Ibid., f.5.

143. Alisa Ogata, O.S.B. "Japanese Benedictine History: A Commentary," (personal copy).

144. Ibid.

145. SBMA: RG 27-3-2, f.10.

146. Ibid.

147. SBMA: OHT 14, 3.

148. SBMA: OHT 14.

149. SBMA: RG 27-3-2, f. 39.

150. Ibid., f. 19.

151. SBMA: OHT 77.

152. Interview: Anne Malerich, O.S.B., 21 June 1995.

153. SBMA: RG 27-3-2 f. 3.

154. Interview: Lydia Erkens,O.S.B., 21 June 1995.

155. SBMA: RG 27-3-2, f. 52.

156. Ibid., f. 53.

157. SBMA: RG 27-3-2, f. 3.

158. SBMA: RG 27-3-2, f. 35.

159. SBMA: RG 27-3-2, f. 3.

160. Carmen Davila, O.S.B. Letter to Sister Mary Reuter. 9 November 1994. Dependent Priory Reports, Puerto Rico. Secretarial Office, Saint Benedict's Monastery, St. Joseph, Minnesota.

161. SBMA: RG P-37, f. 6.

162. Ibid.

163. Interview: Arles Silbernick, O.S.B., 5 July 1997.

164. SBMA: RG P-37, f. 6.

165. Interview: Jean Gibson, O.S.B., 5 July 1997.

166. Ibid.

167. Ibid.

168. Colman J. Barry, *Worship and Work*, 2nd ed. (St. Paul: North Central Publishing, 1980), pp. 205-207.

169. SBMA: RG 27-5A-1.

170. Ibid.

171. Ibid., RG 27-5A-2, f. 5.

172. Ibid.

173. Ibid.

174. Ibid., f.4.

175. Ibid., RG 27-5B-2, f.4.

176. SBMA: OHT 126.

177. SBMA: RG 27-5B-2, f.4.

178. SBMA: OHT 128.

179. SBMA: RG 27-5B-2 f.4.

180. SBMA: RG 27-5B-2 f.4.
181. Ibid.
182. SBMA: RG 27-5B-2 f. 32.
183. Ibid.
184. Ibid.
185. SBMA: OHT 120.
186. SBMA: OHT 128.
187. SBMA: OHT 128.

AFTERWORD

188. McDonald, p. 23.
189. Ephrem Hollermann, O.S.B., Keynote address: Community Renewal, August 4, 2000.

GLOSSARY OF MONASTIC TERMS

ABBESS or ABBOT: the elected leader of a monastic religious
community.

ABBEY: a monastery or convent under an abbess or abbot.

ASPIRANT: a candidate at the beginning stages of entering the
community.

BAND: the starched (or plastic) head-piece that supports the
veil.

BOOK OF CUSTOMS: the specific day-to-day practices of a
religious community in written form.

BREVIARY: the prayers constituting the Divine Office, Liturgy
of the Hours or *Opus Dei*; also the book containing
the prayers.

CELAM: Conference of Latin American bishops.

CMSW/CMSM: Conference of Major Superiors of Religious
Women/Men.

CHAPTER: all perpetually professed members of a monastic
community; also refers to the meetings convened by the
prioress/abbess/abbot to deliberate on community
business.

CHARISM: a gift or power attributed to an individual or group
exercised for the sake of others.

COIF: the pleated head-piece worn around the face covering the hair, ears, and neck.

CONGREGATION (see Federation)

CONVENT: refers to a community of religious or the home in which they live. Monastics most often use the term monastery or abbey.

CONVENT CULTURE: the style of social and artistic expression that characterizes a religious community; especially behavior patterns and language peculiar to such a way of life.

CONVERSION OF LIFE: fidelity to the monastic way of life constantly renewed.

COUNCIL: the representative body of the religious community advisory to the leadership.

DEPENDENT PRIORY: a monastic community in the transitional stage in which a mission begins to take responsibility for itself in view of becoming an autonomous monastery.

DISCERNMENT: decision-making process which incorporates a consideration of all pros and cons, a careful examination of input, a prayerful reflection of options, and finally a reaching of consensus.

DIVINE OFFICE: the traditional prayer of the Church comprised of psalms and readings from scripture prayed by clergy and members of religious orders; also known as Liturgy of the Hours or *Opus Dei.*

FEDERATION: the union of several monasteries organized for the sake of mutual support and communication with Rome.

FORMATION: the formal study and participation in community for candidates to a religious community.

GREGORIAN CHANT: liturgical plainsong of the Church systematized by Pope Gregory I.

HABIT: the religious dress.

HANDBOOK: the guide for the implementation of the elements of the Constitution that are specific for each community.

LCWR: Leadership Conference of Women Religious (formerly CMSW).

LECTIO DIVINA: a meditative reading and reflection on the word of God or other spiritual writings.

LITTLE OFFICE OF THE BLESSED VIRGIN: an abbreviated form of the Divine Office primarily honoring Mary; not considered the official prayer of the Church.

LITURGY: the system of public worship in the Church.

LOCAL MISSION: a community of sisters living away from the central monastery.

MISSIONING DAY: the annual meeting at which the blessing of the prioress and the community is given for the particular service or ministry of each sister.

MONASTERY: the home-base of a community of monastic women or men.

MONASTIC: a member of a religious community living under a leader and following the rule of a founder recognized by Rome.

NOVICE: a neophyte preparing for incorporation into the community.

NOVITIATE: the canonical period, usually one year, of formation for novices discerning commitment to religious life.

OPUS DEI: the work of God, the title Benedict gave to praying the Divine Office or Liturgy of the Hours.

PONTIFICAL HIGH MASS: a Eucharistic celebration with a bishop or abbot officiating and accompanied by pomp, ceremony, and a choir.

PRIORESS: the elected leader of a monastic community of women.

PROFESSION: the formal act of incorporation into a religious community.

QUASI-CHAPTER: the Chapter of a priory dependent on the founding monastery.

RECREATION: the times of the community's schedule not devoted to work and silence; refers not only to physical activities of relaxation and exercise, but also to conversation.

RELIGIOUS LIFE: a public commitment to a community according to a particular rule and leader for sake of service to Christ and the Church.

Rome: designates the authority of the Roman Catholic Church.

Rule of St. Benedict: document prescribing a way of life for monastics, attributed to Benedict of Nursia (c. 480 to 547).

Synod (community): the title given to an experimental, grassroots organization to formally discuss community matters.

Vatican Council II (Vatican II): the ecumenical meeting in Rome (1962 to 1965) of all the bishops in the world to renew the Church.

Vowed living (Benedictine): commitment to God and community to live in obedience, conversion of life, and stability.

ERRATA

1. Page 174
   Full of Fair Hope: A History of St. Mary's Mission at Redlake, by Owen Lindblad, O.S.B.,was commissioned by St. Mary's Mission, not by Studium.
2. Page 367
   "Sister Annette Brophy: pp 194, 212, 346, 350" was omitted in the original list of sister-photographers.

3. The following replaces page 367.

Photograph Acknowledgments

All photographs not acknowledged below are from Saint Benedict's Monastery Archives or personal photos.

Sister-photographers:

Sister Nancy Bauer: pp. 44, 55, 56, 58, 181, 257, 353
Sister Annette Brophy: pp. 194, 212, 346, 350
Sister Linda Dusek: p. 176 (2nd photo)
Sister Verenice Ramler: pp. 99, 187, 229
Sister Mary Reuter: p. 83
Sister Thomasette Scheeler: pp. vii, xx, 18, 21, 31,
   47, 67, 72, 80, 81, 92, 104, 106, 158, 159 (2nd photo),
   169, 178, 180, 185 (2nd photo), 186, 188, 190, 191,
   225, 226, 228

Courtesy of:

College of Saint Benedict, Communications and Marketing, St. Joseph, Minnesota: pp. 62, 196, 198, 211, 213
College of Saint Benedict, Archives, St. Joseph, Minnesota: p. 217
Mount Benedict Monastery, Ogden, Utah: p. 336

4.   The following replaces page 368.

Courtesy of: (continued)

Queen of Peace Hospital, New Prague, Minnesota:
   pp. 256, 259
St. Benedict's Senior Community, St. Cloud,
   Minnesota: p. 242 —1st photo Wayne Torborg
                       —2nd photo Jim Altobell
Saint Benedict's Monastery, Development Office,
   St. Joseph, Minnesota: pp. 73, 172, 183, and
   185 (1st photo) Jim Altobell;
   p.179 (three photos) Dianne Towalski
St. Benedict's Monastery, Sapporo, Japan:
   pp. 317, 318
St. Cloud Hospital, Communications Office,
   St. Cloud, Minnesota: pp. 233 (1st photo), 237,
   238, 245
The St. Cloud Visitor: p. 27 photo Vern Bartos;
   p. 28 photo Dan Musielewicz
Saint Martin Monastery, Nassau, Bahamas:
   pp. 339, 348, 349
St. Paul's Monastery, St. Paul, Minnesota: p. 175
Santa Escolastica Monasterio, Humacao,
   Puerto Rico: pp. 329, 330

Appreciation to:

Thomas Ryan Mulcahy Foundation for a grant
in support of a wide selection of photographs.

WITH HEARTS EXPANDED

PHOTO ACKNOWLEDGMENTS

All photographs not acknowledged below are from Saint Benedict's Monastery Archives or personal photos.

Sister-photographers:

Sister Nancy Bauer: pp. 44, 55, 56, 58, 176
Sister Linda Dusek: p. 144
Sister Verenice Ramler: pp. 188, 229
Sister Mary Reuter: p. 83
Sister Thomasette Scheeler: pp. xx, 18, 21, 31 (three photos) 47, 67, 72, 80, 81, 92, 104, 106, 158, 159 (second photo), 169, 176, 177, 178, 180 (two photos), 181, 185 (two photos), 186, 188 (two photos), 190, 191, 194, 225, 226, 227

Courtesy of:

College of Saint Benedict, Communications and Marketing, St. Joseph, Minnesota: pp. 62, 196, 198, 211, 212, 213
College of Saint Benedict, Archives, St. Joseph, Minnesota: p. 217
Mount Benedict Monastery, Ogden, Utah: p. 336 (two photos)

Appreciation to:

Thomas Ryan Mulcahy Foundation for a grant in support of a wide selection of photographs.

INDEX

For the references to the sisters of St. Benedict's Monastery, see the **Membership List—August 2000** or the **Necrology** following this Index.

MEMBERSHIP LIST
August 2000

Also serves as the Index of the sisters referred to in the book.

NECROLOGY

Also serves as Index for the deceased sisters referred to in the book.

CONTRIBUTORS

"The authors of this book have . . . gifted us with an 'icon of time,' an anniversary story of ever-renewing vision and over-arching meaning. They have given us a landmark that points out the way our Benedictine community has come on the journey of life."

Foreword
Ephrem Hollermann, O.S.B., Prioress

Those who researched, wrote, and edited this book:

Sister Carol Berg: Professor of history
at the College of Saint Benedict and
Saint John's Universtiy.

Sister Olivia Forster: Past missioner to
Japan and author of *Ardent Women:
The History of the Federation of St.
Benedict.*

Sister Shaun O'Meara: Past missioner to
Japan and theology professor at the College
of Saint Benedict and Saint John's University.

Sister Evin Rademacher: Past prioress of Saint Benedict's Monastery and past president of the Federation of St. Benedict.

Sister Emmanuel Renner: Past president of The College of Saint Benedict and Professor Emerita of history at the College of Saint Benedict and Saint John's University.

Sister Stefanie Weisgram: Collection Development Librarian of the College of Saint Benedict and Saint John's University.

A WORD FROM THE EDITOR

In the past forty-three years since our Centennial, the world has changed, the Church has changed, and the sisters of Saint Benedict's Monastery have changed. In the books listed below, pieces of what has happened and who we were and have become are evident. Although the whole story is never known or told, in this book the readers will find a more complete picture of the joys and sorrows, the graces and challenges that have expanded our hearts as we "run the way of the God's commandments with unspeakable sweetness of love."

(RB)
—Stefanie Weisgram, O.S.B., editor

Books Still in Print:

With Lamps Burning (McDonald, Grace, O.S.B.)
The first history of Saint Benedict's Monastery to which this book is a sequel.

Ardent Women: The History of the Federation of St. Benedict (Forster, Olivia, O.S.B.)

401

Behind the Beginnings (Girgen, Incarnata, O.S.B.)

Benedictine Mission to China (Muehlenbein, Wibora, O.S.B.)

Born of Common Hungers: Benedictine Women in Search of Connections (Brophy, Annette, O.S.B., photgraphs; Faulkner, Mara, O.S.B., essays)

Forever Your Sister (Wedl, Janice, O.S.B. and Eileen Maas Nalevanko, editors)

Full of Fair Hope: A History of St. Mary's Mission at Redlake (Lindblad, Owen, O.S.B.)

The Reshaping of a Tradition: American Benedictine Women 1852-1881 (Hollermann, Ephrem, O.S.B.)

Threads from Our Tapestry (Blatz, Imogene, O.S.B. and Zimmer, Alard, O.S.B.)

"This well-documented and clearly articulated history is an engaging account of one community's creative adaptations to the challenges of declining membership, new ministries, founding of new communities, financial strain, and the directives of Vatican II. It is a 'must read' for anyone searching for a model of hope in contemporary society, in that its story of transformations can occur whenever a group combines strong faith, creative energy, compassionate hearts, and trust in God and each other to spread the Good News of commitment to Christ's justice and love."
—Rosemary Rader, O.S.B.,
Benedict Distinguished Professor of Religion,
Carleton College, Northfield, Minnesota

"*With Hearts Expanded* is an astounding, spiritually rich account of the attempt of Saint Benedict's Monastery to remain faithful to its original spirit of Benedictine monasticism. It paints a picture of the community's amazing service outside its walls and gives the reader an inside, up-close look at how the community actually wrestled together in a refocusing of purpose in response to the new understandings of the Vatican II era. *With Hearts Expanded* is a book for anyone who has loved a women's monastic community, has wondered how the evident changes in it over the last forty years have taken place, and pondered the ongoing reality of women's religious life together.
—Roberta Bondi,
Professor of Church History,
Emory University, Atlanta, Georgia.

"*With Hearts Expanded* is a fine example of collaborative scholarship on the part of the women of Saint Benedict's Monastery. It reveals in a studied and insightful way the historical trajectory of one monastic community in a period of change and challenge that was pivotal in shaping the life of American Benedictine women in the third millennium."
—Joel Rippinger, O.S.B.,
Monastic Historian,
Marmion Abbey, Lisle, Illinois

"As one of those Catholic children growing up during the era of Vatican II when everything we believed 'was forever' but actually changing day by day, I witnessed with an outsider's limited view, the dismantling of religious life. *With Hearts Expanded* is a wonderful reading adventure giving the insider's view, answering many of our questions, and satisfying our curiosity. We are taken on this adventure with compassion and zeal; history is presented with an appropriately positive spin. I finished *With Hearts Expanded* knowing that all the hard work of transformation and growth was worth it."

—Laura Swan, O.S.B.,
Prioress, St. Placid's Priory,
Lacey, Washington